Good News for
the Disinherited

Howard Thurman on
Jesus of Nazareth
and Human Liberation

Alonzo Johnson

University Press of America, Inc.
Lanham • New York • London

Copyright © 1997 by
University Press of America,® Inc.
4720 Boston Way
Lanham, Maryland 20706

3 Henrietta Street
London, WC2E 8LU England

Library of Congress Cataloging-in-Publication Data

Johnson, Alonzo.
Good news for the disinherited : Howard Thurman on Jesus of
Nazareth and human liberation / Alonzo Johnson.
p.   cm.
Includes bibliographical references.
1. Jesus Christ--History of doctrines--20th century. 2. Thurman,
Howard, 1900-1981. 3. Liberation theology. I. Title.
BT198.J634   1996   232'.092--dc21   96-45204 CIP

ISBN 0-7618-0607-5 (cloth: alk: ppr.)
ISBN 0-7618-0608-3 (pbk: alk. ppr.)

∞™ The paper used in this publication meets the minimum
requirements of American National Standard for information
Sciences—Permanence of Paper for Printed Library Materials,
ANSI Z39.48—1984

DEDICATED

To The Life, Ministry, And
Enduring Legacy of
Howard Thurman
(1900-1981)

And to
my parents,
Bishop Johnie J. Johnson and Mrs. Thelma B. Johnson

Contents

Acknowledgments

Completing this book could not possibly have been accomplished without the support, prayers, love, and encouragement of a host of persons too numerous to list in this space. A few names must, however, be mentioned.

In 1976 I picked up a book by James H. Cone entitled *A Black Theology of Liberation*. I was a sophomore at Claflin College, Orangeburg, SC. The book was both fascinating and challenging, altering my naive understanding the Christian Gospel and my vision of the life, and of the mission of the Christian Church. Within the next year, I read all of Cone's books, learning as much as I could about black theology. I elected to attend Union Theological Seminary in New York City because Cone was a member of this faculty. I took a course with him in my first year at Union and my future work took shape in that course. The conversations that I subsequently had with him concerning my work convinced me to go on to pursue a Ph.D. in theology at Union. Cone's commitment to mentoring and supporting young scholars, theologians, and ministers is phenomenal. I am humbled to have been one of the persons that he willingly tutored through the arduous theology program at Union. For this, I shall be eternally grateful to him. This book was conceptualized during my endless discussions with him about the possible directions in which my work should proceed.

Latta R. Thomas, retired Chairperson of the Department of Religion and Philosophy at Benedict College, Columbia, S.C., gave me my first teaching job in 1986. I will always owe a debt of gratitude to him, as well as to other Benedict administrators, for giving me a start in the academic marketplace. Latta read and provided helpful responses to earlier drafts of this manuscript. Since the fall of 1990 I have been a member of the faculty of the Department of Religious Studies at the University of South Carolina, Columbia, S.C. I accepted this position because I believed that this was a place where I could grow and be fully appreciated as a theologian and scholar. My colleagues have indeed been very helpful and supportive during these years. Most especially I must mention the current and past chairmen of the Department, respectively, Carl Evans and Harold "Hal" French. They have been untiring in encouraging me and in their patience regarding the pace of my work. Carl, along with Dean Lester Lefton of the College of Liberal Arts, provided the financial support which helped to make this venture possible.

While in graduate school, I visited the Howard Thurman Educational Trust in San Francisco. This visit was very crucial to my research for this book. I am most appreciative of the support they provided during this time. I especially thank Mrs. Sue Bailey-Thurman, Howard Thurman's widow, for her warm hospitality and her faithfulness to the Thurman legacy. George McKechnie, one of Thurman's closest associates during the Boston years, was instrumental in helping me gain access to the Thurman Archives at Boston University's Mugar Library.

Bishop Ithiel C. Clemmons, a member of the General Board of the Churches of God in Christ, has been my pastor, mentor, and friend for nearly twenty years. He is a churchman and a scholar, and I have benefited much from his wisdom, friendship, and encouragement. My interest in Thurman's theology was in part shaped by Clemmons' frequent references to Thurman's writings during the sermons I heard him preach at the First Church of God in Christ, Brooklyn New York. His moral support has strengthened me during some difficult moments in my professional life. I am deeply appreciative of that support.

I have been bivocational for more than ten years. While teaching at Benedict College, Claflin College, and the University of South Carolina, I have simultaneously served as the pastor of the Bowman Temple Church of God in Christ, Bowman, South Carolina. My life has been unalterably shaped both by the religious passion and fervor of my church community and by the intellectual ethos of the academic world. I am thankful to the officers and members of my church for providing the space, experiences, and spiritual ethos wherein my theological views could flourish. I am a folk theologian and the church has provided a context wherein my scholarly interests could thrive and mature.

Despite physical distance and long periods of separation—due largely to the demands of my vocation—my family has always been my greatest source of strength and stability. They mean more to me than words can ever adequately express. In this regard, I have dedicated this book to my parents. For fifty years they have done their best at providing the home environment wherein their children could be nurtured and supported. Moreover, they have always respected what I have attempted to do, even when they did not fully understand my methods or goals. I must also thank Ami McConnell for her editorial assistance.

Finally, and most importantly, I salute my wife and best friend, Richel, who has been my constant companion for the past fourteen years. She has read and critiqued this document more times than either of us cares to mention. She always believed I could and would complete this project. Her love and devotion have never waned. My son, Rendell Omar, and daughter, Ashley Noel, have brought more joy and strength into my life than I could ever have imagined.

Introduction

Howard Thurman (1900-1981) was one of the most respected and prolific religious figures of this century. He was an imaginative thinker, an insightful preacher, and a creative theologian. He was without question one of the more celebrated interpreters of the African-American religious tradition of his generation. Thurman resisted the "theologian" title. Yet he was very adept at offering great theological insights about the nature of human experience, suffering, and religious experience. The deep spirituality of the African-American community resonated within his psyche, and he offered no apologies for this. He often said that "he who seeks to be at home everywhere must be at home somewhere." To Thurman this meant that the religious life is grounded in the particular experiences of a given community. This was a critical point of departure for him, for it speaks of the differences and similarities between religious communities.

Thurman's view of the life, teachings, and religion of Jesus of Nazareth is a centerpiece to his theology. More importantly, however, Thurman's approach to this subject broaches the most fundamental question in the history of Christianity. In one of his more noted encounters with his disciples, Jesus asked Peter, his endeared disciple, "Who do you say that I am?" This question personalizes the meaning of Christian faith in a rather direct way. It demands a response and specific action regarding the response. Christians have answered the question in various ways throughout the centuries. Some of the responses to the question have been classified as "high" Christological claims, because they give priority to the claims about the divinity of Christ. Such approaches can be seen in the Nicene and Chalcedonian Creeds of the fourth and fifth centuries. Other approaches have been classified as "low" Christologies, as they focus upon the humanity of Jesus. Thurman's work would fit within this latter category, and this is what this study will focus upon. Our concern will be to understand Thurman's view of Jesus and to see where it fits within the scope of the history of Christian theology.

Thurman's dislike for theological labels, his disdain for power symbols and titles, such as "theologian", "creed", "dogma", and the like makes the task of analyzing his thought much more daunting. He was an eclectic thinker who drew insights from a wide variety of religious, scientific, philosophical, and general literature. His thoughts on particular subjects are likewise spread throughout the vast corpus of his writings, speeches, sermons, and lectures, as they were compiled over the span of his more than fifty years of active teaching and ministry. Thurman always resisted doctrinal and theological labels and titles, as he attempted to interpret the deepest dimensions of the religious experience. He said:

> I say that creeds, dogmas, and theologies are inventions of the mind. It is the nature of the mind to make sense out of experience, to reduce the conglomerates of experience to its units of comprehension which we call principles, or ideologies or concepts.[1]

He contrasted this approach with his primary interest in religious experiences, which he described as being "dynamic, fluid, effervescent, yeasty."[2] The dynamic and "yeasty" character of religious experiences makes them difficult to capture within a single tradition, doctrine, or religious community. Thurman referred to certain tendencies within religious communities as attempts to "imprison religious experience in some way."[3] In contrast, Thurman's life and thought reflect his passionate sense of the ever-changing nature of religious experience.

At any rate, this study will examine Thurman's work as it developed throughout his more than twenty books, a vast collection of his unpublished sermons, meditations, lectures, and other written material, as well as a huge volume of video and audio cassette tapes. The unpublished material is especially helpful because it helps to provide a more complete picture of Thurman and his work. Despite what has been said thus far about the Thurman's theological method and his penchant for a rather unsystematic style, there is a great degree of consistency in what Thurman said about Jesus over the course of his career. One of Thurman's earlier works, *Jesus and the Disinherited* (1949), is his most thorough statement on the subject, but his principal thesis in this work was, however, outlined much earlier in his career. The thesis of *Jesus and the Disinherited* is that the religion of Jesus is a religion of deliverance for the disinherited peoples of the world. The religion of Jesus spoke directly to the person who lives with his or her "back against the wall."[4] Jesus made poor, oppressed, and disinherited people the priority of his ministry. And in this sense, his ministry was the model for the ministry of the Christian church. The idea of Jesus' relevance to the oppressed has been a major point of emphasis among liberation theologians over the past thirty years.

The methodology employed in this study is primarily hermeneutical and descriptive. Much attention will be given to the task of providing a full exegesis of Thurman's thought and to explaining exactly what he said about the life, teaching, work, and ministry of Jesus. However, we will move beyond this descriptive task to discuss more specifically the theological and practical implications of Thurman's view of Jesus.

Thurman's work is significant to all persons who are interested in the practical aspects of religious faith. Moreover, his work is also significant for theologians seeking to fully comprehend the meaning of human experiences within the context of religious faith. Thurman's theological vision is particularly relevant today, given two key factors: the globalization of the world community, and the growing gap between the rich and the poor in America and elsewhere around the world. Each of these issues occupy much of the focus of Thurman's theology, especially his view of Jesus. He was not concerned about making Jesus of Nazareth or the Christian faith superior to the claims of any religious community. Thus he began his theology without the traditional claims about the divinity, universality, and pre-existence of Christ. Instead he choose to view Jesus as a man who presented a "way" to God. According to Thurman:

> Jesus Christ is a source of inspiration for a faith for living to a generation that has lost its nerve as our generation has because He gave to the people who surrounded Him and to the world, therefore, a vision, a vision of God.[5]

Moreover, Thurman proposed that one should view Jesus' divinity in a non-ontological, anti-metaphysical sense. Jesus' "sonship" was the result of his profound religious experience. To some, such claims bespeak of heresy and anti-Christian ideals. But Thurman believed that it was possible to affirm these ideals without compromising the truths of the Christian faith. He noted:

> [I]t must be remembered that what is true in any religion is found in that religion because it is true. It is not true because it is found in that religion.[6]

Truth is truth, irrespective of the religious tradition or community within which it is found. Thurman was not, however, a universalist; for he continued to emphasize the particular significance that the religion of Jesus has for the oppressed. For them, the religion of Jesus is a "technique of survival."[7] The legitimacy of the Christian witness, Thurman argued, depends on its ability to speak meaningfully to the plight of the oppressed. The true test of a religious idea centers on its relevance as an agency of liberation for the oppressed. Thurman went even further in saying that the religion of Jesus, and all expressions of the true spirit of Christianity contain an inherently liberating motif. Individuals and groups of persons must simply apply and appropriate this motif. This is not a small matter for Thurman, it is at the heart of the Christian gospel.

The relevance of this study centers on the nature of these claims. It is necessary to analyze and assess Thurman's treatment of the life, teachings, ministry, and death of Jesus of Nazareth in order to assess the viability of his project. Moreover, it is necessary to address this aspect of Thurman's thought because it cuts to the heart of the question of the meaning of Christian faith and identity. Is it possible to simultaneously maintain Thurman's type of "low Christology" and remain faithful to depictions of Jesus found in the New Testament, the Christian tradition, and the African-American religious tradition? This study represents my attempt to answer this question. It is my hope that the reader will find Howard Thurman to be a tremendous source of strength and guidance in his/her inward journey.

In Chapter One we will examine the major factors which helped to shape Howard Thurman's life and thought. Specific attention will be given to those persons and traditions which significantly influenced Thurman's understanding of Jesus of Nazareth. The central claim in this chapter is that the African-American religious tradition was the principal influence which shaped Thurman's Christology. We will examine several events and personal experiences of Thurman's life, such as the death of his father, the rejection of Thurman's candidacy for church membership, the influence of his grandmother, and his use of the slave spirituals. Each of these factors helps to demonstrate Thurman's continuity and discontinuity with the black religious tradition.

Chapter Two focuses upon Thurman's view of the humanity of Jesus. The reader will see how Thurman's definition of Jesus' humanity fits within the context of the traditions in biblical studies which are commonly referred to as the old and new quests of the historical Jesus. Thurman's approach to Christology was heavily influenced by his understanding of the historical data presented in the New Testament. The key questions which emerge from Thurman's approach to this issue will be addressed by placing him in dialogue with Rudolf Bultmann. There are several historical facts about Jesus that Thurman regarded as central: Jesus' birth, his Jewish identity, his place in the Jewish religious tradition, his distinction from other religious leaders, his socio-economic and political status, and his death.

Chapter Three continues the discussion which is broached in Chapter Two. It emphasizes the connection between Thurman's reflections on the humanity of Jesus and his ideas about the degree to which Jesus was both human and divine. In this chapter we deal with one of the most controversial issues in Thurman studies, that is, how and to what degree Thurman believed that Jesus was divine. We suggest that this issue can best be addressed by understanding Thurman in relationship to some of the trends in liberal western theology, namely the trend toward synthesizing natural and supernatural reality. Friedrich Schleiermacher and Harry Emerson Fosdick are used as principal examples of the liberal method of understanding the divinity of Jesus. Thurman, we argue, used a non-ontological, anti-metaphysical conception of the divinity of Jesus. In this way he was able to maintain an approach to the divinity of Jesus which did not insult the twentieth century worldview. We examine several texts in order to demonstrate the method utilized by Thurman in this process.

Chapter Four considers the subject at the heart of this study, that is, how Thurman's Christology addressed the questions and concerns of poor and the oppressed. To begin with, I analyze Thurman's view of human oppression. It is out of the context of his view of religious experience that Thurman spoke of Jesus' message to the disinherited. Thus, we look at Thurman's response to his perennial concern, "the significance of the religion of Jesus to people who stand with their backs against the wall."[8] The chapter also examines Thurman's use of the slave spirituals, a theme introduced in the first chapter.

Chapter Five examines Thurman's Christology within the context of the twentieth century quest for a "Black Christ." We begin with a summary statement of the key aspects of Thurman's Christology. Following this we trace the development and maturation of Thurman's thought. Further, we analyze the similarities and dissimilarities between Thurman's "Jesus and the Disinherited" thesis and the claims of other black writers, leaders, and theologians who have addressed the subject of Jesus' identification with the plight of the disinherited. We place Thurman in dialogue with writers such as Henry M. Turner, Marcus Garvey, Countee Cullen, Langston Hughes, Albert Cleage, James H. Cone, and James Deotis Roberts. We will demonstrate that Thurman's work is most relevant to some of the questions which are covered by black liberation theologians.

Chapter Six is the concluding segment of this study. It contains the author's critical assessment and constructive appropriation of Thurman's Christology.

Notes

1   Howard Thurman, "Interview with Ron Eyre," *Critics Corner* p. 211.

2   Ibid.

3   Ibid.

4   Howard Thurman, *Jesus and the Disinherited* (New York: Harper & Row Publishers, 1949; reprint ed., Richmond, IN: Friends United Press, 1969) p. 13.

5   Howard Thuman, "A Faith to Live by—Jesus Christ," September 28, 1953. Sermon delivered at The Church for the Fellowship of All Peoples, San Francisco, CA.

6   Howard Thurman, *The Luminous Darkness: A Personal Interpretation of the Anatomy of Segregation and the Ground of Hope* (New York: Harper & Row Publishers, 1965).

7   Howard Thurman, *Jesus and the Disinherited* p. 13.

8   Ibid., p. 7.

Chapter I

The Impact of the Black Religious Tradition upon Howard Thurman's Interpretation of the Teachings and Life of Jesus of Nazareth

"My own life has been so deeply influenced by the genius of the spirituals that the meaning as distilled into my experience in my early years spills over in much that I have come to think in my maturity."

Deep River and The Negro Spiritual
Speaks of Life and Death
Howard Thurman

The black religious tradition was the principal influence that shaped Howard Thurman's understanding of the teachings and life of Jesus of Nazareth.[1] The purpose of this chapter is to examine the experiences, circumstances, beliefs, and persons, representing aspects of the black religious tradition, which helped to shape Thurman's life and theology. The primary concern, however, is to explain the evolution of Thurman's understanding of the life, teachings, and message of Jesus of Nazareth. The testimonies, songs, biographies, and sermons of the African-

American community emphasized the centrality of Jesus Christ as a source of empowerment and deliverance from all sources of oppression.[2] Black Christians believed that Jesus' death and resurrection conquered the powers of sin and death.[3] This focus on Jesus as deliverer may be called the prophetic impulse in the black religious tradition; our focus here will be upon Thurman's appropriation of this tradition.[4]

The entirety of black religious thought has been shaped by a strong "folk religious heritage." Howard Thurman's theology was a product of this tradition. Our task here is to unfold some of the key themes in this folk tradition, so as to demonstrate its relevance to Howard Thurman's understanding of Jesus. It is unfortunate that this aspect of Thurman's thought has not received much attention. Thurman both extended and challenged the folk tradition of which he was a product.[5]

Formative Factors in the Shaping of Thurman's Theology

The Social Context

The Plight of the Black Community

Before looking at some of the specific folk traditions and experiences that may have helped to shape Thurman's life and thought, we will look at the general socio-political context in which his life was nurtured.[6] The folk experiences and beliefs that we will address are specifically those which seem to have become foundational to his life and to his entire religious vision. In this process we will also note specifically those areas where his understanding of Jesus and the meaning of true religious experience were being shaped.

Thurman was born in Daytona Beach, Florida, in 1900. He spent the first twenty-four years of his life in the South.[7] He was nurtured in its genteel tradition and victimized by its racism towards and economic exploitation of African-Americans. Segregation and oppression were facts of life for the people in his community. Thurman lived with his "back against the wall," and he experienced socio-economic depression firsthand. His parents, Saul and Alice Thurman, were both children of former slaves and they shared the fate of other poor blacks of their day. Jim Crow segregation reigned supreme and few blacks in Florida escaped its domain. Saul Thurman worked as a track man for the Florida

East Coast Railroad Company. This was an unskilled job that paid menial wages, kept him away from his family most of the time, and also caused him to be exposed to the weather for long periods of time. As a result of this exposure, Saul contracted pneumonia, from which he died in 1907. Alice Thurman worked as a domestic for a local white family, leaving the care of her three children—Henrietta, the oldest; Madaline, the youngest; and Howard—to her mother, Nancy Ambrose. The family survived through hard work and thrift.[8] Thurman clearly described the state of race relations in his community as well as the plight of the blacks in Daytona:

> When I was growing up, Daytona had a population of about five thousand permanent residents. The number greatly increased in the wintertime when the tourists arrived. For the most part, they employed local people, black and white, as servants and household retainers, their chauffeurs and personal maids usually traveled with them, returning north at the end of the winter. But the tempering influence of these northern families made contact between the races less abrasive than it might have been otherwise.[9]

His description is more graphic as he described the power dynamics of the racial situation of the town.

> The white community in Daytona itself was "downtown," no place for loitering. Our freedom of movement was carefully circumscribed, a fact so accepted that it was taken for granted . . . white and black worlds were separated by a wall of quiet hostility and overt suspicion. Certain white people could come into our neighborhoods without taking notice. The sheriff often came on "official" business.[10]

Reflections on Racism

As a youngster in Daytona he simply accepted the status quo of race relations as the norm; without questioning in detail the validity of the system of segregation. His religious vision, as a youngster, was not dominated by a concern about the racial exclusiveness of the churches. As he said:

> When I was a boy growing up in Florida, it never occurred to me, nor was I taught either at home or in church, to regard white persons as falling within the scope of the magnetic field of my morality . . . I did not regard them as involved in my religious reference. They were not read out of the human race—they simply did not belong to

it in the first place . . . They were tolerated as a vital part of the environment, but they did not count in. They were a world apart, in another universe of discourse.[11]

The experience of segregation was a central factor that later shaped his understanding of the church. Thurman posited that churches in America have betrayed the religion of Jesus, which, in Thurman's opinion,[12] offers an important method for addressing the concerns of those who must live with oppression. *Jesus and the Disinherited* provides the most conclusive evidence of how Thurman's interpretation of the teachings and life of Jesus is shaped by his experience in the black community in Florida, which he saw as one facet of the experiences of black people in America. In this text, Thurman used the history and experiences of blacks in America as the primary basis of interpreting Jesus' message to the disinherited. Although he also referred to the experiences of other oppressed people, for example Indians and Japanese, the experiences of black Americans dominate his discussion.

Thurman's serious theological reflections on the racial situation in America did not begin until his final year at Morehouse College. His remorse over the segregation and racial disharmony within American religious institutions almost caused him to reject the Christian ministry. Before deciding to attend Rochester Theological Seminary, where he was one of only a couple of black students, he lamented the racial climate of American religious institutions. He noted with great sorrow their inability to counteract the dominance of American racism. In deciding to pursue the Christian ministry, Thurman became passionate about addressing this issue very early on in the process. He began by applying to New Theological Seminary, Newton, Massachusetts, an all-white institution, as his school of choice for his ministerial training. His application was rejected, and he was encouraged by the school's administration to apply instead to Virginia Union Seminary, a black school. Thurman was insulted by this rejection, refused their suggestion, and later enrolled in Rochester Theological Seminary. But he never forgot this experience and it shaped his thinking in a fundamental way.

Thurman entered Rochester Theological Seminary in 1923,[13] where, for the first time in his life, he was in "a totally white world."[14] In this context Thurman began to question his own understanding of the teachings of Jesus of Nazareth, especially regarding the racial situation of the times. He asked himself, how is it possible to believe in the Christian message and not challenge the racial polarization of America? What does my commitment to the gospel suggest about my response to whites? Is a segregated congregation or denomination really a church? These and similar questions plagued him during his first year in seminary. As he said:

> Until I went to Rochester I had accepted the fact that I was a Christian, a practicing Christian. I believed sincerely in the necessity for loving my fellow man. It was a serious commitment; however, it had not ever occurred to me that my magnetic field of ethical awareness applied to other than my own people. Therefore, at Rochester, I found this commitment to brotherhood severely tested.[15]

At Morehouse Thurman had begun to reflect on the race issue and his thinking came full-circle during his stay in Rochester. He concluded that the Christian message for the people of the twentieth century must be interpreted and understood in light of the teachings and life of Jesus.[16] The questions that Thurman posed at the beginning of *Jesus and the Disinherited*, which emerged directly from the thesis of the text, affirmed this point. He asked:

> Why is it that Christianity seems impotent to deal radically, and therefore effectively, with the issues of discrimination and injustice on the basis of race, religion and national origin? Is this impotency due to a betrayal of the genius of the religion, or is it due to a weakness in religion itself?[17]

We should keep in mind, however, Thurman's claim that he did not grasp the full effect of racism until later in his life.

Thurman's Experiences in the Church

The Death of Saul Thurman

In the circumstances surrounding the death of Saul Thurman, Howard's father, we see the foundations being laid for Thurman's revolutionary vision of the African-American religious tradition. These events would bring him into conflict with one of the prized folk traditions of the black church. Mt. Bethel Baptist Church was the spiritual haven in which Howard Thurman's faith was shaped at an early age. Saul Thurman was a very well respected gentleman, but he never joined the family church, Mt. Bethel. He was a family man, a good citizen, but like many males in the community, he was not a practicing Christian.

Like other Baptist congregations, Mt. Bethel adhered to that Radical Reformation principle that indicates that the church should be a society of "visible saints." This is to say that the true church was to consist of "believers", thus the Baptist practice of "believer's baptism."[18] The rights and privileges of membership in this tradition was to be reserved for believers. One such privilege was that of being eulogized in the church building. Persons who, like Saul, died "out of Christ"[19] were often not afforded this privilege. The deacons and officers of Mt. Bethel refused to allow Saul Thurman's funeral to be held in Mt. Bethel church. This decision reflected both the folk traditions of some African-American churches and the puritanical quest for a "pure" church, as is characteristic of the Baptist tradition.

Howard was only seven years old when his father died, but, in reflecting on the event more than a half-century later, he saw it as a pivotal event in his life. It triggered within him some discomfort with his tradition, which would come full circle later in his life. The clear and categorical conclusion that one could draw from the deacons' decisions is that people who die without having become Christians and having a personal faith in Jesus are deemed to be eternally lost. The Jesus of these people was a fierce judge who radically distinguished between saints and sinners. Theirs was a tradition that tended toward, as Thurman would later say, exclusivity and isolation. Commenting on the experience fifty-two years later, Thurman said:

> Perhaps . . . the experience of the death of my father and its consequences . . . gave me an early conditioning against the tendency toward exclusiveness within the Christian Church—to be specific—within our local Baptist Church.[20]

The attitude of the deacons contradicted Thurman's belief that Jesus breaks down barriers that separate people. Thurman recognized that religious exclusivity limits Jesus' true mission, which was designed to create fellowship between all peoples.[21] The focus of Jesus' message was upon love and compassion, but this was the opposite of the church's attitude toward Saul Thurman.[22]

After having been challenged by Nancy Ambrose, Saul Thurman's mother-in-law, the board of deacons reversed their original verdict. The Thurman's family was allowed to have Saul Thurman's funeral in Mt. Bethel Church. The Reverend Sam Cromarte, traveling evangelist, was asked to give the eulogy. Although he did not know the Thurman family, Cromarte gladly accepted the invitation to preach the eulogy.[23]

At the funeral, Cromarte pronounced divine judgment upon the "unregenerate sinner," Saul Thurman, and sentenced him to hell. Howard watched in desperation as Cromarte condemned Saul to an awful fate:

> Under my breath I kept whispering to Mamma, "He didn't know Papa, did he?" Out of her own pain, conflict, and compassionate love, she reached over and gripped my bare knee with her hand, giving a gentle but firm, comforting squeeze. It was sufficient to restrain for the moment my bewildered and outraged spirit.[24]

But the hurt was deep and the rupture in his spirit profound. And, in the days following the funeral, he passionately determined that, "One thing is sure. When I grow up and become a man, I will never have anything to do with the church."[25]

Cromarte showed absolutely no compassion to the family in delivering the eulogy. This is what troubled Thurman the most in the sermon. The redeeming and reconciling love that Thurman had come to associate with the life and teachings of Jesus was absent. Cromarte's harsh distinction between the saved and the damned was more than Thurman could affirm. In this way, the death of Saul Thurman helped to strengthen Thurman's resistance to the practice of making Jesus of Nazareth the object of one's faith or the source of one's experience of justification.[26] Thurman was repulsed by religious exclusivity. Religious exclusivity touted as an affirmation of faith in Jesus of Nazareth was not only uninformed but oppressive. The funeral experience almost caused Thurman to reject the call to the Christian ministry. Three things troubled him:

> One, a vague feeling that somehow I was violating my father's memory by taking leadership responsibility in an institution that had done violence to his spirit. Two, the recognition that I couldn't accept the emphasis upon membership exclusiveness which seemed an authentic part of the genius of the church and the fact that the doctrine of salvation made a gulf between those who belonged to the church as members and those who did not. Three, the examination of the implications of the Christian ministry upon my life and the life around me caused the question of the segregated church to become an issue— how could I in good conscience accept it?[27]

Thurman was called to the ministry during his senior year at Morehouse College. He understood the sociological and theological problems that resulted from segregated religious bodies.

Later in life Thurman encountered Sam Cromarte again. He saw Cromarte in a barbershop one day, without knowing who he was, and was overtaken by a sudden feeling of dread. Thurman went home with that feeling and discussed it with his grandmother.

> She said, "Lord, have mercy, don't you know who that was?" I said, "No I don't know, Grandma." "That was Sam Cromarte, who preached Saul's funeral." I had not seen him since the funeral but—but this, whatever it was, I—I [sic] have no explanation. I don't know anything about that sort of stuff but it—it— [sic] was some rumor or aroma or scent of that tragic experience for me as a little boy . . . the tragic experience at the funeral and that just sort of brooded over my goings and comings and after that, after I saw him and I had this experience without even knowing who he was the whole cloud lifted and it was no longer a psychological problem for me.[28]

The Rejection of Thurman's Candidacy for Church Membership

Thurman's vivid reflections on the circumstances of his father's death—written more than fifty years later—give us a clear indication of why it was such a fundamental event in his life. His experience, approximately five years after his father's death, when his candidacy for church membership was rejected, is another fundamental event. This trauma was particularly accented because the same group of people who had rejected his father, the deacons of Mt. Bethel, then passed judgment on Howard. As was the case in their attitudes about Saul Thurman's lack of church membership, the deacons were equally as traditional and conservative in their understanding of the conversion experience. Their response to young Howard's description of his conversion demonstrate their rootedness in the strong folk traditions of black churches.

Mt. Bethel, steeped in the folk tradition of African-American religion, strongly encourage its children to begin "seekin'" the Lord at the age of twelve, "the age of accountability." After having gone through the period of seekin' the Lord, or mourning, the young Christians were expected to be "converted", saved. The climax of this process was a meeting with the deacons of the church, a conversation with one's mentor, and a corporate baptism with other young initiates.[29] During the meetings with the mentor and the deacons, young converts were instructed on all matters pertaining to life, adulthood, and, most importantly, church membership. In the first several meetings the candidate for membership was indeed the student. In the concluding meeting, however, the roles were somewhat reversed and the candidate was required to address the group directly. The individual was required to give an account of his or her own conversion experience. Young Howard, for example, was required to explain his conversion experience, with the aim of convincing others, namely the deacons, that he had truly been converted.[30] Thurman recounted this of the meeting:

> They examined me, and I answered their questions. When they had finished, the chairman asked, "Howard, why do you come before us?" I said, "I want to be a Christian." Then the chairman said, *"But you must come before us after you have been converted and have already become a Christian. "* [Italics mine][31]

The deacons were obviously not satisfied with his answer. They were in fact not sure that he had actually been converted, since Howard's description of his conversion experience did not meet their expectations. The deacons expected that Howard should have been able to give them specific information about the time, place, and circumstances surrounding his conversion experience. Unable to ascertain enough details of Howard's conversion, the head deacon told Thurman, "You better get yourself straightened out, Howard." The deacons sent him away with a command: "Come back when you can tell us of your conversion."[32]

There is a strong tradition behind the deacons' calling upon young Howard to "tell" of his conversion experience. They wanted more facts, more details, more conviction, and more of a sense of the supernatural transformation of the young lad. Nevertheless, the deacons' rejection made little sense to young Howard, thus he went home feeling dejected, humiliated, and misunderstood. And just as he had done in the past, young Howard confided in his grandmother and mentor, Nancy Ambrose. Grandma Nancy was a pillar of the community, well respected in the church, and the strong spiritual influence in the lives of her grandchildren. She knew her grandson's pain, she understood his spirituality, and she had tutored him in the faith. Therefore, she took the situation in hand and resolved to confront the deacons on the matter. She invited herself into their meeting and staged a direct confrontation with the deacons:

"How dare you turn this boy down? He is a Christian and was one long before he came to you today. Maybe you did not understand his words, but shame on you if you do not know his heart. Now you take this boy into the church right now—before you close this meeting!"[33]

There was, according to Thurman's account of the event, no refutation of Nancy's words. The deacons, tentative though they were about the authenticity of Thurman's testimony, accepted him as a full-member of the church, thereby making him a candidate for baptism.

This solved the immediate problem for Howard, but it left unresolved a much more fundamental issue. Specifically, it left unresolved the strong inner-tensions that we see in the two varying conceptions of the nature of true religious experience, the meaning of conversion, and, most importantly, the meaning of true faith in Jesus Christ. Howard and Grandma Nancy stood on one side of the theological spectrum and on the other was the perspective represented by the deacons of Mt. Bethel. Both positions are rooted in the rich soils of African-American folk religion, and clearly point toward some of the problems that Thurman would have with this tradition later in his life. Thurman's testimony about his conversion showed evidence of his maturing theological perspective. His testimony lacked the specific language, the graphic details, the references to a specific type of feeling, a vision, a voice, and a word of consolation from God or Jesus; all of these were key elements of the conversion narratives of African-American Christians. He had clearly "experienced" something, but his articulation of the meaning of this experience is what would later set him apart. We will see specifically the contrast between these two positions as we examine them more carefully below.

African-American Folk Religious Traditions

Three decades ago, Joseph Washington, an African-American scholar, brought the idea of folk religion to the forefront of the academic discussions of black religion. He created a great stir among African-American theologians when he argued, during that era of Civil Rights demonstrations, that black churches were not truly Christian. Washington argued instead that they were folk institutions, rooted in their distinctive folk religious identities. He posited that black churches made no central contribution to Christian theology, ecclesiology, and ethics. Their primary reason for being was, he noted, for the purpose of racial preservation and serving as a bulwark against the vestiges of American racism. In this sense, Washington stated that the black congregations in America were drawn together by a socio-political agenda, rather than from a genuine commitment to historic Christianity. Thus he concluded that black religion was a "fifth force in American religion," alongside Judaism, Protestantism, Catholicism, and Secularism.[34] He further stated that black folk religion was "the spirit that binds Negroes in a way they are not bound to other Americans. . . It transcends all religious and socio-economic barriers which separate Negroes from other Negroes."[35] James H. Cone later wrote that Washington's description of black religion motivated black theologians to start the black theology movement. Younger black theologians such as Cone wanted to offer a more progressive interpretation of black religion.[36]

Washington's scathing critique of the mission and ministry of black churches and his use of the phrase "folk religion" are radically different from my own use of the phrase. But he did bring the issue of folk theology into the forefront of the discussions of black religion, which is important for our study of Thurman. Unlike Washington, however, I find absolutely nothing pejorative in the "folk" heritage of African-American Christianity. Folk religious traditions demonstrate a universal fact about the religious life, namely that it is a living reflection of the people who espouse the tradition. It mirrors the manner in which individuals and groups of people "put human flesh on their faith." Folk religious practices represent the degree to which Christianity, and all other religions in fact, become meshed in the culture of the believers. Through language, dance, folklore, folktales, popular mythologies, localized customs, and traditions, folk religious expressions allow people to personalize their faith.[37]

Among African-Americans, folk religious practices are varied, representing a "conjecture of many streams—African, European, classic Judeo-Christian, and Amerindian,"[38] and American, as these have all been meshed with the experiences of African-Americans. They represent what Henry Mitchell has called declaring "the gospel in the language and culture of the people [blacks]—the vernacular."[39] African-American folk religion is an aspect of what W. E. B. Du Bois has called the *Gift of Black Folk*.[40] Such gifts include their spirituality, beliefs, and customs.

Folk traditions are by their very nature uncodified, non-systematic, and informal, including a wide spectrum of beliefs and practices within their purview. I include in this category of folk practices such things as folk songs, Pray's Houses, ecstatic trances, Seekin' the Lord, spirit possession, Ring Shouting, dancing. These are couched, with varying degrees of emphasis, together with other phenomena as Brer Rabbit tales, belief in hags, witches, haunts, conjuring, sorcery.[41] These folk traditions do help to make, as Washington suggests, African-American religious communities distinct. They represent a collective body of experiences and beliefs that bind them together more definitively than does their denominational affiliation. These traditions do indeed presently thrive among African-American Christians of various religious traditions. Thus if one seeks to understand why people in these traditions affirm what they affirm and do what they do in their churches and communities, one must look at some of these folk practices. Charles Joyner is more than correct when he says that the folk religious traditions demonstrate that black slaves "did not so much adapt to Christianity (at least not the selective Christianity evangelized to them by their masters) as adapt Christianity to themselves."[42]

Of particular relevance to this study are the folk beliefs about issues such as baptism, church membership, the meaning and significance of the life, ministry, and death of Jesus of Nazareth.

The Meaning of Conversion in African-American Folk Religion

The deacons' response to Howard's description of his conversion experience reveals much about their view of conversion, their understanding of Jesus, and the central role that having faith in Jesus Christ plays in the process. What is demonstrated is very closely linked with what I choose to call the "Seekin' the Lord" tradition in African-American religious history.

The Seekin' the Lord tradition in African-American folk religion would best be understood as a conversion ritual. It presents a model for how people were converted and the key elements which went into this process. A full discussion of the Seekin' the Lord tradition is beyond the scope of this study, but there are some key aspects of it that should be noted before we proceed.[43] The practice of seeking was, according to Margaret Washington Creel, formally introduced to African slaves by white evangelical revivalists.[44] White evangelists in the nineteenth century, such as Charles G. Finney and Phoebe Palmer, made fine use of the "altar service" as a centering point in their worship, hoping for the conversion of more sinners. This was only one of the new "measures" that were popularized by evangelists during this period.[45] At any rate, if Seekin' the Lord began as a conversion ritual, African-Americans transformed it into a full-fledged rite of passage. Sinners were invited to the Christian altar as the place where they would find relief from and forgiveness of sins. As noted above, African-American Christians have traditionally accented the centrality of the conversion experience as a centerpiece of their religious vision. And this religious vision was more often than not linked to their understanding of the role of Jesus of Nazareth as a mediator in human salvation. [46] The conversion was not simply an intellectual experience; it was a dramatic, deeply personal, and transforming event. The conversion experience was a paradigm-shifting moment in the life of an individual.[47] Thus it would be common to hear individuals speak about their conversion experience in the most graphic and categorical terms.

One only has to look casually at the slave Spirituals and the conversion narratives of slaves and ex-slaves to notice the strong Jesus-centered piety. The conversion experience was the centerpiece of the religious life and Jesus was the principal object of religious devotion. Thurman and James H. Cone have correctly noted that in reality the opposite was really the case. The slaves often moved without definite distinctions between statements about God and statements about Jesus of Nazareth.[48] It was always clear that Jesus was a friend of the poor, a liberator of the oppressed, their "Balm in Gilead". He was Emmanuel, God with us, God among us, God for me. In their prayers, songs, sermons, and spirituality they were concerned about the "pragmatic power" of Jesus.[49] Jesus was the slaves' source of deliverance and comfort. Their faith affirmed two central assertions about Jesus: his divine nature and his historical identification with oppressed people. Even when there was an interchange in nomenclature for referring to Jesus, (Lord, God, King of Kings, Master, Son of God) both the divinity and humanity of Jesus were assumed.[50]

Some examples of traditional African-American Christian folk songs, or Spirituals, will illuminate the slaves' conceptualization of Jesus and God's role in their lives.

> When I was a seeker,
> sought both night and day,
> asked de Lord to help me,
> And He show'd me de way.

That Jesus Christ is born.

This song expresses the sense the slaves had of the divine character of Jesus' birth; it was something to be proclaimed and made known everywhere, for it was an answer to prayer. He was King over all.

> He's King of Kings, and Lord of Lords,
> Jesus Christ, the first and last,
> No man works like him.
> He built a platform in the air,
>
> And broke the Roman Kingdom down,
> No man works like him.

The slaves knew that Jesus was not simply another person. Jesus was God visiting them in their trials and tribulations.

> Be with me Lord! Be with me!
> Be with me Lord! Be with me!
> When I'm on my lonesome journey.
> I want Jesus Be with me.

Jesus was the one to have around when one got into trouble. He gave food to the hungry, water to the thirsty and clothes to the naked.

> O Lord, I'm hungry
> I want to be fed,
> O lord, I'm hungry
> I want to be fed,
> O feed me Jesus feed me,
> Feed me all my days.

The Spirituals also remind us—sometimes with the most poetic and intense language—that all persons are sinners and are in need of forgiveness and reconciliation.

> O Lord, I'm sinful
> I want to be saved,
> O Lord, I'm sinful
> I want to be saved.
> O save me Jesus save me
> Save me all my days.

The slaves' hope in Jesus and God was linked to an eschatological hope and vision. They viewed Jesus both as a source of redemption from personal evil and as the source of worldly and eternal freedom. The eschatological dimension of their hope was affirmed in the following song.

> I'm going back with Jesus when He comes, when He comes,
> I'm going back with Jesus when He comes, when He comes,
> O He may not come today,
> But He's coming anyway
> O He may not come today,
> But He's coming anyway
> And we won't die anymore when He comes, when He comes.

For black slaves Jesus was the Son of God, who came to identify with their situation. He brought them freedom and liberation, he was their friend, and he understood their plight. And the salvation that he brought applied to their historic situation and to their hope for eternity. They placed their hope in a God who, acting through Jesus, could and did set them free from the multidimensional sources of oppression and bondage. God freed them from their spiritual as well as their physical sources of oppression; this is why the Spirituals, for example, always carried a dual message. They included a focus on deliverance from slavery and an existential sense of freedom.

The centrality of this experience of deliverance from oppression might account for the strong emphasis that the slaves placed on the importance of conversion. This emphasis is very vividly demonstrated in the conversion narrative of Richard Allen, the famed bishop and founder of the African Methodist Episcopal Church.

> I cried unto Him who delighteth to hear the prayers of a poor sinner, and all of a sudden my dungeon shook, and my chains flew off, and glory to God, I cried. My soul was filled. I cried, enough for me—the Savior died. Now my confidence was strengthened that the Lord, for Christ's sake, had heard my prayers and pardoned all my sins.[51]

Allen was a convert during a Methodist revival, and he articulates the Jesus-centered spirituality that was so strong among African-American Christians, just as it was strong among white evangelicals. The testimony of an eighty-six-year-old black man gives us another example of the conversion experience:

It happened in the fall of the year. I was not yet converted, and my grandmother would not let me forget what she told me. The last time she woke me up, I dozed back off to sleep and commenced to hearing a voice in my ears ringing! "Thank God, you've been redeemed!" That was 4:00 a.m. I told my grandmother who said to me, "Get up from here and go and tell your uncles and relatives, you been redeemed!" Right away my relatives began rejoicing with me. "Thank God, you've been redeemed![52]

In these two testimonies, two aspects of how persons within the black religious tradition conceived of the conversion experience are clear. (1) An emphasis is placed on the centrality of Jesus Christ and (2) there is importance given to remembering the time and place of the event.[53] An examination of Thurman's view shows a contrast with the dominant view of the black religious tradition.[54]

Thurman's View of Conversion

Although Thurman did not totally reject the teachings of his church, he was clear that his experience of God was different. There are several facts about Thurman's treatment of the subject of conversion that help us to grasp the significance of the events surrounding his application for church membership. First, Thurman did not believe that the experience of conversion was contingent upon the life and teachings of Jesus of Nazareth. Second, Thurman neither implied nor suggested that a radical conversion experience was the centerpiece of his religious life. It is noteworthy that there is no account in his writing of ever having a singular, transformative conversion experience and encounter with God, though he was well aware of the popular conception of the conversion event that was espoused by most black Christians. His most thorough discussion of the conversion experience is given in the text *Disciplines of the Spirit*. In that text he described two models of conversion: instantaneous (radical) and gradual (progressive).

Instantaneous Conversion

In *Disciplines of the Spirit*, Thurman discussed conversion in the context of his treatment of the meaning of commitment. He suggested that the goal of commitment to God is the complete surrender of the "very nerve center of one's consent."[55] It is to be able to say "yes" to God with one's entire being, which is possible for all human beings to do, according to Thurman. Instantaneous conversion entails a direct encounter with God. In discussing the biblical view of conversion, Thurman used the ancient song of the black religious tradition:

> My feet looked new,
> My hands looked new,
> The world looked new,
> When I came out the wilderness,
> Leaning on the Lord.[56]

This song suggests that a sudden, radical transformation of the individual took place during the instantaneous conversion encounter with God. Thurman also referred to Paul's Damascus Road experience as a further demonstration of his conception of the instantaneous conversion process. Thurman believed this model of conversion to be consistent with the majority of persons in the Christian tradition. Instantaneous conversion was what the people in church testified about and celebrated. Thurman's conversion experience, however, was gradual and related to his experiences within and outside of the church.

Gradual Conversion

Despite his awareness of the instantaneous, radical view of conversion, Thurman described his personal experience of God in gradualist terms. This sense of surrender to God is less dramatic and sudden than the radical view, but it is equally as complete and transformative. As Thurman said:

> The yielding of the center of consent may be a silent, slow development in the life. The transformation may be so gradual that it passes unnoticed until, one day, everything is seen as different. Somewhere along the road a turn has been taken, a turn so simply a part of the landscape that it did not seem like a change in direction at all.[57]

This is not to deny the positive change taking place within the individual. "A person will notice some things that used to be difficult are now easier; some that seemed all right are no longer possible." This is the case because "There has been a slow invasion of the Spirit of God that marked no place or time."[58] The "invasion" of the Spirit into the human life is the primary focus of Thurman's view of conversion. This "invasion" may indeed be the result of a slow in-coming, but it is an

invasion nonetheless. This is what happens when one experiences a
gradual conversion; there is the sense of one having grown into a
consciousness of God, it is a matter of progressive reorientation of
one's life. Thurman's gradualist view of the conversion experience
and his perception of God emerged from an experience of nature and
the world around him:

> All through my early years I was in subtle and inarticulate conflict
> with what seemed to me to be germane to the religious experience of
> the Christian and what was only a part of the Christian culture or the
> Christian etiquette, of our community.[59]

He was dissatisfied with his church's narrow conception of religious
experience and the conversion event.

Thurman identified three primary ways that persons may encounter
God. One may encounter God directly in an immediate religious
experience; one may meet God through other people; or one may
encounter God through nature.[60] Thurman's religious convictions and
perspectives emerged over a long period of time and developed as he
interacted with the world around him in his native Florida. He expressed
his sense of the presence of God in the following way:

> When I was young, I found more companionship in nature than I did
> among people. The woods befriended me. In the long summer days,
> most of my time was divided between fishing in the Halifax River
> and exploring the woods, where I picked huckleberries and gathered
> orange blossoms from abandoned orange groves. The quiet, even
> the danger, of the woods provided my rather lonely spirit with a
> sense of belonging that did not depend on human relationships. I
> was usually with a group of boys as we explored the woods, but I
> tended to wander away to be alone for a time, for in that way I could
> sense the strength of the quiet and the aliveness of the woods.[61]

During these experiences, Thurman said, he could feel and sense the
very "breath of God." God was both the giver of and a part of this
world, by which Thurman was so fascinated. Thurman was herein
beginning a quest that predisposed him to what he would, later in life,
discover in the mystical religious tradition. He was convinced about
the unity of all things:

> I had the sense that all things—the sand, the sea, the stars, the night,
> and I—were one vine through which all of life was breathing. I saw

the experience as being in itself religious, and even more definitely as being mystical.[62]

His interpretation of these experiences is of great concern to us here. The mystical language and concepts were developed and appropriated later in life, but the foundation of Thurman's religious vision was forged by the religious experiences that we have described. Thurman's experience of God, then, followed the gradual model of conversion.

The gradual conversion experience is not necessarily prompted by a single event. It can be prompted by a variety of things and acts which take place over a period of time. One may be moved by a passage in a text, a piece of poetry, a moment of meditation, a song, a passage of Scripture, or an experience with nature. Thurman argued that it is important to know the source of an individual's experience of God. The key factor was the quality of the person's commitment to God.

Noticeably absent in his remarks regarding this conversion practice, however, are any references to the role of Jesus of Nazareth. For Thurman, Jesus' life and teachings are very important to human beings because they provide an example of what it means to completely surrender one's life to God. The soteriological significance of the life and teachings of Jesus of Nazareth emerged from his example. Jesus was the embodiment of religion at its best. This is why his life is so important to human beings. Jesus demonstrates the all encompassing power of religious experience. In this sense Thurman could posit that Jesus of Nazareth was a model of true conversion. He was totally surrendered to God. But to Thurman, Jesus was neither the source nor the mediator of the conversion experience. According to Thurman, the work of Jesus is to direct human beings to God. Jesus makes human beings aware of the central importance of religious experiences, but Jesus does not mediate this experience.[63]

Thurman's religious experiences were understood and explained—from the earliest periods in his life—in God-centered, as opposed to Christ-centered, terms. A perfect example of this is found in his Statement of Purpose of the Church for the Fellowship of All Peoples:

> The CFAP is a creative venture in interracial, inter-cultural, and interdenominational communion. In faith and genius it is Christian. While it derives its inspiration primarily from the source of Hebrew Christian thought and life, it affirms the validity of spiritual insight wherever found and seeks to recognize, understand, and appreciate every aspect of truth whatever the channel through which it comes . . .

It recognizes and affirms that the God of Life and the God of Religion are one and the same, and that the normal relationship of people as children of God and Father, is one of understanding, confidence, and fellowship.[64]

This is a God-centered statement, which is in keeping with Thurman's vision of religion, which is to be juxtaposed with other approaches which are Christ-centered. This should be kept in mind as we discuss how Thurman's rejection as a candidate for church membership helped to shape his conception of the life and teachings of Jesus. This rejection coupled with the events surrounding the death of Saul Thurman shaped Thurman's resistance to the exclusive faith claims of his church leaders. He rejected the rigid distinction between Christians and non-Christians (those "in Christ" and "out of Christ"), as was made by the deacons of Mt. Bethel and Rev. Cromarte. Thurman never explained his religious experiences in Christocentric terms. Although the full maturation of his perspectives on Jesus were developed over a long period of time, the events at Mt. Bethel did influence his Christology.[65] Nancy Ambrose's influence also provides an essential link in the development of Thurman's understanding of religion and the meaning of the life, ministry, and teachings of Jesus.

Nancy Ambrose

Nancy Ambrose, Thurman's maternal grandmother, was instrumental in shaping the piety and the religious perspective of her grandson. Her influence is especially evident in his interpretation of the life, teachings, and religion of Jesus. Ambrose could neither read nor write, so she left no written documentation of her beliefs. The only indications we have of her beliefs are those indicated in Thurman's writings. The difficulty here results from Thurman's tendency to reinterpret the experiences, beliefs, and ideas of others in light of his own experiences. We currently have no way to determine the degree to which the views that Thurman attributes to Ambrose were shaped by his own opinions. For example, a close parallel exists between Thurman's view of the life and ministry of Jesus and Ambrose's view of the subject.[66]

Ambrose's influence began early in Thurman's life. She and, to a lesser degree, Thurman's mother, Alice Thurman, tutored him in basic matters of religious devotion. Ambrose's impact upon Thurman's thought can be clearly seen in two specific areas. First, Ambrose taught her grandson that an affirmation of the ideal of freedom was a central element in any religious tradition.[67] And second, she taught him that Jesus of Nazareth should not be viewed as an object of religious devotion. Instead, she argued that Christians should seek to follow the religious and ethical example of Jesus.

Nancy Ambrose was born a slave in Florida in the 1850s. Her parents were of black and Seminole Indian heritage. Ambrose played a primary role in the rearing and nurturing of her daughter Alice's three children. In fact, Ambrose was given the sole responsiblity for rearing Howard, despite the fact that Alice remarried twice. Howard was especially dependent upon her as a source of moral support, inspiration, information, and direction. Ambrose instilled her grandchildren with a sense of dignity and industry. Her encouragement helped to motivate and give direction to her grandchildren. A recollection of several episodes of her interactions with Howard will illustrate this point.

Ambrose instilled within Howard a love for education and a thirst for knowledge. She said that "Your only chance is to get an education. The white man will destroy you if you don't."[68] She made sure that he never missed school, and she forced him to take adequate time for study. It was she who made the arrangements for him to become the first black boy from Daytona to receive a high school diploma. After he graduated from high school, she made sure that he pursued a college education, and insisted that education was the only method through which he could escape southern oppression.

Moreover, Ambrose helped to foster Thurman's interest in the plight of black slaves—and especially their religion—as she occasionally reflected upon her experiences as a slave. There was one story that she related to him that lingered long in the mind of the young lad. It seems her master rarely allowed a slave preacher to visit her plantation to preach to the slaves; he feared the preacher would incite a riot among his slaves. So they were mostly forced to listen to the otherworldly, slave-making sermons of white preachers, many of whom were slave owners. These sermons were punctuated with the admonishment of the slaves to obey their masters. When slave preachers were allowed to preach to fellow slaves—an event which happened maybe once or twice per year— the slave preachers would proclaim, "You are not niggers! You are not slaves! You are God's children!''[69]

Some black preachers seemed to intuitively know, despite being illiterate and untutored, that the God of the Bible was a God of freedom, and God was not going to allow God's people to suffer and live in bondage forever. The slave preachers were often the only source of hope that black slaves could expect. Though their homiletical tools were limited in most cases to a bellowing voice, a prophetic imagination, and the indomitable text of the Bible, they painted a picture of freedom that the slaves could grasp. Ambrose, like other black slaves, was greatly encouraged by the slave preachers.

Most white preachers, on the other hand, encouraged black slaves to accept their plight. These ministers often quoted Pauline passages in support of their position: "Servants, obey in all things your masters according to the flesh; not with eye service, as men pleasers; but in singleness of heart, fearing God" (Colossians 3:22). As one former slave put it:

> The first commandment impressed upon our minds was to obey our masters, and the second was like unto it, namely, to do as much work when they or the overseers were not watching us as when they were.[70]

But most slaves knew that this was a bogus message; they knew that they were created to be free by a God of freedom. They knew that whites committed a gross misapplication of the Bible.[71] While white preachers often spoke about obedience to the oppressors, black preachers talked about freedom, human dignity, and liberation.

Ambrose's experience with the white preachers' presentation of the gospel, as they interpreted the Pauline Epistles, caused her to develop a radically anti-Pauline stance. Many black slaves, as did Ambrose, developed a passionate dislike for anyone or anything that made them feel that their status as slaves was inevitable.[72] They maintained a hermeneutic of freedom, which said that only that which seeks to express and enhance their legitimate quest for freedom was worthy of their commitment. They believed that there had to be a "Bible in the Bible,"[73] for the message that their masters taught was not the message in which they believed. This practice of appropriating scriptures that addressed and enhanced their quest for freedom, as seen in the religion of black slaves, was a dominant factor in the shaping of Ambrose's faith perspective.

Since Ambrose was an illiterate woman, it was her custom to have her grandchildren read to her, a task that Howard enjoyed. She loved the great stories of the Old Testament, but her favorite passages were found in the Gospels. She was intrigued by the life of Jesus. According to her, he was the most important person in the Bible. Thurman also recalled that Ambrose only allowed him to read one passage from the entire Pauline corpus, I Corinthians 13.[74] Her personal dissatisfaction with Paul was passed on to her grandson, and this dissatisfaction is later reflected in his Christology.

Ambrose believed and taught her family that the most important aspects of any religious tradition were its ethical claims. She argued that the quality of one's faith in God has to be measured in relation to how it influences one's relationships with other human beings. Religion, as she envisioned it, should always enhance the lives of people who are powerless. Religion, at its best, compels people to love, and to break down barriers between each other. As for Thurman, he posited that there are three primary things that religion does for human beings. First, it is a basis for integrated action. Second, it inspires persons to surrender their lives. Third, religion provides a sense of wholeness.[75] The guiding norms of Ambrose's faith were freedom and inclusivity. [76] These were the motivating factors in her decision to challenge the decisions of the deacons of Mt. Bethel Church regarding the funeral of Saul Thurman and Howard Thurman's candidacy for church membership. In both cases the deacons, according to Ambrose, had betrayed the freedom and inclusivity norms of genuine religious faith. The deacons attempted to limit rather than enhance the fellowship of the church.

Ambrose's conception of religion and religious norms emerged directly from her understanding of the religion of Jesus. Jesus' life and message embodied ideals of freedom and inclusivity. He was the champion of the poor and the disinherited. He taught people how to love and respect each other. He spent his time with poor people. He healed the sick, fed the hungry, clothed the naked, forgave the sinners, gave sight to the blind, and lived among the outcasts. Jesus could speak to the conditions of the oppressed people of his day because he had compassion upon them. Ambrose loved Jesus, and she attempted to follow his principles. Elizabeth Yates aptly described Ambrose's view of Jesus:

> As God was real to Jesus, so was God real to her. She took time
> often to talk with God, not just telling Him her troubles but listening
> to what He had to say about them. She had not the slightest doubt
> but that He loved her enough to care for her. Her grandson was
> increasingly aware of this relationship, and it had its own effect on
> his life.[77]

Ambrose's understanding of God was forged from her perception of Jesus—the man who cared for poor people, the down-trodden, people who, like her, were trying to make the best of the insanity in their socio-political environment. She believed that Jesus of Nazareth was a friend of the poor, a champion of the cause of the oppressed.

Though Ambrose's understanding of God was forged from her perception of Jesus, she never made Jesus an object of worship. She never prayed to him or saw him as an intercessor of any sort; he was simply our best example of a religious person, one whose life was totally surrendered to God. She would say that Jesus demonstrates the best of human religious and moral capacities. Thurman said that she "felt her way into Jesus," she had a "feeling about Jesus," she grasped the essence of the life and teachings of Jesus. Thurman offered a graphic statement on her piety:

> I learned more, for instance, about the genius of the religion of Jesus from my grandmother than from all the men who taught me . . . Greek and all the rest of it. Because she moved inside the experience and lived out of that kind of center . . . [78]

He elaborated on this point further:

> [Nancy Ambrose] couldn't read her name if it was as big as this chapel. But she had stood inside of Jesus and looked out on the world through his eyes. And she knew by heart what I could never know.[79]

Thurman later described his grandmother's piety in mystical terms though he did not necessarily fully understand it as a child when she taught him about the Bible. Ambrose resisted the popular biblical title for Jesus, "Lord," because it was contrary to her view of Jesus. Thurman said of her, "I was never sure that Jesus was my grandmother's Lord."[80] Mrs. Ambrose's faith was experientially based, as opposed to being rooted in the Christological and Trinitarian dogmas of the Christian tradition. Ambrose clearly did not affirm the doctrine of the divinity of Jesus Christ as the basis of her faith. There was no God/man synthesis in Ambrose's thought. Moreover, Jesus was not an object of worship; rather Jesus was a model of how human beings should live. This was a central point of departure from the Christian tradition in her understanding of Jesus.

Thurman's description of the contrast between the devotional practices of Ambrose and Alice Thurman provides valuable information for our attempt to understand the former's influence on his thought. He described the issue in the following way:

> Fortunately for me, the influence of my mother tutored me in a kind of Christian experience that was less limiting than the teachings of our particular church. It is difficult to make clear precisely what happened to me during those formative years. Very early I distinguished between the demand to surrender my life and thus become a follower of Jesus, on the one hand, and the more prescribed demands of our local church, on the other hand.[81]

Thurman's grandmother and mother instilled within him a passionate love for religious devotion. They differed, however, in terms of their understanding of the object of their religious devotions.

Alice Thurman's piety and belief were more in line with the traditions of her church. She was a dedicated worker and believed strongly in her church. Thurman described her in the following manner:

> My mother loved the church... Yet my mother did not talk about religion very much. She read the Bible constantly but kept her prayer life to herself. I discovered the key to her inner religious life at the weekly prayer meeting . . .The first time I heard her pray aloud in a meeting, I did not even recognize her voice . . . She spread her life out before God, telling him of her anxieties and dreams for me and my sisters, and of her weariness.[82]

Jesus Christ was the object of Alice Thurman's devotions; she believed in him as both Lord and Savior. The same cannot be said of Ambrose. Thurman's reflections emphasize this point:

> . . . [Nancy] had a feeling about Jesus that was a little like my own. Or mine was a little like hers, I don't know how you say it. But, but, as over against my mother. . . my mother had a different faith. Jesus was a friend and her Lord you see. I was never sure that Jesus was my grandmother's Lord. [83]

We can better understand Nancy Ambrose's discontinuity with the faith claims of the black religious tradition by examining certain themes in that tradition.[84]

The sermons, slave songs, testimonies, and life stories of persons within the Christian segment of the black religious tradition were intricately linked to their view of Jesus Christ. They believed that Jesus was God, Emmanuel; his message of liberation was for persons who were oppressed by socio-political, moral, spiritual, and psychological evil. Jesus was a friend of the disinherited. Ambrose, in her clever way of thinking, held to the latter half of this equation. Her piety was definitely Jesus-centered[85] and anchored in his message of love, reconciliation, and justice for the poor. Jesus could talk to her and she to him because they were fellow victims of oppression. This was the line of continuity which Ambrose kept with the slave religious tradition, the source of her religious faith. She fostered her family's belief in the liberating message of Jesus as the key element in the biblical record. She belonged to a long line of black people (like Henry Highland Garnet), who argued that no faith principle that limits the dignity and freedom of individuals is worthy of their acceptance and belief.[86] Nancy Ambrose's model of faith suggests that it is possible to draw strength and insight from Jesus' life and teachings without "worshipping" him, as such.

This focus upon the centrality of the historical Jesus as a participant in the historical struggles of the poor, a comrade of the oppressed, and a model of religious piety became the preeminent theme in Howard Thurman's Christology. Thurman also adhered to Ambrose's rejection of the practice of viewing Jesus Christ as an object of worship. In the next segment of the study, we will look more specifically at how the black religious tradition influenced Thurman's interpretation of the life and teachings of Jesus of Nazareth.

Thurman's Selective Appropriation of African-American Folk Beliefs

Having discussed some of the ways in which black people have expressed their understanding of Jesus of Nazareth, we must further verify our claim that the black religious tradition indeed influenced Thurman's view of the life and teachings of Jesus. This task will be accomplished through an examination of Thurman's interpretation of the religious motifs of the Spirituals. At this juncture I will compare his interpretation of the Spirituals, as found in *Deep River and The Negro Spiritual Speaks of Life and Death*, with what he says about the life and teachings of Jesus, as articulated in *Jesus and The Disinherited*.

Thurman was a student of the Spirituals, having been tutored in them as a child at Mt. Bethel Baptist Church. His words best express the long-term affect that the Spirituals had on his life.

> [T]hese essays [on black Spirituals] are intimate and personal. They lay bare in my hand the gift which these songs, centuries old, are to my own spirit. For me, they are watering places for my own spirit and have enabled me to affirm life when its denial would be more ego satisfying, to honor my own heritage and rejoice in it. [I] was deeply influenced by the genius of the spirituals . . . in my early years.[87]

These words, coupled with what we have been examining in this section, suggest to us that Thurman's interest in the Spirituals was not merely academic or intellectual. The Spirituals were central elements in the shaping of his religious experiences.

Thurman's first formal treatment of the religious and theological insights of the Spirituals was done during his tenure at Morehouse and Spelman Colleges in the academic year 1929-30. He did not, however, offer an extensive written study on the subject until the mid-forties. *Deep River* was published in 1945 and *The Negro Spiritual Speaks of Life and Death* in 1947. Both texts predate his first book-length study of the life and teachings of Jesus, *Jesus and the Disinherited* (1949), the thesis he first developed in 1935 in a lecture at Boston University School of Theology, first published under the title "Good News for the Disinherited," in *Religion in Life* (Summer, 1935). This thesis was also restated as a poem about Jesus in 1944, "The Greatest of These."

The central issue in *Jesus and the Disinherited, Deep River and The Negro Spiritual Speaks of Life and Death* is that religious insights should and do serve as a positive social force in the survival and liberation of oppressed persons. Thurman's definition of religion and religious experience are important here. He defined religious experience—appropriating the definition of Rufus Jones—as "the finding of man by God and the finding of God by man."[88] Religion, Thurman said, emerges from religious experiences. Religion is "religious experience as it has impact on the world."[89] Or, in other words, religious experience is the content of religion, and religion is the form of religious experience. The principal issue that Thurman pointed to is that genuine religious experiences are liberating and powerful. Religious experiences, coupled with the knowledge that emerges from them, make it possible for human beings to transcend the multi-dimensional sources of oppression which afflict them. Thurman actually believed that the test of religious experience "turns on what word it has to share about God with men who are the disinherited, the outsiders, the fringe dwellers removed from the citadels of power and control in the society."[90]

In *Jesus and the Disinherited*, the liberating power of religion is seen in the life, teachings, and religion of Jesus,[91] all of which address the socio-political, religious, and ethical interests of the disinherited. Thurman's study of the Spirituals offers the same insight; the only difference is that he uses the religious life of the slaves as his point of departure and as the example of his view of liberation.

> My own life has been so deeply influenced by the genius of the spirituals that the meaning as distilled into my experience in my early years spills over in much that I have come to think in my maturity. The reader who is acquainted with *Jesus and the Disinherited* or with the Ingersoll lecture on "The Immortality of Man" under the title *The Negro Spiritual Speaks of Life and Death* will recognize at once some of the basic ideas expressed in this volume.[92]

The similarity in emphasis in *Jesus and the Disinherited, Deep River and The Negro Spiritual Speaks of Life and Death* is more than a mere coincidence. Thurman believed that God is the object of all true religious experiences, and that the power of religious experiences is derived from the *self-revealing* power of God, which is made known in the religious experience. God guarantees the authenticity and potency of religious experience. Jesus' religious insights were powerful and meaningful because they were indeed "experiences" of God. God was the only object of Jesus' religious devotion. Jesus' religious experiences—as can be seen in his baptism—demonstrate that he got power from God.

Similarly, Thurman said that God was the object of the slaves' religious devotion. Their experience revealed a power that comes from such experiences. Moreover, he noted that the similarities between the religious experiences of the slaves and the religion of Jesus—just as would be the case with other genuine religious experiences—lie in the object, goal, and reference point: God.[93] A religious experience that does not have an ultimate point of reference beyond the individual is incomplete and limited.[94] Thurman made a similar point in his preface to *Deep River*:

> In what is written here, there is at work the movement of the creative
> spirit of God as it has sought under great odds to tutor my rebellious
> spirit in conflict with some of the tragedies of my social experience.
> I believe, with my forefathers, that this is God's world. This faith
> has had to fight against disillusionment, despair, and the vicissitudes
> of American history.[95]

Thurman believed that the religious insights of the slaves were shaped
against the same socio-political, psychological, and spiritual background
as Jesus' religious insights. Both perspectives emerged from oppressive
socio-economic and political circumstances. Thurman began *Jesus and
the Disinherited* as follows:

> The significance of the religion of Jesus to people who stand with
> their backs against the wall has always seemed to me to be crucial.
> This is the question which individuals and groups who live in our
> land always under the threat of profound social and psychological
> displacement face: Why is it that Christianity seems impotent to deal
> radically, and therefore effectively, with the issues of discrimination
> and injustice on the basis of race, religion and national origin?[96]

The religion of the slaves provided an answer to this need because it
demonstrated what people could do, despite their social situation, when
their faith was based primarily on the life and teachings of Jesus.[97]
Aside from this connection, we can also see a specific correlation
between what Thurman says here and what he says in *Jesus and the
Disinherited* (which contains his interpretation of Jesus) and *Deep River
and The Negro Spiritual Speaks of Life and Death*. We will return to
this theme in Chapter Four.

We have seen that the black religious tradition was the most
influential factor in the shaping of Howard Thurman's view of the life
and teachings of Jesus of Nazareth.[98] This thesis has been based upon
several key facts.

First, two primary experiences (the events surrounding his father's
death and surrounding his own candidacy for church membership) were
central to Thurman's early views on religion and the life and teachings
of Jesus. Second, Thurman inherited his grandmother's distaste for the
Pauline Epistles and the misappropriation of Scripture for the purpose
of oppression. Third, Ambrose also helped him to see that the ethical
and spiritual aspects of the life and teachings of Jesus were the most
important elements in the Bible because through Him, liberation is

possible. In order to know Jesus, one has to "stand within" Jesus—to look out on the world through the eyes of Jesus. Since Jesus is the friend of the oppressed, by "looking out on the world through the eyes of Jesus,"[99] the believer can experience existential freedom from the psycho-spiritual and intellectual sources of human oppression. She/he is thereby given the freedom and strength to address all the socio-economic and political factors that limit human freedom. Fourth, Thurman learned from Nancy Ambrose that Jesus should never be the object of one's religious devotion: he should instead be admired as one who showed us the way to God. Though Jesus was the subject of a tremendous religious experience, his experience was not unique; any other person who surrenders to God in a like manner could feel the same affirmation from God that Jesus felt. Fifth, the black religious tradition, as defined in the slave religious experience, helped to shape Thurman's belief in the idea that a valid religious perspective must address the socio-political and ethical conditions of oppressed people. His treatment of the themes of fear, deception, hate, and love help to demonstrate this point.[100] In Thurman's thought, people are always more important than any creed or dogma; just as his father's memory was more crucial than the church's attitude towards non-members, and conversion was more essential than the deacons' narrow conception of religious experience.[101]

Notes

1   For an excellent discussion of the different sources of Thurman's thought, see Walter Fluker, "A Comparative Analysis of the Ideal of Community in the Thought of Martin Luther King Jr. and Howard Thurman" (Ph.D. dissertation, Boston University, 1988); see also the published version of this dissertation, *They Looked For a City: A Comparative Analysis of the Ideal of Community in the Thought of Howard Thurman and Martin Luther King, Jr.* (Washington, DC..: University Press of America, 1989); Alton B. Pollard, III, "Howard Thurman and the Challenge of Social Regeneration: Transformed, Always Transforming" (Ph.D. dissertation, Duke University, 1987); see his published version of this work, *Mysticism and Social Change: The Witness of Howard Thurman,* Martin Luther King, Jr. Memorial Studies in Religion, Culture, and Social Development, (New York: Peter Lang, 1992); Luther E. Smith, Jr., *Howard Thurman: Mystic as Prophet* (Washington: University Press of America, Inc., 1981).

2   This is not to suggest that black people did not understand Jesus in other ways and with other symbols. We have simply presented one of the more important themes.

3   For a discussion of this issue, see Joseph Washington's text, *Black Religion* (Boston: Beacon Press, 1964); James H. Cone, *Black Theology and Black Power* (New York: Seabury Press, 1969). Cone continues the process of using the black religious tradition as a source for his theological reflections in *A Black Theology of Liberation* (Philadelphia: Lippincott Co., 1970) and *God of the Oppressed* (New York: Seabury Press, 1975).

4   More will be said on this issue below.

5   I think here of works such as: Luther E. Smith's *Howard Thurman: The Mystic as Prophet*; Walter E. Fluker's *They Looked For a City*; Pollard's *Mysticism and Social Change;* Mozella G. Mitchell's texts, *Spiritual Dynamics of Howard Thurman's Theology* (Bristol, IN.: Wyndham Hall Press, 1985) and *The Human Search: Howard Thurman and the Quest for Freedom*, Martin Luther King, Jr. Memorial Studies in Religion, Culture and Social Development (New York: Peter Lang, 1992); Carlyle Felding Stewart III's *God, Being and Liberation* (Washington, D.C.: University of America Press, 1989).

6   The experience of the Thurman family in Florida was only one facet of the black experience of suffering in America.

7   An exception to this would be the short stay that Thurman had in Washington, DC. during the Summer of 1918. He attended a Student Army Training Corps Camp at Howard University during that Summer. He also spent one half of the Summer of 1921 in Cleveland, Ohio and the other half at Columbia University, New York. Howard Thurman, *With Head and Heart* (New York: Harcourt Brace & Jovanovich, 1979), pp. 33, 43.

8   Although it is true that the trip to India in 1936 had a profound affect on Thurman's theological vision, his reflections on the liberating significance of the life and teachings of Jesus began before that time. The thesis of *Jesus and the Disinherited* was developed during a lecture at the School of Theology of Boston University in 1935. In the final section of this study we will note why Thurman's conception of Jesus should not be traced back to the liberal theological tradition. Ibid., p. 46.

9   Thurman, *With Head and Heart* (New York: Harcourt Brace Jovanovich, 1979), p. 9.

10 Ibid., p. 10.

11 Howard Thurman, *The Luminous Darkness: A Personal Interpretation of the Anatomy of Segregation and the Ground of Hope* (New York: Harper & Row, 1965), p. 3.

12 More will be said on this issue below.

13 Howard Thurman, *The Luminous Darkness*, p. 45.

14 Ibid., p.. 46.

15 Ibid., p. 51.

16 The terms disinherited, dispossessed, outcast, and oppressed, are used in a socio-political and economic sense. They refer specifically to persons who are victims of unjust socio-political arrangements. This understanding of the terms is consistent with Thurman's use of them.

17 Howard Thurman, *Jesus and the Disinherited* (Nashville: Abingdon-Cokesbury Press, 1949; reprint ed., Richmond, In.: Friends United Press, 1981), p. 7.; Howard Thurman, *The Luminous Darkness: A Personal Interpretation of the Anatomy of Segregation and the Ground of Hope* (New York: Harper & Row, 1965), p. 3. See his discussion of racism and the church in *Footprints of a Dream: The Story of Church for the Fellowship of All Peoples* (New York: Harper & Row, 1959). Also see Dennis W. Wiley, "The Concept of the Church in the Works of Howard Thurman" (Ph.D. dissertation, Union Theological Seminary, 1988), Chapter 2.

18 For a thorough discussion of these issues see Robert G. Torbet's *A History of the Baptists*, 3rd ed. (Valley Forge: Judson Press, 1963), note especially chapter XVIII.

19 Thurman, *With Head and Heart,* p. 9.

20 "Transcript of Howard Thurman Documentary," January 8 & 9, 1976, interviewer: Landrum Bolling, prepared on January 22, 1976, p. 10. The film script and the transcription are housed at the Mugar Library, Boston University, Boston, MA.

21 See, Wiley, "The Concept of Church in the Works of Howard Thurman."

22 Thurman did not grasp the full theological significance of the event at that early stage in his life. But the event did cause him to resist interpretations of the gospel which seemed to have a harsh attitude towards persons who did not adhere to a particular view of the biblical message.

23 Dennis W. Wiley calls this an example of the religious experiences of non-church persons, see his "Church," p. 40; see also Thurman, *With Head and Heart*, p. 5.

24 Thurman, *With Head and Heart*,p. 6.

25 Ibid.

26 For a discussion of this issue, see Van A. Harvey, *A Handbook of Theological Terms* (New York: Macmillan Publishing Co., Inc.), pp. 135-36; Karl Rahner and Herbert Vorgrimler, *Dictionary of Theology* (New York: Crossroad, 1981), pp. 260-61. 32 Thurman, *Footprints of a Dream*, pp. 17-18.

27 Thurman, *Footprints of a Dream,* pp. 17-18.

28 "Transcript of Howard Thurman Documentary," January 8 & 9, 1976, interviewer: Landrum Bolling, prepared on January 22, 1976, p. 10.

29 "Transcript of Howard Thurman Documentary," January 8 & 9, 1976, interviewer: Landrum Bolling, prepared on January 22, 1976, p. 10.

30 We must look beyond the event and examine other areas of Thurman's thought if we are to grasp the full significance of this event.

31 Thurman, *With Head and Heart,* p. 18.

32 Ibid. The author is solely responsible for this emphasis. This idea of requiring youngsters and adults to testify about their religious convictions has roots in the American evangelical tradition. It was popularized by nineteenth century revivalists, and it was a part of the black religious tradition. Albert J. Raboteau, *Slave Religion.* p. 266f. See also, Charles G. Finney, *Revivals of Religion. The Christian Classics*; (Virginia Beach: CBN University Press, 1978), Lecture XIV.

33 Thurman, *With Head and Heart,* p. 18.

34 Joseph Washington, Jr., "Folk Religion and Negro Congregations: The Fifth Religion," in Gayraud S. Wilmore, ed. *African American Religious Studies* (Durham, NC: Duke University Press, 1989), p. 50.

35 Joseph Washington, Jr., *Black Religion.*

36 James H. Cone, *My Soul Looks Back* (Maryknoll, NY: Orbis Books, 1984), pp. 8f.

37 See for example Kofi Appiah-Kubi and Sergio Torres, editors, *African Theology en Route* (Maryknoll, N.Y.: Orbis Books, 1979). Note the chapter by Appiah-Kubi.

38 Eugene Genovese, *Roll, Jordan, Roll: The World the Slaves Made* (New York: Vintage Books, 1976), p. 209.

39 Henry Mitchell, *Black Preaching* (San Francisco: Harper & Row, Publishers, 1970), 29.

40 See W. E. B. Du Bois *The Gift of Black Folk* (New York: John Reprint Corp., 1924, 1968).

41 For more discussion of this subject, see Alonzo Johnson and Paul Jersild, *Ain't Gonna Lay My 'Ligion Down: African American Religion in the South* (Columbia, S.C.: The University of South Carolina Press, 1996).

42 Charles Joyner, *Down by the Riverside* (Urbana: University of Illinois Press, 1984). There are many current studies that are focused on the aspects of the black folk religious heritage. We note, for example, Riggins Earl, *Dark Symbols, Obscure Signs* (Maryknoll, N.Y.: Orbis Books, 1993); Dwight N. Hopkins, *Shoes that Fit Our Feet* (Maryknoll, N.Y.: Orbis Books, 1993); Theopholis Smith, *Conjuring Culture* (New York: Oxford University Press, 1994; Emilie M. Townes, *A Troublin in My Soul* (Maryknoll, N.Y.: Orbis Books, 1993); Delores Williams, *Sisters in the Wilderness* (Maryknoll, N.Y.: Orbis Books, 1993). Other relevant texts would include Walter F. Pitts, Jr., *Old Ship of Zion* (New York: Oxford University Press, 1993); Peter Goldsmith, *When I Rise Crying Holy* (New York: AMS Press, Inc., 1989).

43 For a thorough discussion of this issue see my chapter, Chapter One, in Alonzo Johnson & Paul Jersild, eds. *Ain't Gonna Lay My 'Ligion Down."*

44 See Margaret Washington Creel's *A Peculiar People: Slave Religion and Community Culture Among the Gullahs* (New York: New York University Press, 1988), note particularly chapter nine.

45 William Mcloughlin provides an excellent survey of this subject. See his *Modern Revivalism: Charles Grandison Finney to Billy Graham* (New York: The Roland Press Company, 1959).

46 This claim can be verified by examining the testimonies, songs, sermons, and theological statements of blacks Christians and religious organizations. African-American womanist theologians such as Kelly Brown-Douglass and Jacquelyn Grant have accented the centrality of the person and work of Jesus of Nazareth in the religious reflections of African-American Christians in general and especially women. See, for example, Brown-Douglas' *The Black Christ* (Maryknoll, NY: Orbis Books, 1994) and Grant's *White Women's Christ, Black Women's Jesus* (Atlanta: Scholars Press, 1988). Both emphasize that African-American faith is "Jesus-centered", as strong emphasis is placed upon Him as a source of power, salvation, and deliverance.

47 More will be said about this below as we discuss the variety of ways that blacks have understood their conversion experiences. See footnote 44.

48 James H. Cone, *The Spirituals and the Blues: An Interpretation* (New York: The Seabury Press, 1972), p. 47. Thurman, *Deep River & The Negro Spirituals Speak of Life and Death* (Richmond, IN: Friends United Press, 1977), p. 126.

49 Harold Carter, *The Prayer Tradition of Black People* (Valley Forge: Judson Press, 1976), p. 36, 47.

50 In the black religious tradition the humanity and divinity of Jesus have been held in creative tension. What is said about the humanity of Jesus presupposes the divinity of Jesus. Also when blacks, particularly in the slave religious tradition, speak of the divinity of Jesus they presuppose that he was the fully human person who lived and was crucified in first

century Palestine. James H. Cone has made this point forcefully in his *Liberation*, Chapter 6, and *God of the Oppressed*, Chapter 6. See also J. DeOtis Roberts, *A Black Political Theology*. Philadelphia: Westminster Press, 1974) Chapter 5.

51 Richard Allen, *The Life and Gospel Labors of the Right Reverend Richard Allen* (Philadelphia: F. Ford and M.A. Ripley, 1880), p. 5.

52 Quoted in Harold Carter, *The Prayer Tradition of Black People* , p. 36. For an excellent study of the variety of black conversion experiences see Clifton F. Johnson, ed., *God Struck Me Dead* (Boston: Pilgrim Press, 1969). See also Albert J. Raboteau, *Slave Religion: The Invisible Institution in the Ante-bellum South* (New York: Oxford University Press, 1978), p. 266f. See also the very fascinating account of black slaves' view of their master being converted in Norman R. Yetman, ed., *Life Under the Peculiar Institution* (New York: Holt, Rinehart and Winston Inc. 1970), p. 215.

53 What is said here does not implicitly suggest that there are no other ways of expressing this event in the black religious tradition. The themes that we have examined have been used because of their support of the thesis of this study.

54 See Wiley, "Church," chapter 2, for an excellent discussion of Thurman's views of Jesus' religious experiences. Mozella Mitchell's dissertation, which has been published, offers the most thorough assessment of Thurman's view of conversion. See "The Dynamics of Howard Thurman's Relationship to Literature and Theology" (Ph.D. dissertation, Emory University, 1980). See chapter 1 of the published version of this study, *Spiritual Dynamics of a Howard Thurman's Theology* (Bristol, IN.: Wyndham Hall Press, 1985).

55 Howard Thurman, *The Creative Encounter* (New York: Harper & Row, 1954; reprint Richmond, In.: Friends United Press, 1972), p. 73.

56 Howard Thurman, *Disciplines of the Spirit* (New York: Harper & Row, 1963; Richmond, In.: Friends United Press, 1977),p. 24.

57 Ibid., p. 2.

58 As quoted in Mitchell, *Spiritual Dynamics of Howard Thurman's Theology*, Chapter 1.

59 Thurman, *Footprints of a Dream*, p. 18.

60 See *The Creative Encounter* for his most thorough discussion of this issue.

61 For a discussion of the development of his mystical consciousness see Thurman, *With Head and Heart*, p. 7; see also the lectures, "Mysticism and Social Action."

62 Thurman, "Mysticism and Social Action," 13 October 1978, The Lawrence Lectures on Religion and Society, First Unitarian Church of Berkeley, CA., p. 3.

63 Howard Thurman, "Mysticism and Social Action."

64 Howard Thurman, "The Church for the Fellowship of All Peoples," Howard Thurman Archives, Mugar Library, Boston University.

65 The spirit of Rev. Cromarte's eulogy of Saul Thurman, coupled with the Mt. Bethel deacons' rejection of Howard's candidacy for membership, reflected a rejection of the religion of Jesus.

66 In this study, at any rate, we accept Thurman's statements about Ambrose at face value. More will be said about this issue in the next chapter as we study Thurman's method of biblical interpretation.

67 In this section we will discuss the subject of Ambrose's continuity and discontinuity within the black religious tradition.

68 Elizabeth Yates, *Howard Thurman: Portrait of a Practical Dreamer* (New York: The John Day Co., 1964), p. 23.

69 Thurman, *With Head and Heart*, p. 21.

70 William Lerone Katz, ed., *Five Slave Narratives* (New York: Arno Press and the New York Times, 1969), p. 21.

71 Thurman, *Jesus and the Disinherited*, pp. 29-39.

72 Katz, *Five Slave Narratives*, p. 20.

73 Raboteau, *Slave Religion*, p. 293.

74 Ambrose's approach to Paul, given the circumstances under which her view evolved, is certainly understandable, even if it does not reflect full wisdom of Pauline literature on this subject.

75 See Thurman's "The Church, the State and Human Welfare".

76 Here the terms faith and religion are being used synonymously; both refer to particular patterns of belief and practices. Paper presented at the 34th Annual Convocation of the School of Religion, Howard University (Washington, DC., 14 November 1950.)

77 Yates, *Howard Thurman: Portrait of a Practical Dreamer*, p. 23.

78 As quoted in Smith, *Howard Thurman: The Mystic as Prophet*, p. 33.

79 Ibid.

80 Bolling, "Documentary," p.39. This issue will be discussed more below.

81 Bolling, "Documentary," pp. 38-39.

82 Thurman, *With Head and Heart*, p. 16.

83 Bolling, "Documentary," p. 39.

84 See the discussion of this issue below.

85 We label her faith as Jesus-centered because she believed so strongly in the centrality of the life and teachings of Jesus.

86 A liberationist biblical hermeneutic has always been part of the black religious tradition as blacks have been selective in their appropriation of Scripture as a source of strength in the their socio-political struggles. They would go to the boarders of agnosticism before espousing a faith that did not seek to perpetuate their freedom. See Wilmore, *Radicalism*, Chapter 3.

87 Thurman, *Deep River*, pp. 6, 13.

88 Howard Thurman, *The Creative Encounter* (New York: Harper & Row, 1954; reprint, Richmond, In.: Friends United Press, 1972), p. 39.

89 See Ibid., and Thurman's "The Church, The State and Human Welfare," n.p., 1950 November 14-16; see also his reference in "Mysticism and Social Change," *Eden Theological Seminary Bulletin* (Spring 1939).

90 Howard Thurman, Introduction to *Why I Believe There Is A God: Sixteen Essays by Negro Clergymen* (Chicago: Johnson Publishing Company, Inc., 1965), p. xi.

91 See my discussion of this in Chapter Four.

92 Thurman, *Deep River and The Negro Spiritual Speaks of Life and Death*, p. 13.

93 The idea that God is the primary factor in all true religious experiences goes hand in hand with the belief, as Thurman suggested, that all truly religious experiences must aid in the human quest for freedom and community.

94 This idea emerges directly from Thurman's belief in the Universality of God.

95 Thurman, *Deep River and The Negro Spiritual Speaks of Life and Death*, p. 13.

96 Thurman, *Jesus and the Disinherited*, p. 7.

97 Please note what is said earlier about the implicit Christology of the black religious tradition.

98 Luther Smith has provided a thoughtful examination of the question of how the liberal and mystical theological traditions affected Thurman's thought. Among the persons who have made a significant effect upon some areas of Thurman's thought are: Rufus Jones (the Quaker mystic); George Cross; Henry Robins; and Conrad Moehlman. See the following studies for interpretations of the intellectual sources of Thurman's thought: Pollard provides a helpful interpretation of Thurman's mysticism. On social issues, Smith provides the most comprehensive study of Thurman's thought; see his *Howard Thurman: The Mystic as Prophet*. Carlyle Felding Stewart III offers the best analysis of Thurman's view of liberation; see his "A Comparative Analysis of Ontology and Ethical Method in the Theologies of James H. Cone and Howard Thurman" (Ph.D. dissertation, Northwestern University, 1982). This issue will be discussed further in the following chapters.

99 Thurman, "Standing Inside with Christ," a lecture given at Bishop College: Lacey Kirk Institute April 21, 1970).

100 Thurman, *The Growing Edge* (New York: Harper & Row Publishers, 1951; reprint Richmond, In.: Friends United Press, 1981), p. 97.

101 In no way is what we have said in this chapter designed to minimize the originality of Thurman's theological contribution. We have simply attempted to note some of the influences upon his thought. The final shape and form of his views, however, result from his own creativity and genius.

Chapter II

Jesus of Nazareth: Towards a Definition of Humanity

Despite all the merit that there is in the scholarly and reverential researches into the facts concerning the historical Jesus, they do not, nor can they, explain him adequately. Spiritual genius, or any kind of genius for that matter, cannot ever be explained in any complete sense.

—Howard Thurman

Howard Thurman was a practical theologian with a very pragmatic theological vision. He was interested in all aspects of the religious life, particularly the ethical, the spiritual, the doctrinal, and the socio-political dimensions. However, as a mystic, he was intensely concerned about exploring the direct connection between personal religious experiences and the socio-political world in which people live and work. The true test of the meaning of Christian and religious experience, he would say, rests upon the relevance of its message to those people who "live with their backs against the walls of life." For Thurman, "religious truth," "power," "genius," and "doctrine" were central tools for the promotion of social wholeness. This practical vision has direct implications for what Thurman said about the life and work of Jesus.

This chapter will focus specifically on Thurman's claims about the humanity of Jesus, beginning with what it means to say that Jesus was a true human being. We will begin with a discussion of how the issue of Jesus' humanity has been dealt with in the history of the Christian church.

Defining the Parameters of Christological Discussions in the History of the Christian Church

In the history of the Christian church, Christological doctrines have defined Jesus' humanity and divinity. There are two major approaches to the subject of Christology which are dominant in the tradition. These two are commonly referred to as "high Christology" and "low Christology," or "Christology from above" and "Christology from below." Richard A. Norris writes that these approaches attempt to do two things:

> . . . on the one hand, to ask about [Jesus'] relation to God and, on the other, to seek a way of expressing his representative character as a human being—his status as the one in whom humanities' common destiny is both summed up and determined.[1]

High Christologies argue, with some variation, that Jesus' divine nature—his god-likeness—is the criterion for understanding the meaning of his humanity. They argue that Jesus was essentially God, and as such, he was different from other human beings because of his "nature." He was distinguished from other human beings because he was the God-man, God in the flesh, God incarnate. Clearly, high Christologies give priority to Jesus' divine nature, in seeking to determine who he was. Thus in describing the life and work of Jesus they most often begin with a discussion of his pre-existence, virgin birth, and incarnation. In high Christologies, what is said of Jesus' human nature is subordinate to claims about his divine nature.

By contrast, low Christologies, or Christologies from below, contend that Jesus was human in every sense of the term, only to be distinguished from other human beings by the quality of his religious experience. Low Christologies place most emphasis on Jesus' human intellect, personality, consciousness, will, and experiences as the categories within which to speak of his divinity.[2]

The common bond between the high and low Christologies is their mutual concern for human salvation, or soteriology. This is to say that they mean to demonstrate how Jesus' life, teaching, death, and resurrection brought salvation to human beings.[3] From the beginning of Christian history, soteriological questions have shaped what the church has said about who Jesus was and his significance to the human family. Soteriological questions have always taken precedence over abstract questions about the two natures (divine and human) of Jesus, his pre-existence, or his virgin birth. For example, among the four gospels, only Luke and Matthew contain narratives describing Jesus' infancy. But all of the gospels and epistles of the New Testament exhibit a strong soteriological concern.

In the epistles and gospels we see the soteriological emphasis as writers proclaimed Jesus Christ as the Savior of the world.[4] In the New Testament, Jesus is declared to be the mediator between God and humanity, God's answer to all human questions and problems.[5] No one proclaims this message more forcefully than Paul: "For I am not ashamed of the gospel: it is the power of God for salvation to every one who has faith, to the Jew first and also to the Greek" (Romans 1:16, RSV). The "gospel" was the proclaimed good news about Jesus, the Christ, the one who brought salvation to all human beings. The primary concern for Paul, as for other biblical writers, was to "know Him and to make Him known" as the Savior of the world. This focus was maintained in the early church as her leaders fought heresies and attempted to save the church from lapsing into chaos. Some of the earliest controversies within the early church centered on Christological questions, as the church attempted to clarify and expand its message about Jesus.

The Nicene Controversy of the fourth century is a graphic demonstration of this fact. The principal positions in this controversy were represented by two individuals, Athanasius and Arius. While their conclusions differed, both Athanasius and Arius were principally concerned about explaining how and why Jesus was the savior of the world. Athanasius stated:

> He, Jesus, became man so that we might be made God; and he manifested himself in the flesh, so that we might grasp the idea of the unseen Father; and he endured the insolence of men, so that we might receive the inheritance of immortality.[6]

The emphasis here is on what Jesus made possible for human beings. He "became" human in order that human beings might "be made God." This is a soteriological issue. (We will return to this theme below.)

The soteriological and Christological issues that I have noted here are closely akin to the structure and content of Thurman's Christology. This is particularly true of what he wrote in *Jesus and the Disinherited.* First and foremost Thurman wanted to demonstrate how the historical Jesus helped to bring deliverance and salvation to those persons who "lived with their backs against the wall." This concern for the relevancy of gospel to the conditions of oppressed people was always a perennial issue for Thurman. This practical concern always took precedent over abstract questions about doctrine and theology. Dealing with the subject of Jesus' humanity and divinity in isolation from discussions of the plight of the poor and the oppressed would have been an effort in futility for Thurman. Soteriological matters—dealing with human salvation—took precedence for Thurman over other types of theological questions divorced from matters of socio-communal relevance.

Such is the case with Thurman's approach to the study of the life, teachings, and work of Jesus. Questions about the two natures of Jesus, his miracles, his death and resurrection were all sublimated to Thurman's primary concern about Jesus' relevance to the oppressed. So Thurman's was a low Christology at best. Thurman's low Christological focus inevitably leads us back to the point of identifying Thurman with a particular tradition of Christian theological reflections. The one which comes closest in this regard is the "quest of the historical Jesus," with which Thurman's Christology is so closely linked, at least in terms of emphasis.

The Quest of the Historical Jesus

Thurman's discussions about the relevancy of Jesus' life, teachings, and message to the conditions of the oppressed rely heavily on his own understanding of the accuracy and significance of historical data presented in the four gospels. Thurman clearly believed that there is enough data there to reconstruct an accurate picture of who Jesus was and what he did. This is not to say that Thurman was a biblical literalist— far from it; but he believed in the possibility of constructing an adequate story of Jesus. The gospel of Mark was Thurman's favorite among the four gospels. He preferred its style, its theology, and its message, and he gave it priority because it is commonly regarded as the oldest of the four gospels. Mark, Thurman believed, helped to present the most realistic picture of Jesus, giving us a full picture of his life and his interaction with his environment.

> It is utterly fantastic to assume that Jesus grew to manhood untouched by the surging currents of the common life that made up the climate of Palestine. Not only must he have been aware of them; that he was affected by them is a most natural observation.[7]

The power of Jesus' ideas can only be understood and appreciated when viewed in context. Jesus' teachings "were directed to the House of Israel, which was . . . haunted by the dream of restoration of a lost glory and a former greatness."[8] The historical context of the first century gives credibility to Jesus' claims regarding the oppressed.[9]

One gains a greater appreciation for Thurman's claims when he is placed in dialogue with some of the great liberal theologians of this century on the subject of Christology. This provides a context within which to locate and assess his work.

In 1906 Albert Schweitzer's *The Quest of the Historical Jesus* pronounced the end of the so-called "old quest" of the historical Jesus, a tradition which was dominant in the nineteenth century. The "quest" was in essence a search for the "life of Jesus." It attempted to offer a picture of the life of the historical Jesus which would be understandable to modern minds. Schweitzer plowed through the works of "old questers" such as Hermann Samuel Reimarus, David Friedrich Strauss, and Bruno Bauer. After studying them in great detail, Schweitzer concluded these works offered more information about the values, philosophies, and religious perspectives of their authors than they did about the life and beliefs of Jesus.[10] Moreover, he concluded that the attempt to write a "biography" of Jesus was futile. He stated that the New Testament does not offer enough historical data to make a reconstruction of the life of Jesus possible.

However, Schweitzer was by no means disinterested in the centrality of Jesus as a subject of inquiry; he was a noted New Testament scholar. His focus shifted from the life of Jesus to the centrality of his preaching and message. Following Johannes Weiss, Schweitzer concluded that, contrary to the depictions of the liberal, life-of-Jesus biographers, the historical Jesus was a radical preacher. As a preacher, Jesus' message centered on the immanent and actual in-breaking of the Kingdom of God in history. It proclaimed a radical end to this world order, which he clearly expected to happen in his lifetime and not in the distant future and not merely in a "spiritual" manner. According to Schweitzer, Jesus was almost obsessed with his radical vision and as such died in despair, as this vision was never fulfilled. Schweitzer's work helped to significantly shape the course of research into the life of Jesus, but it also had a sobering impact on the field of New Testament studies in general.

In the wake of Schweitzer's startling findings, New Testament scholars faced the difficult task of finding a way to discuss the significance of the historical material in the New Testament gospels. The old quest of the historical Jesus was over, but the challenge of determining the validity and value of the narrative material in the gospels remained. Schweitzer's mantle in New Testament fell upon the shoulders of his younger contemporary, Rudolph Bultmann. Bultmann, a renowned German biblical scholar, rekindled the debates surrounding the old quest.[11] Bultmann stood in the middle between Schweitzer and the new generation of biblical scholars emerging in the post-World War II period—those who initiated the new quest of the historical Jesus.[12] Like Schweitzer, Bultmann thought it impossible to reconstruct a "life of Jesus" from New Testament sources. And he downplayed the significance of the historical data presented in gospels. In extending Schweitzer's thesis, Bultmann's exegetical program entailed an extensive effort to "demythologize" the New Testament. This process extended Schweitzer's thesis and, taking Schweitzer's project to heart, extended it to its logical conclusion. Thus Bultmann set out on a program of "demythologization" as the basis of his New Testament scholarship. Demythologizing the New Testament was necessary, said Bultmann, precisely because the world-view depicted in Scripture is radically different from the modern scientific world-view.

> Myths speak about gods and demons as powers on which man knows himself to be dependent, powers whose favor he needs, powers whose wrath he fears. Myths express the knowledge that man is not master of the world and of his life, that the world within which he lives is full of riddles and mysteries and that human life also is full of riddles and mysteries.[13]

Demythologizing entailed uncovering the mythological dimensions of Scripture, which color and shape all of the so-called historical data contained therein. The classic reference Bultmann made in demonstrating this point was to the pre-scientific, tripartite view of the universe existing in the New Testament in which the universe was understood as a three-layered structure with earth suspended in space between heaven and hell.

As a result of his form-critical research on the gospels, Bultmann reached the conclusion that we can learn very little, if anything, about the historical Jesus from reading the New Testament. The gospels in particular and the New Testament in general do, however, reveal much about Jesus' preaching. And it is this kerygmatic preaching which should be at the center of the identity of the Christian church. So Bultmann was satisfied with a faith which rested solely on the efficacy of the Christian doctrine of justification by faith, and trust in the truth of New Testament kerygma. Bultmann was satisfied with his findings but for other New Testament scholars, some of whom were his former students, he had gone too far. Bultmann's radical existentialist methodology severed the tie between the historical Jesus and the kerygma of the church. In this way, Bultmann undermined—according to his critics—the foundation of the Gospel. The question emerging in the minds of many, was whether Bultmann had "thrown out the baby with the bathwater." Had he jettisoned the essence of the Christian gospel in the interest of exegesis of demythologization? Had he seriously considered the implications of his project, its centrality in protecting the integrity of the faith? These were the issues that motivated his former students.

The person who is accredited with raising the red flag against Bultmann is Ernst Kasemann, the New Testament scholar. His 1953 address on the "Problem of the Historical Jesus" prompted two key developments. To begin with, Kasemann argued that Bultmann's thesis about the historical Jesus was potentially destructive to the Christian message. In severing the connection between the New Testament proclamation of Jesus as Christ and the message of the historical Jesus, Bultmann was effectively undermining the heart of the Christian faith. If the church cannot indeed claim knowledge of the historical Jesus, he could in effect be deemed a mythical or fictional figure. This would be a deathblow to the Christian faith. Based upon this fundamental claim, Kasemann went on to say that it is without question possible for students of Scripture to reach behind the claims of the New Testament church to find the real historical Jesus. In so saying, Kasemann helped to initiate the so-called "new quest of the historical Jesus."[14] Kasemann was not alone in this assessment of Bultmann and in the desire to reconvene a quest of the historical Jesus.

Thurman's Method and the Quest

Thurman's treatment of the life and teachings of Jesus echo Kasemann's claims. In fact, his *Jesus and the Disinherited* was written several years prior to Kasemann's 1953 address. In any case, the core of Thurman's Christology rests on his claims about Jesus' rootedness in the socio-political realities of first century Palestine. Without a proper understanding of the life and social environment in which Jesus lived, it would be impossible to speak meaningfully of his role as the "Christ." And in this sense, it would be impossible to speak of the relevance and potency of Jesus' message of liberation to the oppressed. So our discussion here will examine Thurman's attempts to link Jesus' message with other first century religious options in the Jewish community.[15]

This question of the whether or not of the facts and circumstances of the life of Jesus can be known reached an even more fundamental point for Thurman, further accenting the differences between his approach to the subject and that of the Bultmannians. If, as Bultmann believed, it is impossible to know the true historical Jesus, it follows that one cannot know anything about Jesus' dispositions. The same would hold true of any attempt to describe Jesus' religious experiences. Earlier efforts to do so were rendered incredible by Albert Schweitzer's scathing critique of the life-of-Jesus proponents, some of whom had attempted to offer psychological profiles of Jesus. In any case, for Thurman the subject of religion and the realm of religious experience in general provided the hermeneutical framework within which to understand the religion of Jesus. In fact, Thurman would argue that our knowledge of Jesus' religious experience and his attitude towards religion is the basis upon which we can speak about his relevance to the oppressed.

As we will see, Thurman emphasized the need to see Jesus' religious vision as one alongside other first century Jewish options.[16] In order to understand the historical Jesus, Thurman would argue, we must see the interconnectedness between his religious experience and every other aspect of his life. As he said:

> [T]he religious insight of the Master and the categorical insistence derived from his religious experience is that what God requires of man, always, under all circumstances, is sincerity. Sincerity is one of the virtues found in all religions, whatever category.[17]

So it was of central importance to Thurman that we know something about the "psychological climate [in which] Jesus began his teaching and his ministry."[18] In *Jesus and the Disinherited* is Thurman's statement about how the "psychology of Jesus" addresses the principal psychological forces which affect oppressed people. (These facts simply confirm what we have already said about Thurman's low Christology and the priority that he gave to the humanity of Jesus as the foundation of his Christology).

Jesus and the Jewish Community

Howard Thurman identified three primary factors that helped to delineate the life of the historical Jesus. First, Jesus must be viewed within the context of his religious and ethnic identity: his Jewishness. Second, we should recognize Jesus as a poor, underprivileged, Jewish person. Third, we should see Jesus as a human being. Thurman examines these facts as the key to providing a true picture of who Jesus was and his status as the son of God.

Jesus of Nazareth was, according to Thurman, the founder of Christianity. Christianity evolved out of the fertile soil of Jesus' personal religious experience. And Jesus' life, message, and religious experience were rooted in the soul of the Jewish community of first century Palestine.[19] As a first century Jew, Jesus was a part of a socio-religious community, which Thurman has described as a having a "unique sense of community"[20] with God. As a member of this community, Jesus was "a member of a minority group in the midst of a larger dominant group."[21] As the founder of Christianity, Jesus offered to his generation an alternative vision of God, of human life, and of the nature of human relationships. In his discussion of the meaning and significance of the religion of Jesus, however, Thurman's primary emphasis is upon the socio-political relevance of this message. In comparing Jesus' views with those of his contemporaries, Thurman left untouched some of the tough exegetical problems surrounding Jesus' differences with them on questions such as the meaning of the resurrection. Such differences are given quite a bit of attention in several of the gospels, for example Mark 12:18-47; Matthew 22:19, 23:33; Luke 20:27-41. In any case, it is instructive to note what Thurman did emphasize, that is the significance of the religion of Jesus as a source of power to the oppressed. We will shift our focus now in order to examine Thurman's discussion of the relationship between Jesus' religious vision and that of other first century Jewish sects. In this context, we get a true sense, according to Thurman, of how we speak of the "humanity of Jesus."

The Sadducee Sect

Thurman said that the Sadducees represented the priestly class in the Jewish community. They were a part of the oppressed Jewish community within the Roman Empire. However, the Sadducees were an elite group within the Jewish community. They enjoyed a measure of freedom, privilege, and leadership opportunity within their society. The Sadducee party built their ethic and religious system on a compromised foundation:

> They did not represent the masses of people. Any disturbance of the
> established order meant upsetting their position. They loved Israel,
> but they seem to have loved security more.[22]

The Sadducees emulated the social and political position of the Romans, and they shared the amoral fate of the Romans. As a class of leaders within their community, they had actual power. As such, they were capable of contributing to the oppression their people, even if they were not totally free themselves.

The Sadducees were troublesome to Thurman: "They saw only two roads open before them—become like the Romans or be destroyed by the Romans. They choose the former."[23] Thurman's standard for assessing the Sadducees, as with groups such as the Pharisees and Zealots, centered on the relevance of their message to the conditions of oppressed Jews. Thurman questioned whether these groups provided an adequate "technique of survival" for poor Jews. Which system, he asked, provided the most meaningful method of helping oppressed people to relate to the authorities and the social realities of their generation? The Sadducee method of survival was problematic because they compromised the legitimate strivings of the poor masses in order to protect their own place in the community. They stood against the revolutionaries and any legitimate attempt by the poor to dramatically change their circumstances.[24] Thurman suggests, therefore, that the Sadducee socio-political and ethical vision does not provide an adequate model of survival for the people of that era because they, the Sadducees, had a disdain for the poor. The Sadducee ethic was based on deception and deceit, as they compromised their values as a means of accommodating the Romans. The third chapter of *Jesus and the Disinherited*, which focuses on Jesus' attitude toward the practice of deception, is addressed specifically to the art of moral compromise which characterizes groups such as the Sadducees.[25]

The Pharisee Sect

The Pharisees were the guardians of the Mosaic Law. They were viewed as the interpreters of the tradition.[26] Jesus' conflict with the Pharisees centered around the differences in their conception of the Law and his. We see this emphasis in Mark 3:6 in which Pharisees conspire against Jesus because of his refusal to adhere to the Sabbath Laws. Jesus' repeated confrontations with the Pharisees reveal the numerous ways that he attempted to correct what he perceived to be their misunderstanding of the Law. Thurman's assessment of the Pharisees did not focus on these obvious theological differences. Rather, he focused upon the question of the adequacy of their social vision for oppressed people. The key to the Pharisee system was their disdain and contempt for the Romans. Their resistance to the Romans was nonviolent and nonphysical. Thurman notes that, aside from compromise, the alternative to cooperation with the Romans available to the Pharisees was "to reduce contact with the enemy to a minimum." Theirs was,

> . . . . the attitude of cultural isolation in the midst of a rejected culture. Cunning the mood may be—one of bitterness and hatred, but also one of deep, calculating fear. To take up active resistance would be foolhardy, for a thousand reasons. The only way out is to keep one's resentment under rigid control and censorship.[27]

The Pharisee philosophy made room for no quality interaction with the enemy. They refused to passively accept their subjugation to the Romans. Instead, they choose to resist their oppressors by hating them.

The ethic of the Pharisee was not applicable to the poor masses because it was based on hatred. According to Thurman, hatred is always spiritually, psychologically, and morally destructive. It is as devastating to the person who hates as it is to the one who does the hating. In *Jesus and the Disinherited* Thurman explains why hatred, just as fear, was destructive to the oppressed. An atmosphere that is dominated by a Pharisaic hatred-type of ethic is always on the brink of eruption from socio-political strife and violence. Thurman described the Pharisees' contempt as a "powder keg."

> One nameless incident may cause to burst into flame the whole gamut of smoldering passion, leaving nothing in its wake but charred corpses, mute reminders of the tragedy of life.[28]

The Zealot Sect

The Zealot sect was the last of the three groups that Thurman analyzed among Jesus' contemporaries, the first century Jews. The Zealots were the only major group that systematically practiced armed resistance and violence against the Romans. They believed in and practiced a policy of active and violent resistance to Roman oppression. They went far beyond the Pharisees in their contempt for their Roman oppressors; they were prepared for physical resistance. Pushed to the edge by their depressed circumstances, Zealots resolved to solve their problem with the sharp edge of the sword. They were the revolutionaries within the Jewish community, determined to overthrow their Roman detractors. Thurman described the Zealots as persons who insisted on wanting to "do something" about their predicament. For the Zealots,

> "Why can't we do something? Something must be done!" [was] the recurring cry. By "something" is meant action, direct action, as over against words, subtleties, threats, and innuendoes. It is better to die fighting for freedom than to rot away in one's chains, the argument runs.[29]

Thurman argued that the Zealots represent the frustrations of all other oppressed people who have decided to take up the fight against their oppressors in an armed struggle. Their motto was similar to that of the African-American slaves who came centuries after them, as they sang in their Spiritual:

> Before I'd be a slave
> I'd be buried in my grave,
>
> And go home to my God
>
> And be free!

This reference to the slave experience is a common pattern in Thurman's work, as he used the African-American situation as an analogy for the Jewish situation in Jesus' time. Thurman expressed sympathy towards the Zealot philosophy and method of interaction with the oppressor, admiring their will to survive. But he believed that their philosophy was fundamentally flawed, it was fatalistic and nihilistic at best.[30] As Thurman noted, "Armed resistance is apt to be a tragic last resort in the life of the disinherited."[31] And as such, it was doomed to fail, just as the revolutionary rhetoric and actions of African-American slaves such as Nat Turner. Like Turner's, the Zealot philosophy was not viable because it had no hopes of succeeding. Their desire for freedom was noble, but it was doomed for failure. As Thurman said, "The fact that the ruler has available to him the power of the state and complete access to all arms" was not taken into consideration by the Zealots.[32] There was an irrational element in the Zealot ideal, which refused to accept the almost impossible odds against which they had to strive. To the Jewish Zealots, any failure was "regarded as temporary and, to the devoted, as a testing of character."[33] According to Thurman, this philosophy will ultimately lead to the destruction of all persons who are involved in the conflict. Physical violence against the oppressor is no more desirable than the physical violence of the strong against the weak. Moreover, the Zealot ethic was flawed, just as was the Pharisee ethic, because it was built upon and supported by hatred of the enemy. It was a philosophy which dehumanized and vilified other human beings by making them objects of hate.

Jesus and the Jewish Sects

Our next challenge is to understand the relationship between Jesus' philosophy and that of the Sadduccees, the Pharisees, and the Zealots. Jesus' teachings represent one of the living options available to the oppressed Jews of his generation. Thurman said, for example, that the key difference between Jesus and Paul was in their approaches to the Jewish religious heritage. Jesus identified totally with the Jewish tradition. This is clearly seen in the fact that Jesus submitted himself to the prophetic preaching of John the Baptist. In adhering to John's preaching, Jesus

> identified himself with the most creative and significant religious and spiritual expression of Israel at this time. [John the Baptist was]. . . the growing edge within Israel.[34]

Another important issue in Jesus' adherence to the preaching of John the Baptist is that it locates his ministry with the "mingling mass of human beings who felt the stirring in their hearts in response to the message of God."[35] The ministry of John the Baptist represented the latest phase of God's dynamic revelation to Israel. This is a significant point for Thurman because he insisted that Jesus did not start a new "religion" as such; his religious faith was rather an extension of Israel's vision of God.

As an adherent of John's prophetic preaching, Jesus came as "a son of Israel, involved in the struggles of Israel."[36] Jesus identified himself with John the Baptist's tradition of Jewish religion. Jesus was, according to Thurman, "the creative fulfillment of the meaning of the heart of the law and the genius of the covenant."[37] Jesus' ministry was addressed to the house of Israel and he was an extension of this community.[38] Thurman always attempted to depict the inner dimensions of Jesus' religious experience and self-consciousness. He provided, for example, the following description of how Jesus might have viewed himself in relation to the faith of Israel:

> . . . [I]n me [Jesus] at last all that God has been saying, and the prophets, all that has been meant by the peculiar relationship of Israel to God, if it is true that all of these things are rushing upon me, and in some sense I seem to be the fulfillment of the law of Israel (and mark you! the fulfillment of the law of Israel, not the beginning of a new religion, not the making of something new, but the fulfillment of the law, of the unfolding of the mind and heart of God to Israel), the climatic moment of the divine declaration in the heart of these people."[39]

Thurman makes a further point about Jesus' rootedness in the tradition of John the Baptist. Jesus' baptism at the hand of John the Baptist was a necessary preparation for the beginning of his own public ministry and the great revelation upon which it would be based. After the baptism, Jesus experienced a true theophany, a "great illumination." In this moment:

> . . . . it seemed as the heavens opened and the spirit of God descended upon him. . . He felt the most wonderful thing that a human being can ever feel in life—and what is that? that [sic] the thing you are doing, your dream, your hope, your life, has the ultimate approval of God.[40]

Again, it is important to note here that Thurman's main concern is to anchor Jesus' life and ministry in a particular time and place in human history: Jesus was a man whose religious vision emerged in the context of a particular religio-ethnic community. (We will return to this theme in the next chapter.)

At any rate, Thurman goes further in this direction by noting the difference between Jesus' message—as an extension of God's revelation to Israel— and that of the Apostle Paul. Jesus' message centered on the Kingdom of God, as revealed to and founded in Israel's religious vision. The message of Paul, on the other hand, centered on his kerygmatic Christology. Paul was the architect of the theology and philosophy of the tradition which became Christianity. He was in part responsible, Thurman argued, for severing Christianity's ties with the Jewish community. Thus Thurman declared that Paul was "the first great interpreter of Christianity."[41] Jesus maintained his rootedness in the Jewish community, but Paul, contrary to Jesus, broke with the religion of his Jewish foreparents.

Jesus' Economic Status

Another aspect of Jesus' life that Thurman examined is the economic dimension. As a human being, Jesus' life was shaped by specific socio-economic forces. In this context, the actual event of Jesus' birth is secondary to the significance of his having been born into economically impoverished circumstances. This approach runs counter to other high Christological approaches, but Thurman's statements about Jesus' socio-economic status help to shape his claims about Jesus' birth and death. The discussion up to this juncture in the chapter has centered on the context within which Jesus' life was shaped and nurtured. I have chosen this approach because it reflects Thurman's own approach to the issue. He begins with the Jesus' social environment, and only later shifts to talk about his birth and death. This is one distinguishing feature of Thurman's theology. He understood Jesus' life in connection with the socio-political background from which he emerged. Again, this approach is important because we can see Jesus in a context analogous to the conditions of oppressed people in every era of human history.[42] The aim of Thurman's method is to show that "The economic predicament with which [Jesus] was identified in birth placed him initially with the great mass of men on the earth."[43]

Jesus' identity as an agent of divine revelation is greatly enhanced by socio-economic realities. Thurman declared that:

> If we dare take the position that in Jesus there was at work some radical destiny, it would be safe to say that in his poverty he was more truly Son of Man than he would have been if the incident of family or birth had made him a rich son of Israel.[44]

Three claims emerge from this statement, each of which is central to Thurman's thought: Jesus' chosenness and "radical destiny", the significance of the title "Son of Man", and the fact of Jesus' poverty. The key for Thurman is that Jesus' economic status provided the context within which to understand his messianic mission. The title that Thurman used, "Son of Man," reveals his preference and his belief in titles for Jesus. But for Thurman, the title addresses the issue of Jesus' place in human history. Thurman's reflections on the birth and death of Jesus emerge within the context of this discussion of these economic matters. It remains our task at this juncture to discuss how Thurman's statements about Jesus' socio-economic status helped to shape his claims about Jesus' birth and his death.

Thurman and the New Testament Writers on the Birth and Death of Jesus

Despite their differences on particular points, all New Testament writers agree categorically on one Christological point, namely that Jesus of Nazareth was God in the flesh. Using both Hebrew and Greek sources as reference points, these writers were unapologetic in the belief in the uniqueness and superiority of Jesus Christ. He was God *pro nobis*, God for us, and "Emmanuel", God with us. He was called God in the flesh, the "Messiah", and "Savior of the world."[45] Two of the central components of this belief were the writers' conception of the pre-existence and birth of Jesus and their understanding of the meaning and significance of his death and resurrection.

The New Testament writers' view of the uniqueness of Jesus also influenced their understanding of the meaning and significance of Jesus' birth, life, and death. It is clear, for example, that while there is no elaborate doctrinal statement on the Virgin birth and the pre-existence of Jesus Christ in the New Testament, both are alluded to in Scripture.[46] One passage which expresses the supernaturalist view of the birth of Jesus is found in Matthew 1:18-21 RSV:

> Now the birth of Jesus Christ took place in this way. When his mother Mary had been betrothed to Joseph, before they came together she was found to be with child of the Holy Spirit; and her husband Joseph, being a just man and unwilling to put her to shame, resolved to divorce her quietly. But as he considered this, behold, an angel of the Lord appeared to him in a dream, saying, "Joseph, son of David, do not fear to take Mary your wife, for that which is conceived in her is of the Holy Spirit; she will bear a son, and you shall call his name Jesus, for he will save his people from their sins."

The idea of the Virgin birth, which is a central theme in the development of many Christological debates, is aptly stated in this passage. Matthew's thesis is reaffirmed in the gospel of Luke, which gives an account of an angel who spoke to the Virgin Mary. He says:

> The Holy Spirit will come upon you, and the power of the Most High will overshadow you; therefore the child to be born will be called holy, the Son of God. (Luke 1:35, RSV)

In the Gospel of John and in the Pauline epistles, the idea of the pre-existence of Jesus comes into play. John 1:1-2,14 says:

> In the beginning was the Word, and the Word was with God, and the Word was God. He was in the beginning with God . . . And the Word became flesh and dwelt among us, full of grace and truth; we have beheld his glory, glory as of the only Son from the Father. (RSV)

Paul makes a similar suggestion in Philippians 2: 6-8:

> [Jesus,] Who though he was in form of God, did not count equality with God a thing to be grasped, but emptied himself, taking the form of a servant, being born in the likeness of men. And being found in human form he humbled himself and became obedient unto death, even death on a cross. (RSV)

All of these Christological claims were worked out in relationship to Jewish messianic ideas which were dominant in that era, as well as in prior centuries.

The Christological questions which are raised and answered in New Testament writings—and perhaps, more importantly, those which are not raised and answered—provide the central basis for many of the Christological debates which emerged in the Christian tradition during the early centuries of the Christian era.[47]

Our concern here is simply to note that the post-New Testament Christological developments—up to the confirmation of the Chalcedonian doctrine in 451 AD—helped to establish the standards of orthodoxy for the Christian community since the fifth century. Several issues were central in this process: (1) that Jesus had a pre-existence as the son of God; (2) that he was literally born of a virgin (3) that Jesus had two related but distinct natures, one divine and one human (4) that he was co-equal with God (5) that the death of Jesus was a vicarious and forensic event, providing atonement for all human sins, both past and present. While particular interpretations of these themes vary, they remain central to most traditional Christological affirmations. We must consider whether or not these claims were reflected in Thurman's Christology.

Thurman never totally rejected the views and treatments of Jesus' life and death found in the New Testament. His approach to them, however, was radically different. To begin with, he viewed the birth as a "symbolic" event. He posited that the facts given in the New Testament which surround the birth of Jesus help us to better envision Jesus as God's "symbol of the dignity and the inherent worthfullness of the common man."[48] According to Thurman, Jesus' message to the common person is reflected in the facts surrounding his birth. His birth was first announced to poor peasant shepherds, as opposed to either the Jewish or Roman aristocracy. Thurman described it in the following manner:

> Stripped bare of art forms and liturgy, the literal substance of the story remains, Jesus Christ was born in a stable, he was born of humble parentage in surroundings that are the common lot of those who earn their living by the sweat of their brows.[49]

Thurman affirmed that this is the definitive starting point for understanding who Jesus was: we must begin with a statement about Jesus' relevance to the oppressed. The task that Thurman identifies is that of helping the oppressed to grasp the meaning of Jesus' birth and to draw strength from it. In viewing Jesus, the oppressed may see themselves. According to Thurman, "when [the disinherited] beholds Jesus, he sees in him the possibilities of life even for the humblest and a dramatic resolution of the meaning of God."[50]

The birth of Jesus was an event which had great and cosmic implications for human beings in every era. The incarnation, if we choose to call it such, refers to the specific manner in which the divine became united with the conditions of oppressed people. In the person of Jesus, God chose the oppressed as his own people, giving them special "prerogatives as children of God."[51] The birth of Jesus is a part of the growing edge in human history, and it is a paradigm for understanding how God is revealed in history:

> The Birth of the Child in China, Japan, the Philippines, Russia, India, America, and all over the world, is the breathless moment like the stillness of absolute motion, when something new, fresh, whole, may be ushered into the nations that will be the rallying point for the whole human race to move in solid phalanx into the city of God, into the Kingdom of Heaven on the earth. . .[52]

Thurman's is a radical reinterpretation of the meaning and significance of the birth of Jesus. For him it was primarily a symbolic event. It was a clear manifestation of God's election of poor Jews in general and of Jesus in particular as a medium of his revelation. The birth of Jesus was thus symbolic of God's election of every poor child and every poor people in all of human history. Jesus' birth created within human beings a special "mood". Thurman described it as the mood of Christmas, which is a spiritual experience. The true meaning of Jesus' birth is expressed in this mood.[53] He made no attempt to distinguish the "biological facts" surrounding Jesus' birth from the birth of any other human person. There was no need, in Thurman's view, to give "proof of a virgin birth" or to literally affirm this idea. Instead, Thurman saw the New Testament accounts of the birth of Jesus as a statement about Jesus' inclusiveness in the human family. Jesus, Thurman argued, was born of a woman just as is any other person.

Thurman rejected the high Christological approaches which begin their interpretation of Jesus with claims about his virgin birth and pre-existence. These were troubling claims to him because they too easily separate Jesus from the facts of history and the laws of nature. In so doing they limit the symbolic potential of the events of the birth.

Thurman broached this subject in a rhetorical question that he raised on the issue.

> Was the sonship of Jesus a gift placed upon the first-born of Mary
> and Joseph when he first stirred in the womb, or was it something he
> earned in great fulfillment?[54]

Thurman looked at the life and experiences of Jesus in order to find an answer to this question. He demonstrated that Jesus' distinctiveness from other human beings was the result of his growth in relationship to God the Father.[55]

In discussing the meaning of the crucifixion, therefore, Thurman described it first as a political event with direct political consequences.

> The crucifixion of Jesus Christ reminds us once again of the penalty
> which any highly organized society exacts of those who violate its
> laws. . . those who resist the established order because its
> requirements are too low, too unworthy of the highest and best in
> man. . . Behold then the hill outside of the city of Jerusalem, the
> criminal and the Holy Man sharing common judgment, because one
> rose as high above the conventions of his age as the other descended
> below.[56]

As a symbolic event, the crucifixion had relevance for all persons who suffer from unjust political oppression. In viewing the crucifixion, we learn much about the nature of the universal human experience of suffering. Again Thurman referred to the experience of black slaves in order to illustrate this point. Black slaves saw themselves as participants in the sufferings of Jesus, and they attached great psychological significance to his death. Thurman noted that in the slave songs,

> . . . . the death of Jesus took on a deep and personal poignancy. It
> was not merely the death of a man or a God, but there was in it a
> quality of identification in experience that continues to burn its way
> deep into the heart even of the most unemotional. The suffering of
> Jesus on the cross was something more. He suffered, He died, but
> not alone—[the slaves] were with Him.[57]

The principal song Thurman used in his study of this aspect of slave religion is "Were You There When They Crucified My Lord?". The slaves' approach to the death of Jesus began with their experience. That is to say their own personal sufferings provided the primary framework for their interpretation of Jesus' death. Thurman called the slaves' reflections "an experimental grasping of the quality of Jesus' experience, by virtue of the racial frustrations of the Singers."[58]

Thurman's reflections on the crucifixion are passionately articulated in his poem on the subject:

> He was dying! . . .
> There was the sense of pure relief
> That he and the dogging shadow were face to face!
> Nothing could reach him now.
> He was beyond the violence of all his foes,
> He thought.
> He gripped the pain!
> He established its place and bade it stay!
> Death was at hand, he knew:
> A zone of peace holds fast the place
> Where pain and death are met.
>
> ————————————————
>
> This is the Cup; not Death!
> To yield the right to prove the Truth
> As if it could not stand alone.
> This is the Cup; not Death!
> Father, into Thy Hands, I give my life.[59]

Just as the birth symbolized God's election of the poor, the crucifixion declared God's identification with those oppressed because of political corruption. We will talk about how Thurman relates his view of the death of Jesus to ideas about the resurrection in the next chapter, when we turn to Thurman's view of the divinity of Jesus.

Jesus' Minority Status

Thurman argued that Jesus' participation in a politically oppressed minority community was also a primary element in the shaping of his view of God and humanity. The economic and racial disadvantages with which Jesus lived were compounded by his membership in a minority community.

In sum, we can see that Thurman's Christology takes the historical Jesus as the principal point of departure. Thurman affirmed that it is essential to view the historical Jesus in connection with the socio-political facts of the first century since Jesus was a product of his socio-religious environment. Several factors are crucial in this regard. First, Thurman accented the centrality of Jesus' Jewishness in determining his identity. In fulfilling this task, Thurman said that one must juxtapose Jesus with other Jewish sects of the first century (such as the Sadducees, Pharisees, and Zealots). Second, a key factor in Thurman's understanding of Jesus was the "economic" factor; Jesus was a "poor Jew." This underscores Jesus' identification with the poor and oppressed masses of the black community. Thurman said, for example, that the birth and death of Jesus should be understood socially and politically, as opposed to being viewed as supernatural interventions into human history. Third, Thurman wanted to demonstrate that Jesus should be seen as a full human being with all of the limitations of true humanity. He had, accordingly, no doctrine of the virgin birth or theory of how Jesus grew into favor with God as a result of his obedience to God. These issues will be looked at in greater detail in the next chapter when we discuss their implications upon Thurman's view of Jesus' divinity.

Notes

1   Richard A. Norris, ed. & trans. *The Christological Controversy*, Sources of Early Christian Thought (Philadelphia: Fortress Press, 1980), p. 2.

2   Karl Rahner & Herbert Vorgrimler, *Dictionary of Theology*, 2nd ed. (New York: Crossroad, 1981), pp. 70-71. Wolf hart Pannenberg, *Jesus God and Man*, trans. Duane A. Priebe & Lewis L. Wilkens, 2nd ed. (Philadelphia: The Westminster Press, 1977), p. 33. See especially the first chapter of his work. Pannenberg also argues that the high christological approach is the dominant approach in the history of the Christian church.

3   Soteriology is the branch of theology which covers the meaning of the atonement of Jesus Christ. See Van A. Harvey, *A Handbook of Theological Terms* (New York: Macmillan Publishing Co.), pp. 224-225. The close connection between Christology and soteriology in Christian thought is well documented in the tradition. See Wolf hart Pannenberg's, *Jesus, God and Man.* chapter 2.

4   Ibid.

5   Robins Scroggs, *Christology in Paul and John,* Proclamation Commentaries (Philadelphia: Fortress Press, 1988), p. 6.

6   St. Athanasius, "Treatise on the Incarnation of the Word," in *The Faith of Our Fathers*, ed. William A. Jurgens, Vol. 1. (Collegeville, MN.: The Liturgical Press, 1970), p. 322.

7   Thurman, *Jesus and the Disinherited,* pp. 18-19.

8   Ibid. p. 21.

9   James H. Cone makes a similar claim about the centrality of the historical Jesus in the doing of black theology. See his *God of The Oppressed* (New York: Seabury Press, 1974), p. 115.

10 Schweitzer's central contribution in this text lies in his thorough review of the life-of-Jesus movement of the nineteenth century. Moreover, he offered his own interpretation of the eschatological message of the historical Jesus. See Albert Schweitzer, *The Quest of the Historical Jesus*, trans. (New York: Macmillan Publishing Co. Inc., 1968).

11 Bultmann is also important here because he helps us to better grasp the place and significance of Thurman's conception of Jesus.

12 See Robin Scroggs' *Christology.* Also see *The Basic Writings of Saint Augustine*, Whitney J. Oates ed. Vol. 2 (New York: Random House Publishers, 1948), and see Van A. Harvey, *A Handbook of Theological Terms* (New York: Macmillan Publishing Co., Inc., 1964), p. 27.

13 Rudolph Bultmann, *Jesus Christ and Mythology* (New York: Charles Scribner's and Sons, New York, 1958), p. 19.

14 For an excellent discussion of the issues surrounding this development see James M. Robinson's *A New Quest of the Historical Jesus*, (Philadelphia: Fortress Press, 1958).

15   It is of interest to note that Thurman's *Jesus and the Disinherited* was
      originally published four years prior to Kasemann's noted lecture on the
      historical Jesus. He was very much in step with the direction in which
      New Testament scholarship would later move.

16   Please note our discussion of this in the first chapter.

17   Howard Thurman, "Lectures on Jesus and the Disinherited," #9, p. 2.

18   Thurman, *Jesus and the Disinherited,* p. 21.

19   Howard Thurman, "The Moment of Crisis, Paul," p. 4. We will give
      more detailed attention to this issue in chapter five.

20   Thurman, *Jesus and the Disinherited,* p.16.

21   The study of Jewish sects of the first century has been a hotly debated
      issue in New Testament scholarship. While some scholars have stressed
      the radical differences between the teachings of Jesus and the beliefs of
      other first century sects, others have argued that Jesus' views are much
      closer to his contemporaries than many Christians care to assert. Thurman's
      best discussion of this subject is contained in *Jesus and the Disinherited.*
      Three of the more important texts in this area are E. P. Sanders, *Jesus
      and Judaism* (Philadelphia: Fortress Press, 1986); see especially Chapter
      10. See also Geza Vermes, *Jesus the Jew: "A Historian's Reading of the
      Gospels"* (Philadelphia: Fortress Press, 1973); and Paula Fredriksen,
      From Jesus to Christ (New Haven: Yale University Press, 1988), especially
      Part II.

22   Thurman, *Jesus and the Disinherited,* p. 24.

23   Ibid.

24   Ibid.

25   More will be said about this issue below.

26   I find Sanders' discussion of this issue to be helpful. See his *Jesus and
      Judaism;* note especially Chapters 9-10.

27   Thurman, *Jesus and the Disinherited,* p. 24.

28   Ibid. p. 25.

29   Ibid.

30   Thurman's views on this issue are similar to Martin King's critique of the
      practical and the moral aspects of the black power slogan. See King's
      text, *Where Do We Go From Here: Chaos or Community?* (Boston: Beacon
      Press, 1967).

31   Thurman, *Jesus and the Disinherited,* p. 26.

32   Ibid. p. 26.

33   Ibid. pp. 26-27.

34   Thurman, "Moment of Crisis," #3, p.2.

35   Ibid. p. 2

36   Thurman, "Man and the Moral Struggle (Jesus)", p. 2.

37   Thurman, "Moment of Crisis, Paul" p. 4. Thurman is consistent with
      Bultmann's starting point in studying the message of Jesus. Bultmann, in
      Jesus and the Word, begins his analysis with a study of the historical and

theological background of the ministry of Jesus, which entailed a study of the Jewish religion and culture of that day.

38 Recent New Testament scholarship also affirms the idea that Jesus' ministry was confined to the house of Israel. See. E. P. Sanders, *Judaism;* see the Introduction.

39 Thurman, "Man and the Moral Struggle (Jesus", p. 4.

40 Ibid.

41 Ibid. p. 4. Thurman's claim on this subject is consistent with the distinction that scholars such as Schweitzer and Bultmann have made between the teachings of the historical Jesus and the kerygmatic proclamation of the New Testament Church.

42 His claims here are similar to those of persons such as Walter Rauschenbusch. The key difference is that Thurman is particularly concerned about demonstrating Jesus' relevance to oppressed African-Americans, as he develops his focus. See, for example, Rauschenbusch's *A Theology of the Social Gospel.*

43 Thurman, *Jesus and the Disinherited*, p. 17. Some interesting research is going on in this area of New Testament scholarship today; this will help us to better grasp the similarities. Geza Vermes' text, *Jesus the Jew* is central to this area of scholarship. See also Richard A. Horsley with John S. Hanson, *Bandits, Prophets, and Messiahs* (New York: Harper & Row, 1985).

44 Thurman, *Jesus and the Disinherited*, p. 17

45 Oscar Cullman makes a very important and significant point in suggesting that some New Testament scholars are misguided in their failure to realize the degree to which the Christologies of the New Testament were shaped by the original thinking and claims of Jesus and early Christian community. See his *Christology of the New Testament*, trans. Shirley C. Guthrie & Charles A. M. Hall, Revised ed., (Philadelphia: The Westminster Press, 1955).

46 Cullman provides an excellent account of the diverse Christological perspectives found in the New Testament.

47 John H. Leith, *Creeds of the Churches* (Atlanta: John Knox Press, 1973), p. 31. The development of the theology and creeds of the Christian Church was not a simple and pristine process. Many political, ecclesiastical, personal, and socio-cultural factors shaped the emergence and formation of what the church has said on these matters. Many of the issues are still debated and there is no one way to interpret the creeds and the beliefs which they influence; these are beyond the scope of our study. For a more detailed account and some ideas about the other issues, see Maurice Wiles' text, *The Making of Christian Doctrine* (Cambridge: Cambridge University Press, 1967) and *The Remaking of Christian Doctrine* (London: SCM Press, 1974). Please see the full discussion of this issue in chapter six of this study.

48 Howard Thurman, *The Mood of Christmas* (New York: Harper & Row, 1973; reprint ed., Richmond; Ind.: Friends United Press, 1985), p. 11.

49 Ibid. p. 11.

50 Ibid.

51 Ibid.

52 Ibid. p. 16.

53 See for example his text, *The Mood of Christmas*. This issue will be examined more closely in the next chapter.

54 Thurman, *Deep is the Hunger* (New York: Harper, 1951; reprint ed., Friends United Press, 1975), p. 172.

55 This issue will be covered in the next chapter. The subject of the uniqueness of Jesus will be covered in the context of a discussion of his divinity.

56 Thurman, *Deep Is the Hunger,* p. 31.

57 Thurman, *Deep River,* p. 26.

58 Ibid. p. 27.

59 Howard Thurman, *The Inward Journey* (New York: Harper & Row, 1961; reprint ed., Richmond, Ind.: Friends United Press, 1980), p. 59.

Chapter III

The Divinity of Jesus of Nazareth

Jesus approached all of life from within the tremendous
vitality of his religious experience. The incentive in his
mind was always spiritual and religious. Therefore, his
attack upon the problems of human existence and human
destiny was from within the meaning of religion and
religious experience rather than from any within the context
of morality, of ethics, or of any kind of reform.

—Howard Thurman

In the preceding chapter we examined Thurman's conception of the
humanity of Jesus. Thurman made a convincing case for the
significance of understanding Jesus in strictly historical terms, as a
man alongside of all human beings. The question that we must now
ask, however, is specifically "how, and to what degree, [Thurman]
consider[ed] Jesus to be divine."[1] This question brings us to the other
half of the Christological equation introduced above, which centers on
the humanity and divinity of Jesus. Thurman's approach to this subject
follows a long line of revisionist Christologies, all of which call into
question the traditional interpretations of Jesus' divinity. In this tradition
the principal goal is to depict Jesus' life and ministry within the
parameters of modern historical and theological perspectives. Here

more than in any other area of Thurman's thought, we see evidence of his rootedness in the liberal Western theological tradition.[2]

The Divinity of Jesus in Liberal Theology

Liberal Protestant theology is a by-product of modern science, philosophy, and history in the Western world. More specifically, modern liberal theology developed under the influence of the Enlightenment. Since the eighteenth century, liberal theologians have radically re-interpreted the core beliefs and doctrines of the Christian tradition. Since the late eighteenth century and early nineteenth century, liberal theology has attempted to rid itself of layers of history, tradition, and dogma and to return to the "essence of Christianity", to use Adolf Harnack's phrase.[3] No aspect of the corpus of Christian doctrine receives more attention in this regard than the Christological dogmas that have been in place since the early Middle Ages. Western Christological orthodoxy was shaped under the influence of Greek philosophy and the world-view emerging from the first through the fifth centuries. While there are other issues at stake, the core of Christological orthodoxy revolves around several fundamental claims: (1) that Jesus had a pre-existence as the son of God; (2) that he was literally born of a virgin (3) that Jesus had two related but distinct natures, one divine and one human (4) that he was co-equal with God (5) that the death of Jesus was a vicarious and forensic event, providing atonement for all human sins, both past and present.

The liberal assault on these beliefs began with the fundamental assumption upon which they were built, namely their claims about the meaning and nature of true "divinity". Moreover, liberalism called into question the traditional interpretation of the connection between the supernatural world (God) and the natural (physical) world, including human beings. The subject of Jesus' divinity is crucial to this area. In the modern liberal tradition, the divinity of Jesus is understood primarily in light of his religious experiences, psychological strength, God-consciousness, personality, and moral wisdom, as opposed to his "nature."[4] Theologians from this school espouse a "low" Christology, radically de-emphasizing any notion of the "two natures" of Christ.

Kenneth Cauthen posits that there are two dominant streams in modern, liberal, Christological reflections. The first begins with Friedrich Schleiermacher, whose Christology focuses upon the "dynamic, personal, ethical categories"[5] of Jesus, as opposed to metaphysical categories. The second pole is represented in the works of Albrecht Ritschl, who chose to focus on the "practical side of the [Christological] issues."[6] Both of these perspectives are rooted in strong presuppositions about the nature of God's relationship to the created order. Orthodox theologians tend to radically separate God from the created order. Liberals, on the other hand, tend to blur this distinction, often equating the natural world with the supernatural. The entire structure of liberal religious thought is based upon this tendency to bring together—if not synthesize—the realm of nature with the divine. The focus is upon the immanence of God in nature, human life, human personality, the human spirit, intellect, will, religious experience, etc. Liberalism comes closest to what was traditionally known as pantheism, which assumes that the divine is completely united with the natural world.[7] Pantheists move beyond the simple idea that God is revealed in nature and affirm that God has become one with God's creation. [8]

We see examples of this tendency towards pantheism in liberal theologians such as Friedrich Schleiermacher, the great luminary of Protestant liberalism. Schliermacher argued, for example, that every "act" of God can be understood and explained totally in physical, social, and historical terms. This is true because God places within human beings, human history, and within the physical world the "capacity" to receive these divine "eruptions". But if God's actions are to be viewed as eruptions, they are always eruptions from within the ebb and flow of history. Thus events such as the virgin birth, the miracles of Jesus, or other such "miracles" represent "eruptions" from within the cause-effect nexus of human history and within the natural laws of physics. They are God's actions embodied in human and physical actions and activities. As such, Schleriemacher's miracles never entail a suspension of the laws of nature in order to prove their facticity. Miracles are distinguished from other historical, social, or physical acts only in the sense that they meet us as something significant, something that we do not understand or control. They meet us as revelations of the mind of God. Miracles are, in this sense, simultaneously human acts, acts of God, and supernatural acts.[9] This equation is clearly demonstrated in the following statement:

> So, too, in relation to the Redeemer Himself, the new corporate life is no miracle, but simply the supernatural becoming natural, since every exceptional force attracts mass to itself and holds it fast . . . In relation to the new creation itself such a passage is not supernatural.[10]

Supernatural acts are "natural," immanent, then, because of their inevitable connection with other historical events. And further:

> To sum up: in this whole matter we posit, on the one side, an initial divine activity that is supernatural, but at the same time a vital human receptivity in virtue of which alone that supernatural can become a natural fact of history.[11]

Schleiermacher's proposal represented the beginning of a long tradition of liberal interpretations of this idea.[12] Theologians such as Harry Emerson Fosdick, the great pastoral theologian of this century, would follow Schleiermacher's liberal interpretation of Jesus' life and ministry. His discussion of the subject of the unity of the divine and human illustrates this point:

> In our theology no longer are the divine and human like oil and water that cannot mix; rather, all the best in us is God in us. This makes faith in the divine Christ infinitely easier than it was under the old regime.[13]

In the man Jesus we see the best of humanity united with the divine, revealing that "divinity hedges us all about like . . . vital forces."[14]

With these things in mind we can now begin to examine the implications of the liberal theological tradition upon the substance of Howard Thurman's Christology.

Howard Thurman and the Liberal Christological Model

The themes that we have noted thus far from the liberal Christological tradition provide an essential link to Thurman's Christology. This is particularly true for understanding Thurman's treatment of the issue of Jesus' divinity. Like Schleiermacher and Fosdick, Thurman's point of departure in examining the divinity of Jesus was strongly anthropocentric. To understand how and in what sense Jesus was different from other human persons, it is necessary, Thurman would contend, to look at the broader subject of God's workings in nature.

Thurman's description of the relationship between God and nature is very mystical. This mysticism runs throughout his work. For example,

Thurman describes nature as God's "working paper." It is God's handiwork, in which we see the essence and majesty of God, evoking within human beings a "mood of reverence."[15] The mood of reverence is created within human beings because the human spirit intuitively recognizes a kinship between itself and the natural world. The human spirit marvels at "the greatness of God at work in the world of nature. It heightens the spirit and enriches the awareness of values."[16] This sense of awareness of the fundamental kinship between human beings and nature has a strong mystical component to it. Thurman's personal experiences demonstrate this mystical bent.

An example of this can clearly be seen in Thurman's recollection of his early experiences as a child growing up in Daytona, Florida, where he took deep solace in walking along the beaches of the Atlantic Ocean. These moments had deep mystical meaning for him.

> Here I found, alone, a special benediction. The ocean and the night together surrounded my little life with a reassurance that could not be affronted by the behavior of human beings. The ocean at night gave me a sense of timelessness, of existing beyond the reach of the ebb and flow of circumstances. Death would be a minor thing. I felt, in the sweep of that natural embrace.[17]

He goes further with this theme in discussing his early reactions to the frequent storms that would come in from the ocean:

> Unafraid, I was held by the storm's embrace. The experience of these storms gave me a certain overriding immunity against much of the pain with which I would have to deal in the years ahead when the ocean was only a memory. The sense held: I felt rooted in life, in nature, in existence.[18]

During his childhood the woods and the night were his "earliest companions."[19]

> There seems to be in the very nature of the human mind, the insistence that everything everywhere belongs. This sense of the wholeness in the universe gives us an immeasurable sense of security. And this is God, very God.[20]

The presence of God, for Thurman, lurked and loomed large everywhere. He believed human beings only need to perceive this presence.

This discussion of Thurman's mysticism is very much relevant to the subject of Christology because it uncovers the basis upon which the discussion of Jesus' uniqueness and divinity took place. And the common bond between Jesus' uniqueness and his divinity is, for Thurman, religious experience. It is through religious experience that we come to know both the nature of the cosmic order and the source of Jesus' uniqueness. In his book *Search for Common Ground*, Thurman argued that there is a common ground of unity in all of life and nature, indeed in the entire cosmic order.[21]

Religious Experience, Moral Excellence, and Suffering: The Foundations of Divinity

The question with which we began this chapter was, simply put, "how, and to what degree, he [Thurman] considers Jesus to be divine."[22] In addressing this question we must return again to the area of religious experience. In the religious experience, we learn what is distinctive about Jesus, as well as how he is similar to other persons. Thurman began with the fundamental assumption that Jesus' religious experience and "God consciousness" grew more profound and meaningful as he matured into adolescence and adulthood. In this sense, we might say that Thurman offered a developmental understanding of Jesus' religious experience. As Jesus matured in his experience of God, his primary knowledge of God increased likewise.[23] Out of the depths of his experience, Jesus discovered that,

> God . . . cares for the sparrow—a sparrow, you can't even eat it, it's all bones and feathers; even is he mindful of the hairs on your head: that all of life is one. This is what he says.[24]

Aside from being strongly developmental, Thurman's depiction of Jesus' religious experience is also strongly mystical in scope.

The developmental and mystical aspects of Jesus' religious experience strongly resonate with Thurman's personal experiences. In describing the far-reaching implications of Jesus' religious experience, Thurman said:

> To Jesus, God breathed through all that is: the sparrow overcome by sudden death in its flight; the lily blossoming on the rocky hillside;

the grass of the field and the clouds, light and burdenless or weighted down with unshed waters; . . . to Jesus, God breathed through all that is.[25]

As a youngster too, Thurman had a profoundly mystical understanding of God's work in nature.

> As a boy, in Florida, I walked along the beach of the Atlantic Ocean in the quiet stillness that can only be completely felt, where the murmur of the ocean is stilled and the tide moves stealthily along the shore. . . . Many years later, in the growth of my own knowledge and the probing of the mysteries of religious experience, or any experience for that matter, did I recognize the experience as being in itself religious, and more definitely as being mystical.[26]

The common bond between the two descriptions is the strong experiential and mystical bent, at the heart of which is the affirmation of trust in God. In each case, the encounter with nature yields forth a sense of unity and mystery. To the recipients, in these cases Thurman and Jesus, the experience evokes a feeling of profound trust and security in life. As Thurman wrote:

> To relax . . . and to trust God—not to run His world, not to people His Universe, not to hold things in some kind of all-encompassing grasp. . . It was the experience of the Master, I think after trying and doing it here and there a little, that when he finally made the supreme and transcendent discovery that when a man is sure of God in that way, he can stand anything that life can do to him, and even death becomes a little thing.[27]

There are several pivotal points in Jesus' life to which Thurman referred in tracing the development of his religious experience and in explaining its profundity. These areas include his early experiences in life and ministry, his baptismal revelation, his temptation, his passion, and his crucifixion. Throughout his life, Jesus drew strength from the experiences, representing the zenith of his religious maturation and encounters. Fundamental to each of these realms is Thurman's insistence that Jesus was a man who "worshipped God."[28] As a worshipping person, Jesus demonstrated to other human beings what it means to completely surrender to God. In elaborating on his perspective, Thurman wrote that Jesus "earned" his divinity in "great fulfillment."[29] In saying that Jesus earned his sonship, Thurman suggested that Jesus did not

have "privileged status" with God. He had no special capacity, nor
was he born with a distinct nature which would have predisposed him
to God's actions. To suggest that the "sonship" of Jesus was given as
a supernatural gift either at or before his birth, as expressed in the
Chalcedonian doctrine of the dual natures of Christ, would in essence
remove Jesus from the realm of true humanity. Thurman rejected this
approach because, as he said, it would assign other human beings an
"irreducible handicap that puts them forever at a disadvantage."[30] In
linking Jesus more closely to the experiences and lives of other persons,
however, we see him as one who:

> . . . . won the approval of God in some special sense that sets him
> apart in his own right, then it would follow that his life presents both
> a challenge and a judgment.[31]

Thurman shied away from making claims about the early religious
experiences for which there is no direct support in Scripture.
Nevertheless, he proposed that what happened to Jesus early in his life
was a "truing" of his spirit, which would prepare him for the tumultuous
events which were to take place in his adult life. In discussing what
might have been on Jesus' mind during his Triumphant Entry into
Jerusalem, Thurman said:

> Perhaps his mind was far away to the scenes of his childhood, feeling
> the sawdust between his toes, in his father's shop. He may have
> been remembering the high holy days in the synagogue, when his
> whole body quickened by the echo of the ram's horn as it sounded.[32]

Jesus' "quickening" experience represented an essential moment in his
lifelong preparation for ministry. And this continued as Jesus began
his public ministry and continued to live out his calling. We should
recall, for example, what was said in the preceding chapter about
Thurman's discussion of Jesus' baptism. On the occasion of his baptism,
Jesus had a true experience of God; he had a theophany, a revelation
of God. In this moment:

> it seemed as the heavens opened and the spirit of God descended
> upon him. . . He felt the most wonderful thing that a human being
> can ever feel in life—and what is that? that [sic] the thing you are
> doing, your dream, your hope, your life, has the ultimate approval
> of God.[33]

This was a foundational event in Jesus, signifying the deepening of his religious consciousness and commitment to God. From this experience, Jesus came to know in a personal way that "God was" and that God "was near."[34] Indeed God could be trusted with the most delicate details of human life.

Later in Jesus' ministry, he likewise felt a burst of energy for doing the will of God. Jesus' understanding of God grew as he lived and grew within the Jewish community, as he continued to experience God. In addition to the fundamental claims Thurman made concerning Jesus' religious experiences, Thurman linked the divinity of Jesus to the question of morality. Aside from distinguishing himself as one who worshipped God and who totally surrendered to God, Jesus' distinctiveness is also demonstrated in the strength of his moral will. Thurman pointed to morality and suffering as key indicators of the manner in which Jesus gained God's approval and earned his distinction as the son of God.[35] In any case, it was important for Thurman to note that Jesus was indeed a "moral personality."[36] He was essentially a moral personality because his entire vision for life emerged from his religious experience, his experience of God—the Supreme moral agent.

> [I]n Jesus and in Israel God was Righteous Will and at the same time, without loss of personality or persons, He was the creator of existence.[37]

For Thurman, Jesus' religious experience revealed "the ultimate sense of responsibility that the individual has for his life before God."[38]

In the preceding chapter, we examined Thurman's interpretation of the meaning of Jesus' death. It is no small matter to note that Thurman attached the same epistemological significance to the death of Jesus as he did to Jesus' religious experiences in general. Thurman posited that Jesus learned more about God and became more certain of God as a result of his crucifixion than he did at any other moment in his life. Through his suffering, Jesus reached the ultimate level to which the human spirit can soar; he was released from the power of fear. According to Thurman, in suffering, which he describes as "the great moral struggle", human beings come closest to God because they are "stripped to the literal substance of themselves." They have "no pretentions in life, with no props left, just the naked spirit laid bare to the Mind of God." The end result of this is a feeling of desolation, which results in a more profound "consciousness that God is articulate in them."[39] From Jesus' experience of suffering on the cross, Thurman concluded the following:

> Out of the depth of that tremendous agony [on the cross] Jesus cries, "My God, my God, why hast Thou forsaken me?"—the most audacious utterance in the entire literature of religion, for here is one who declares that he is surer of God than God is of him.[40]

What do we conclude from Jesus' experience of agony on the cross? For Thurman it was very clear: in his suffering, as Jesus uttered the fateful words "My God, my God, why hast Thou forsaken me?" (Mark 15: 35, NEB) he was most sure of God and of His presence. He could be sure of God's presence because human history reveals that

> in the religious experience of men, they have discovered that they are closest to God when in their moments of agony, in their moments of desolation, they seem to be the farthest away from Him.[41]

This passionate belief lead Thurman to conclude that Jesus' suffering made it possible that even death became for him a "little thing." It was a "little thing" because here too Jesus could remember the words proclaimed to him during his baptism: "Thou art my Son, my Beloved." (Luke 3:22, NEB). But again, we note that this experience was not, for Thurman, unique to Jesus; other human beings can and do have such assurances from God.

If it is true, in any case, that Jesus was more aware and sure of God, more completely surrendered to God during his time of suffering, Thurman made an essential connection. He did not simply suggest that unmerited suffering is redemptive. Rather, the experience of suffering is in itself a religious experience. It is religious precisely for the reasons mentioned above, namely that suffering strongly reveals the presence of God in human life and experience.

Thurman described suffering as one of the "disciplines of the spirit."[42] As a discipline of the spirit, suffering creates space in human life where God is revealed. Thurman was radical in this regard, he went beyond liberals such as Fosdick and Schleiermacher, actually making the category of suffering a criterion for understanding Jesus' divinity, arguing that Jesus was "closest" to and most sure of God during the times of his suffering and temptations. (This would later have strong implications for what Thurman wrote concerning human suffering in general). In making suffering a primary category for understanding divinity, Thurman made a distinctive contribution to western theology on the whole and not simply to Christology.

We see then that, for Thurman, the primary basis for speaking about the uniqueness of Jesus is the religious experience. And the depth of this experience is linked to Jesus' willingness to follow the logic of his obedience to a direct conclusion, even to death. The challenge that Jesus presents to other persons is the demand and the necessity of being obedient to God. In this sense, Thurman is consistent with his mentor, Henry B. Robins, who said that "the uniqueness of Jesus' sonship . . .is a sense of dependence [on God]."[43]

The major assumption that Thurman made is that there is within each human person a "potential for divinity," a potential for divine sonship/daughtership. The idea of divinity for Thurman refers to the degree to which human beings share the will and purposes of God. Again this theme in Thurman's thought is similar to what we have noted about liberal theologians such as Fosdick and Schleiermacher.

Likewise, in Thurman's thought, the distinction between the supernatural and the natural world are blurred. In each, the idea of divinity has been "naturalized" and rendered more practical. As Fosdick put it:

> Divinity is not something supernatural that ever and again invades the natural order in a crashing miracle. Divinity is not in some remote heaven, seated on a throne. Divinity is Love. Here and now it shines through the highest spiritual experiences we know. Wherever goodness, beauty, truth, and love are there is the divine.[44]

Divinity, in Fosdick's understanding, is the practical embodiment of a metaphysical concept. He went on to say that "the divinity of Jesus became not only an assertion about Jesus but about divinity." For Fosdick, Jesus' divinity was defined by his personality, religious experience, and ethical vision. This is to say that the divinity of Jesus, which was an expression of "his spiritual life,"[45] was the embodiment of the metaphysical idea of divinity. Jesus' ideal personality and his ethical vision were concrete manifestations of his divinity. Here we notice that Fosdick's position is nuanced in a slightly different way than Schleiermacher (who argued that Jesus was distinguished by his "absolutely powerful God-consciousness,"[46] or the "veritable existence of God in Him"[47]) or Thurman.

Fosdick identified the personality and ethical vision of Jesus as the central indicators of his divinity. He made this very obvious in the following remarks:

> When, however, we love men, are merciful to the ungrateful and
> undeserving, forgive our enemies, reclaim the lost, and help the
> fallen, when, in a word, we respect personality, wherever we find it
> as the supreme treasure, then in the eternal love behind our love, the
> divine behind our service, we find Jesus' God.[48]

This "respect for personality" is summed up in the expression of love
towards the neighbor. Jesus' fulfillment of the mandate to love is one
aspect of his personality and ethical vision and is, therefore, also central
to what can be said about his divinity and his relationship to other
persons. According to Fosdick, "Jesus has given the world its most
significant idea of God."[49] One aspect of the distinctiveness of Jesus
was his revelation of God as the universal moral will. Jesus revealed
the moral core of the universe in a way that no other human being had
ever done. Fosdick wrote:

> A moral grandeur is exhibited in Jesus' obedience to the divine will,
> from the first struggle in the desert until it led him through
> Gethsemane to the cross, which to many of us makes his relationship
> to God the most impressive spiritual phenomena in history.[50]

Jesus made obedience to God the fundamental element of the religious
life. He was, as such, the fulfillment of the law of God, providing
humanity with its "loftiest ethical ideal."[51] This fact, Fosdick and
Thurman would argue, distinguished Jesus from other human persons.

Divine Adoption and Divine Begetting: The Special "Sonship" of Jesus

All of the themes of Thurman's Christology discussed thus far
have categorically linked him to a tradition of Christological reflections
which can be traced to the beginnings of Christian history. As was
mentioned, his views were similar to those of the Adoptionist tradition.
Adoptionism is one of the oldest Christological heresies in Christian
history. In its most basic expression Adoptionism is that tradition which:

> regards Jesus Christ as simply a human being, [who] in a special
> manner possessed the divine spirit and was adopted by God as his
> Son.[52]

To say that Jesus was "adopted" as the son of God suggests that Jesus was not born with a divine nature. In this way, he cannot be regarded as a pre-existent, almighty being, co-equal and co-eternal with God. Rather, he was adopted to be the son of God. He was "begotten" by God.

There are several New Testament passages that seem to support the claims that adoptionists make about Jesus. Among them Matthew 3:17b; Mark1:11b; and Luke 3:22b. Here we find the phrases, "Thou art my beloved Son; with thee I am well pleased," and "Thou art my beloved Son; today I have begotten thee."[53]

The great controversy that led to the formation of the Nicene Creed centered on the question of whether the "begotteness" of Jesus signified that he was "created" by God or whether his "begotteness" simply indicated that he stood in special relationship to God.[54] Arius—who was declared to be the archheritic in this controversy—used the two terms synonymously. To say that Jesus was "begotten" meant, in Arius' opinion, that Jesus was created by God. Arius explained his position in the following manner:

> But what is it that we say and believe and did teach and do teach? That the Son is not unoriginated (4), neither in any way partially unoriginated (5), nor from any essential substratum (6). Rather, that by will and counsel He subsisted before time and before ages, fully God, only-begotten, unchangeable: and before He was begotten—that is, created—or separated or established, He did not exist. For He was not unoriginated.[55]

The problem with the Arian position, according to the framers of the Nicene Creed, was its denial of the doctrine of the eternal existence of the Son; if the Son had to be created, there must have been a time when he did not exist. To the orthodox defenders of the faith, this seemed to undermine the Christian teaching on Jesus Christ as the Savior of humankind.

The Nicene Creed, which became the standard of orthodoxy, speaks of the "begotteness" of Jesus as a way of demonstrating his subordination to God, without, however, positing that Jesus was ever "created."

> God from God, Light from Light, true God from true God, begotten not created [poiethenta], of the same essence [reality] as the Father. . .
> But, those who say, *once he was not* [italics mine], or he was not before his generation, or he came to be out of nothing, or who assert

that he, the Son of God, is of a different hypostasis or ousia, or that he is a creature, or changeable, or mutable, the Catholic and Apostolic Church anathematizes them.[56]

Two principal Christological affirmations emerge from this creed. First, the "Son of God" was neither created nor made, such as were other human beings and creatures. Rather, he is co-equal and co-eternal with God. Second, Jesus of Nazareth was identified as the eternal son of God. These themes are diametrically opposed to the Adoptionist approach to Christology, which posits that Jesus was chosen to be the son of God at some point during his earthly existence. According to the Nicene Creed, any discussion of Jesus having "become", or having been "made" to be the son of God is a misrepresentation of the truth of the Gospel.

The idea of Jesus being "adopted" and "begotten" by God did not, however, present any contradictions for Thurman. He did not perceive either of these as being opposed to his view of the divinity of Jesus. At any rate, Thurman rejected both the Arianism, with its notion of Jesus having been created at an earlier, pre-existent stage, and the Nicene Creed, which says that Jesus was at one and the same time begotten by God and co-eternal with God. Thurman spoke instead of the "begotteness of Jesus" in a spiritual sense. He pointed to the baptism of Jesus as the point at which this adoption took place. Clearly Jesus was chosen at that time to be a son of God.[57] The baptism of Jesus represented his public identification with things pertaining to the Kingdom of God. The other aspect of Thurman's treatment of the divinity of Jesus can be linked to his statements about Jesus' "anointing". Jesus' religious experience, coupled with his anointing, confirmed his special mission.

> [Jesus] was the Anointed One of God, the one who, as a result of his religious experience, had glimpsed in some full-orbed manner the living mind of living God and was so imbued with the glory of that vision that he dared to believe that in the details of his living this revelation could find a fulfillment.[58]

Religious experience is also crucial here.

The Maturation of Jesus' Divine Consciousness

The fact that Jesus was "adopted" to be the son of God and the fact of his humanity further confirm what we have said about the manner in which he attained his divinity. Thurman circumvented questions about Jesus' sinless perfection. He focused instead on the nature of Jesus' spiritual development. As he said:

> [Jesus] grew into manhood exhibiting in word and deed a fresh new quality of the age-old response of the spirit of man to the call of God. God was everything to him.[59]

As Jesus grew in life, his vision of God became more clear, as did his mission. According to Thurman:

> [Jesus'] was a vision of a great ideal that all men are children of God, that the normal relation of one man to another is love (anything else is against life), and that there is a personal Power, God, equally available to the rich and poor, to Jew and Gentile, to men and women, to the wise and the foolish, to the just and the unjust.[60]

Jesus' development was not, however, void of great struggle and adversity. Thurman wrote *Temptations of Jesus* in order to reveal the moral and spiritual dilemmas that Jesus faced during his life and ministry. Thurman wrote:

> [T]he Master. . . struggled to find a way [which would] be for him The Way in which he [could] walk in utter harmony with the Will of his Father and the purpose of life.[61]

In this sense, Thurman noted that Jesus' struggle and quest were the same as those of every other human being who seeks to learn to do the will of God. Thurman felt that Jesus experienced a degree of struggle with sin. Just as any other human being, Jesus had the freedom to sin and disobey God if he chose to. Thurman offers the following fictional narrative in describing Jesus' temptations:

> With all the embodiment that I feel of the very living Spirit of God,
> with all the for instances of His Kingdom, . . . nevertheless, I still
> must operate within the structure that holds. When I get out of it,
> life becomes the Enemy. When I am in it, life becomes the Resource.
> When I get out of it, I experience the Wrath of god. When I am
> within it I experience the Love of God.[62]

This quote provides an indication of the "inner sense" of the struggle
that Jesus felt as he was tempted. The hermeneutical question remains
to be asked: Could we assume that this temptation was indeed "real"?

> If the dilemma were real, if the temptations were real, Jesus could
> have failed. If he could not have failed, there is no meaning in his
> freedom. I am so very glad that he struggled and triumphed. And so
> he speaks to me all the time that I might struggle, if, happily, I too
> might triumph.[63]

Jesus' struggles with the powers of death and destruction indicate the
degree to which he was like other human beings and shared a similar
plight with them.

But the key issue for Thurman was that Jesus did not sin, he did
not succumb to the powers of evil. In this sense, Jesus exhibited a
degree of spiritual and moral superiority over other human beings. He
had the power to withstand the temptation. But this too was the result
of and an indication of the profundity of his religious experiences.
These experiences—progressing in accordance with the degree of his
surrender to God—gave meaning and power to Jesus' life. Nothing
more clearly depicts the reason for Jesus' identity as he witnessed the
"trueing his spirit and his whole life by the will of his Father."[64] The
depth of Jesus' experience and surrender is characterized by the fact
that he seems to have become completely absolved in fulfilling the will
of God. Thurman's description of Jesus' Triumphant Entry into
Jerusalem makes this point very clearly:

> So close had [Jesus] worked with God that the line of demarcation
> between his will and God's Will would fade and reappear, fade and
> reappear. Step by resolute step, he had come to the great city.[65]

This is the context wherein Jesus achieved distinction as an individual
who lived before God. This brings us to the final aspect of Thurman's
treatment of the divinity of Jesus.

We have noted earlier that Thurman's views were very similar to those of Harry Emerson Fosdick who was a part of what, according to Kenneth Cauthen, was called the "back to Jesus" movement in liberal theology.[66] While Fosdick and others saw no need to prove or defend the notion of the Second Person of the Trinity, they did believe that Jesus' life and personality were the highest expression of religious consciousness. Fosdick affirmed that Jesus of Nazareth provides the principal means whereby human beings come to know God. Christocentric liberals see Jesus as the embodiment of religious truth.[67] Other individuals may approximate the way of life that Jesus espoused, but they are not to be equated with the primacy of Jesus of Nazareth.

Unlike the Christocentric liberals, Thurman was much more "open-ended" about his assessment of the primacy of Jesus of Nazareth as the conduit of religious truth. Thurman believed that Jesus was indeed a conduit of religious truth but not the source of that truth. Thurman's position is closer to Cauthen's definition of modernistic liberalism.[68] Thurman actually argued that Jesus was unique; he represented "life at its best.[69] But Thurman would never extend this argument to suggest that Jesus' was the only way to God, or the only embodiment of God that we have in human history. For Thurman, Jesus was one example in a long tradition of persons who were living testimonies of what it means to "walk with God".

People Who Have Walked With God

In discussing his view of Jesus' divinity Thurman went to great lengths to demonstrate the commonality between Jesus' religious experience and the experiences of other persons. He posited that there are other individuals who embody the same type of religious experience and genius as did Jesus. He believed this to be true even for persons outside of the Christian tradition. He pointed to the lives of individuals such as Buddha, the Brahmin Mystics, and Mahatma Gandhi.[70] In each of these persons we find examples of how individuals surrender their lives to God in a complete sense. They embodied the highest form of spiritual and moral idealism. Like Jesus, "they provided a vision of the way life ought to be between man and man, even between man and animals."[71] Each individual had a different set of experiences but their contributions to life emerged directly from their inner experiences.

We see an example of this in Thurman's analysis of Buddha's spiritual and ethical contributions to humanity. He portrays the Buddha as a perennial seeker: a seeker of inner-peace, spiritual illumination, justice for the poor, peace among people, and peace within the self. The Buddha's genius rested in the strength of the "ethical insights" which emerged from his moments of inner-illumination. He provided to the world an ethic that was steeped in the highest form of religious self-consciousness. Thurman explains this in the following manner:

> Now the ethic that is a derivative from the discovery of Buddha is this: it is the ethic of self purification. . .But now this is the wonderfully glorious thing about his insight, he discovered that if an individual becomes sufficiently pure in his life that the purity of this life radiates automatically without the movement of his will, even the purity of his life radiates a quality that is moral in character, that affects the lives of other people.[72]

The logical outcome of the Buddha's religious experience was his strong, life-affirming movement back into the chaos of the world as an agent of transformation. In so doing the Buddha challenged all human being's to

> . . . make an attack on moral disorder in the world by the purification of one's own life on the theory and the faith that something can be radiated from that that is redemptive in character. And until we test that how dare we set up our faith, whatever it may be, with arrogance and pride and look with judgment upon the face of the Buddha.[73]

The comparison between the Buddha and Jesus is not without some complications. Thurman did not avoid these complications. For instance, the Buddha's religious vision was non-theistic; there was not a supreme deity in his vision. This is certainly radically different from Jesus' strong monotheistic religious experience. Yet the two are brought together in Thurman's thought under the umbrella of his broad vision of religious experience. If, as we have said, Jesus' divinity was in essence anchored in the profundity of his experience of God, Buddha attained a like degree of divinity in his self-purification and inner-illumination. The Buddha attained an absolute perfection of consciousness; he reached a state of self-transcendence that is rare among human beings. So the object of their religious affections may have been radically different, but the Buddha and Jesus both demonstrated the true nature and meaning of religious experience. Both introduced an ethic that was radical, powerful, and redemptive for all human beings. Moreover, the key to Thurman's treatment of this subject was his assumption about the nature of their ethical contributions. Jesus and Buddha were similar in that each garnered his ethical vision from his religious experience. They demonstrated that the religious experience was to be validated by its impact on the world, its social relevance. Each man's vision is life-affirming and life-transforming.

A few references to Thurman's statements about the religious visions of the Brahman mystics will also help us in this discussion. These mystics, operating from within the wellsprings of Hindu spirituality, offer another eastern vision of the holy life. Thurman described them in the same manner as he described Jesus and Buddha; they were religious pioneers, people whose religious visions transcended the normal limits known to other human beings. The Brahman mystics embodied the religious ideals that others only dream about. They saw and experienced what others desire, but the others "don't have their patience, don't have their courage".[74] In discussing this issue, Thurman went back to the idea that we have discussed above, the belief in the universality of God and the oneness of all truth. Here he discussed the Hindu notion of the world-soul, the idea that all of reality is essentially spiritual. In the Brahman ethic, as in Hinduism in general, there is an assumed kinship between human beings, the animal kingdom, and the natural world. The universal presence of God is expressed and seen in each sphere. Thurman was convinced that this emphasis was one of the revolutionary aspects of Hinduism. Revolutionary because it supports the liberal Protestant notion of the infinite worth of the human soul. Both the Brahman and the Christian tradition affirm the idea of the "sacredness of all personalities." The line of continuity between Buddhism and the religion of Jesus is the accent that each places on the ultimate responsibility that each individual has for the other. Each envisions a pattern of human ethical responsibility that grows out of their religious visions. Again, this underscores Thurman's belief in the revolutionary power inherent in true religious experience. Thurman concluded that persons and groups such as Jesus, the Buddha, and the Braman mystics found the secret to the meaning of life and that their witness sheds light on all human pathways to God.

These examples should show us how Thurman's understanding of Jesus' divinity is linked to his view of religious experience in general. And in so doing light is shed on what I have suggested about the universal implications of this notion in his theology. Before concluding this chapter, I will reference the doctrinal statement of the Church for the Fellowship of all Peoples as a further demonstration of this point. The Faith Statement that Thurman helped to develop for the Church for the Fellowship of All Peoples, the San Francisco church co-founded by Thurman, helps to illustrate this point:

> I affirm my need for a growing understanding of all men as sons of God, and I seek after a vital experience of God as revealed in Jesus of Nazareth and other great religious spirits whose fellowship with God was the foundation of their fellowship with man.[75]

This statement expresses the essence of Thurman's conception of the universality of religious truth. Thurman discovered a way to acknowledge the definitive status of Jesus of Nazareth without becoming Christocentric.[76] In chapter one of *Jesus and the Disinherited*, for example, Thurman quotes an epigram from a text written by Heinrich Weinel and Alban G. Widgery. Weinel and Wigdery say that:

> To some God and Jesus may appeal in a way other than to us: some may come to faith in God and to love, without a conscious attachment to Jesus. Both Nature and good men besides Jesus may lead us to God. They who seek God with all their hearts must, however, some day on their way meet Jesus. [77]

According to Thurman, God does not imply that knowing Jesus is a prerequisite for human salvation. Rather, Thurman contended that any person who had a true experience of God would inevitably come to know the same kind of illumination evidenced in Jesus. Thus all true seekers come to know Jesus as a fellow traveler along the way. They know and experience the revelation that we see in Jesus, Buddha, Gandhi, the Braman mystics, and a host of other seekers we see in human history. Thurman was by no means imperialist or exclusive in this regard. Other persons and religious traditions provide different "paths" to God, but to Thurman they were not inferior to Jesus' path. In fact, Thurman went out of the way to avoid the evolutionary view of non-Western religious traditions even though this perspective, which regards non-Western religions as lower forms of religious development, is a common one among many liberal theologians of the last two centuries.[78]

One more fact needs to be considered before concluding our reflections on Thurman's view of the divinity of Jesus. Thurman believed that religious experiences provide truth that is operative in all religious encounters. This is why Thurman found no reason to make Jesus' claims binding on all persons. He believed that there is truth in all genuine expressions of religious faith. Thurman agreed with Rufus M. Jones' description of religious truth:

> Truth is never some dead thing which can be laid out; it is living, moving, quickening, outgrowing its old forms, taking on new expressions and preserving itself, as life does, by endless variations and by infinite embodiments.[79]

This sense of the universality of truth is what operates in Thurman's work. Given this assumption, he would not limit religious truth to one particular tradition, community, or individual. This would go against his belief in the fundamental sense of "unity" and "aliveness" in all of life. Thurman believed that truth must be celebrated and espoused irrespective of where it is found.[80] This belief, coupled with what was said above, accounts for why Thurman was not a Christocentric thinker.

There are several factors which should be noted before concluding this chapter on Thurman's view of the divinity of Jesus. Firstly, Thurman unquestionably believed that Jesus of Nazareth was fully human and fully divine. Secondly, he refused, however, to base his understanding of the humanity and divinity of Jesus on the "two natures" doctrine of the Chalcedonian Creed.[81] Instead, he choose to interpret the divinity of Jesus in terms of Jesus' spiritual and experiential accomplishments. He followed the liberal tradition in insisting that Jesus earned his special sonship and divinity through his experience of and obedience to God. This is the centerpiece of Thurman's treatment of the divinity of Jesus. He insisted on depicting Jesus as a person who was "hungry for God." Thirdly, while Thurman acknowledged the uniqueness and divinity of Jesus, he was not a Christocentric thinker. He refused to suggest that the religion of Jesus nullified the claims of all other religious leaders and traditions. Fourthly, Thurman viewed Jesus' response to and experience of suffering as true signs of his divinity. Fifth, the liberal emphasis on the immanent presence of God within the realm of human experience and in nature had a direct impact upon Thurman's understanding of what the belief in the divinity of Jesus actually meant. Finally, in this chapter we have demonstrated that the liberal Western theological tradition played a central role in shaping Thurman's assessment of the divinity of Jesus.

Notes

1   Dennis W. Wiley, "The Concept of the Church in the Works of Howard Thurman" p. 74.
2   See the beginning of chapter one.
3   See Adolf Harnack, *What is Christianity?* (Gloucester, Mass.: Peter Smith, 1978).
4   Please note that we will not cover these themes in the same order that they are listed here. We will cover them in a way that helps us to better understand Thurman's work.
5   Kenneth Cauthen, *The Impact of American Religious Liberalism* (New York: Harper and Row, 1962; Washington, DC: University Press of America, 1983), p. 104.
6   See Cauthen for a description of some of the more significant liberal approaches to christology. Our concern here is simply to focus upon those thinkers whose Christologies help us to grasp Thurman's work. Ibid.
7   Howard Thurman, "The Idea of God and Modern Thought," paper presented at the 25th annual Garvin Lecture on the Idea of God as Affected by Modern Knowledge at the Church of Our Father (Unitarian), Lancaster, PA, 23 November 1965. He also delivered another lecture that was a variation on the earlier article. See his, "God an the Modern World," paper presented n.p., Seattle, WA, 29 June 1970.
     Van Harvey, *Handbook of Theological Terms* (New York: Macmillan Publishing Co., Inc. 1964), p. 172.
8   Schleiermacher, *Christian*, p. 365. See Kenneth Cauthen, *Liberalism*. Also see Henry P. Van Dusen's article in George F. Thomas, ed., *The Vitality of the Christian Tradition* (New York: Harper and Brothers, 1944). We should also remember Karl Barth's critique of the liberal approach to the distinction between the immanence and the transcendence of God. See his, *The Theology of Schleiermacher*, ed. Dietrich Ritschl, trans. Geoffrey W. Bromiley, (Grand Rapids: William B. Eerdmans Publishing Company, 1982), p.
9   Schleiermacher, *Christian*, p. 365.
10   Friedrich Schleiermacher, *The Christian Faith*, ed. H. R. Mackintosh and J. S. Stewart, (Philadelphia: Fortress Press, 1976), p. 365.
11   Ibid. p. 365.
12   We speak here specifically of Bultmann's characterization of first century cosmology with its pre-scientific explanation of nature and natural phenomena. See his discussion of this subject in Rudolf Bultmann, *Jesus Christ and Mythology;* see also Schleiermacher's more detailed discussion of this issue in *The Christian Faith*, pp. 62f, 365f. Richard R. Niebuhr notes that Schleiermacher's description of the supernatural is written in contradiction to the Deist view of natural and the supernatural. See his

text for a more thorough discussion of the development of Schleiermacher's Christology as this is reflected in his major writings. See his *Schleiermacher on Christ and Religion* (New York: Charles Scribner's Sons, 1964), p. 166; Schleiermacher, *Christ*. p. 365.

13   Harry Emerson Fosdick, *The Modern Use of the Bible* (New York: The MacMillan Company, 1924), pp. 266-267.

14   Ibid. p. 270.

15   Howard Thurman, *Disciplines of the Spirit* (Richmond, IN.: Friends United Press, 1977; p. 89; New York: Harper & Row, 1963)

16   Ibid.

17   Thurman, *With Head and Heart,* p. 8.

18   Ibid. p. 8.

19   Thurman, *With Head and Heart,* p. 9.

20   From "The Growing Edge," quoted in Mozella Mitchell's "The Dynamics of Howard Thurman's Relationship to Literature and Theology" (Ph.D. Dissertation, Emory University, 1980) later published under the title, *The Spiritual Dynamics of Howard Thurman's Theology* p. 24. Mitchell demonstrates that the search for universality and unity within reality represents one facet of Olive Schreiner's impact upon Thurman's thought. See her short article on this subject, "Howard Thurman and Olive Schreiner: Post-Modern Marriage Post-mortem," in *Journal of Religious Thought* 38 no. 1 (Spring 1981): 67.

21   Note also Wiley's claim that Thurman makes "everyone" a mystic in the sense that he himself was to liberal leanings. See his "Church"; note especially chapter 3. For a discussion of these and other related issues see also Howard Thurman, *Search for Common Ground,* (New York: Harper & Row, 1971); see also Wiley, "Church;" and Pollard, "Social."

22   Dennis W. Wiley, "Church." p. 74.

23   Howard Thurman, "The Religion of Jesus—Jesus and God," 6 November 1978, 2nd Christian Church, Indianapolis, IN. No liberal theologian accents this point more emphatically than Schleiermacher, who refused to develop an elaborate doctrine of the Trinity because the knowledge that is required for such a doctrine was not available through religious experience. Schleiermacher believed that what one says about the being of God must be validated through experience. See Schleiermacher, Christian. The final segment of the study gives a very short, in relation to other sections of the book, discussion of what he believes can be said about the doctrine of the Trinity. As a matter of fact, Schleiermacher believed that the knowledge of its dependency on God is the most fundamental element of human awareness. No theologian more radically rejects the liberal focus on the primacy of "religion" versus "revelation" as a foundation for the Christian faith than did Karl Barth. Barth, representing the dominant neo-orthodox reaction to the liberal tradition, regarded religion as "criminal arrogance" against God. See Richard R. Niebuhr, *Schleiermacher*, p.179. This emphasis is a consistent theme in

the neo-orthodox tradition. It represents a total rejection of the notion of a "primal ground" of God consciousness or knowledge to which human beings can appeal for an understanding of God. For a more detailed discussion of this subject see Chapter 4 of Niebuhr's text.

24 Howard Thurman, "Standing Inside with Christ," An Address Delivered at the Kirkland Institute of Bishop College, 70 April 21, p. 4.

25 Thurman, *Disciplines of the Spirit,* p. 89.

26 Quoted in Mitchell, *Dynamics.* p. 12.

27 Howard Thurman, *The Temptations of Jesus* (San Francisco: Lawton Kennedy, 1962; reprint ed. Richmond, In.: Friends United Press, 1978), p. 67.

28 Thurman, "A Faith to Live By—Jesus Christ," n.p., 28 September 1952.

29 Thurman, *Deep River,* p. 172.

30 Ibid.

31 Ibid. p. 173.

32 Howard Thurman, "The Soundless Passion of a Single Mind," (58, January 29), p. 7.

33 Thurman, "Man and the Moral Struggle (Jesus", p. 4

34 Howard Thurman, "The Religion of Jesus—Jesus and God" (n.d.), p. 3.

35 We will discuss the subject of Jesus' moral imparatives in the next chapter.

36 This emphasis on the centrality of "morality" and "personality" in the doing of Christology is also a consistent theme in the works of George Cross, one of Thurman's mentors. See for example, his *What is Christianity: A Study of Rival Interpretations* (Chicago: University of Chicago Press, 1918), p. 193. See also Luther Smith's discussion of Cross' impact upon Thurman's work, *Howard Thurman: The Mystic as Prophet*, Chapter 2.

37 Howard Thurman, "Jesus and the Disinherited," Part II. p. 7.

38 Thurman, "Religion of Jesus," Vol. II., p. 3.

39 Thurman, "Man and the Moral Struggle," n.p., n.d., p. 11.

40 Ibid.

41 Ibid.

42 Howard Thurman, *Disciplines of the Spirit* (New York: Harper & Row, 1963; reprint ed. Richmond, IN.: Friends United Press, 1977), see chapter 3.

43 Henry B. Robins, *Aspects of Authority in the Christian Religion* (Boston: The Griffith & Rowland Press, 1927), p. 128.

44 Harry Emerson Fosdick, *A Guide to Understanding the Bible* (New York: Harper & Brothers, 1938), p. 42; quoted in Cauthen, *Liberalism*, p. 80.

45 Quoted in Cauthen, p. 80.

46 See Schleiermacher's full discussion of this issue in his treatment of the person of Jesus in his *The Christian Faith.* p. 374.

47 Ibid. p. 385.

48 Fosdick, *Modern Use of the Bible,* p. 223.

49 Ibid. p. 222.

50 Ibid.

51 Ibid. p. 226.

52 Rahner, *Dictionary of Theology,* p. 4.

53 Both Wiley and Smith have noted the adoptionist element in Thurman's thought. See Wiley's "Church" and Smith's *Howard Thurman: The Mystic as Prophet.* Lk.. 3.11. *The New Oxford Annotated Bible.* See the explanatory notes on this passage, p. 1245.

54 For a more thorough discussion of this see, William A. Jurgens, *Early Fathers* p. 277f.

55 Ibid. p. 279.

56 Leith, *Creeds of the Churches,* p. 31.

57 We will discuss this issue in greater detail below. Wiley makes this point in his study, "Church," p. 87.

58 Howard Thurman, "Man and the Moral Struggle, Jesus," p. 8.

59 Howard Thurman, *The Inward Journey,* p. 27.

60 Ibid.

61 Howard Thurman, *Temptations of Jesus* (San Francisco: Lawton Kennedy, 1962; reprint ed., Richmond, IN.: Friends United Press, 1978), p. 7.

62 Ibid. p. 37.

63 Ibid.

64 Thurman, *The Inward Journey,* p. 31.

65 Ibid.

66 Kenneth Cauthen, *Liberalism.* See Chapter 1.

67 See the definition of Christocentricism in Cauthen, *Liberalism,* Chapter 2. Luther Smith provides a very good discussion of this subject and he gives specific attention to Thurman's connection with his mentors' views of the finality of Jesus. See his *Howard Thurman: The Mystic as Prophet.*

68 See Chapter 2 of Smith, *Howard Thurman: The Mystic as Prophet.*

69 Thurman, *The Mood of Christmas.* p. 8.

70 See his series entitled, "Men Who Walked with God, Buddha," n.p. , 5 May 1953.

71 Thurman, "Standing Inside With Christ", p. 8; 21 April, 1970.

72 Thurman, "Buddha", p. 7.

73 Ibid. p. 8.

74 Thurman, "Men Who Have Walked With God, The Braman Mystics," 26 April, 1953; p. 3.

75 See Howard Thurman, *With Head and Heart,* p. 143. See also his record of the founding of Fellowship Church, *Footprints of A Dream* (New York: Harper & Row, 1959); as well as his edited collection of letters that tells the story of the church, *The First Footprints: The Dawn of the Idea of the Church for the Fellowship of All Peoples* (San Francisco: Lawton and Alfred Kennedy, 1975).

76 See Luther Smith's assessment of Thurman's place in the liberal approach to Christology. Smith classifies Thurman within what Cauthen has called the "modernistic" liberal tradition. See *Liberalism* p. 29; and Smith's *Howard Thurman: The Mystic as Prophet,* p. 74.

77 Quoted in Howard Thurman, *Jesus and the Disinherited.* p. 11.

78 One sees this ambiguity in Schleiermacher's attitude towards other religions. In the prolegomena to his systematic theology he admits that there are other forms of piety outside of Christianity. But he also argues that they are "inferior" to Christianity. Moreover he says that "monotheistic" expressions of piety represent the highest form of development of religious self-consciousness. Thus polytheistic faiths are regarded as a lower form of religious self-consciousness. He refers to Greek and Indian religions as examples of polytheism, and uses Judaism, Islam, and Christianity as the three great expressions of monotheism. Note, however, that he readily discredits Judaism and Islam because of their lack of a universal ethic and the overemphasis on the emotional aspects of religion respectively. Christianity is seen as the most significant of all three forms. See his *Christian.* See especially rubrics 7-8. This approach, in my opinion, represents a form of intellectual and cultural arrogance which is not uncommon in western religion. On the one hand they recognize the contributions of other religions but are not willing to give them equal credibility with Christianity. This same limitation is also seen in the brilliant but highly biased work of Ernst Troeltsch, the great history of religion specialist. See James Luther Adams' introduction to Troeltsch's *The Absoluteness of Christianity and the History of Religions,* with introduction by James Luther Adams, trans. David Reid, (Richmond: John Knox Press, 1971), p. 15.

79 Rufus Jones, *Practical Christianity* (Philadelphia: The John C. Winston Co., 1899), p. 22.

80 See Thurman, *Common Ground.* Note the discussion of the "universality" of human experience that runs throughout this text.

81 It is essential to note that while Athanasius said that the ultimate purpose of the Incarnation was to make human beings "divine," said he: "He [Logos] became man so that we might be God; and He manifested Himself in the flesh, so that we might grasp the idea of the unseen Father; and He endured the insolence of men, so that we might receive the inheritance of immortality." This does not imply that individuals are said to be divine in a metaphysical sense, namely in the same sense of the persons of the Godhead, or in the sense of possessing a divine nature. Rather he suggests that individuals share in the divine life. See Jurgens, *The Faith of the Early Fathers*, p. 322.

Chapter IV

Good News for the Disinherited: Jesus of Nazareth and Human Liberation

> Wherever [Jesus'] spirit appears, the oppressed gather fresh courage; for he announced the good news that fear, hypocrisy, and hatred, the three hounds of hell that tract the trail of the disinherited, need have no dominion over them.

—Howard Thurman

This chapter brings us to the crux of the issue in Thurman's treatment of the life, teachings, and ministry of Jesus. The key concern here is the question of how Jesus empowers, strengthens, and liberates the oppressed, those persons who live with their "backs against the wall."[1] Thurman's entire theological project reflected his interest in this practical issue. He wanted more than anything else to demonstrate the relevance of religious faith to the socio-political concerns of oppressed people. He indeed argued that the moral and spiritual integrity of the Christian church rests on its ability to meaningfully relate the truths of the gospel to the plight of the poor and the dispossessed in society. This mandate emerged from Thurman's understanding of Christianity as a religion of liberation.

In this chapter we will focus on the mission of Jesus and his word of liberation for the oppressed. We will examine Thurman's analysis of the multidimensional nature of the human oppression from which Jesus delivers. Much attention will be given to the subject of Thurman's rootedness in the African-American community and his appropriation of themes and ideas emerging from this tradition. In addition, we will specifically examine those aspects of the life, message, and ministry of Jesus which Thurman used in addressing the issue of oppression.

African-American liberation theologians have helped to change the course of Christian thought over the past three decades. They have insisted, as James H. Cone notes, that the Christian message is a message of liberation. For theologians such as Cone, oppression is defined in terms of racial matters. At any rate, the emphasis on the meaning of the Christian message for the oppressed echoes Thurman's theology. In this sense, Thurman was a forerunner to the black theology movement. His active career ended before the black theology movement began.[2] Thus the most productive period of his intellectual development was actually behind him before the liberation theology movement began. Yet there are very strong correlations between Thurman's work and the theology of James H. Cone, the leading black liberation theologian. Carlyle Felding Stewart, III has accurately demonstrated this point.[3] The term liberation does not appear in Thurman's writings, as it does, for example, in the works of Cone and Roberts. For liberation theologians, the term "liberation" has always had reference to socio-economic and political matters. It meant primarily freedom from immediate social and economic bondage. Thurman, however, used terms such as "wholeness" and "self-actualization" in order to express this same idea. His use of these terms corresponds to what liberation theologians say about the liberation process.[4] Thurman's thesis about Jesus' relevance to the oppressed is at the heart of his view of human self-actualization and wholeness.

Towards an Interpretation of Human Oppression and Liberation

If we are to talk about the religion of Jesus as "good news for the disinherited", we must begin with an understanding of the meaning and experience of oppression. Thurman's *Jesus and the Disinherited* provides an excellent starting point for a discussion of human oppression. He wrote the text in order to show "[t]he significance of the religion of Jesus to people who stand with their backs against the wall."[5] This issue is central. Thurman wrote:

> This is the question which individuals and groups who live in our land always under the threat of profound social and psychological displacement face: Why is it that Christianity seems impotent to deal radically, and therefore effectively, with the issues of discrimination and injustice on the basis of race, religion and national origin? Is this impotency due to a betrayal of the genius of the religion, or is it due to a weakness in religion itself?[6]

Two central points are revealed here. First, Thurman believed that Christianity, which originated in Jesus' religion and religious experiences, is a religion for the oppressed. Moreover, Thurman also revealed his belief in the inherent, liberating power of religious experience.

Discussions of Thurman on the subject of human oppression must begin with a statement about this phrase: "people who stand with their backs against the wall."[7] This phrase expresses the essence of Thurman's definition of oppression. People who live with their "backs against the wall" are persons who live in situations where they are not, in his words, "self-actualized." Self-actualized people are socially and psychologically whole. They may have some problems but their lives are fundamentally whole. Persons who are not self-actualized lack this sense of wholeness and fulfillment. Thurman understood wholeness and fulfillment in a complete sense. Every facet of human existence would be including the socio-economic, political, moral, and physical. In discussing the plight of the first century Jewish community, for example, Thurman talked about the total climate within which they lived. The principal context for understanding oppression begins with an analysis of the socio-economic and political structure under which people live. The other levels of their existence emerge from these.

Thurman's interpretation of the experience of individual and communal oppression does not end here. It also extends to the psycho-spiritual[8] and the ethical dimensions of human experience. He depicted the multidimensional nature and sources of human oppression. It is this emphasis, focusing on the internal—the psycho-spiritual and the ethical—dimensions of oppression, which constitutes one of Thurman's central contributions to the African-American religious tradition.[9] This is corroborated somewhat by Cornel West, the renowned African-American intellectual of the 1990s, in two of his works, *Prophesy Deliverance: An Afro-American Revolutionary Christianity*, and later in *Race Matters*. West says that black liberation theologians have failed to fully grasp the deep sense of existential crisis and dread which helps to define the existence of oppressed people, and black liberation theologians have acknowledged this negligence.[10] In *Race Matters*, West discusses the subject of nihilism. He proposes that nihilism is the most destructive force in the African-American community, eating away at its very soul. Nihilism represents the convergence of socio-cultural, political, spiritual, and economic forces upon the black community. It represents a loss of meaning, purpose, values, and identity, reducing the significance of life to the most petty episodes of personal gratification and self-indulgence.

West's discussion of nihilism broaches the subject of the multidimensional nature of oppression, as Thurman described it. Oppression touches the deepest and most fundamental dimensions of human life. It is not simply a matter of social, economic, and political powerlessness. It is also a matter of psycho-spiritual values, attitudes, and experiences, all of which are central to the question of the meaning of human life. Thurman's view of human oppression goes beyond questions of racial and gender oppression, which would later become so central to black and feminist theology.[11] He wanted to deal with oppression's core or its soul rather than merely its manifestations in issues such as gender and race.[12]

One example of this fact is the manner in which Thurman dealt with segregation, describing it as a spiritual/moral problem. For Thurman, it went beyond the legal concerns. *The Luminous Darkness*, 1966, unpacks the meaning of segregation, discrimination, and prejudice at a personal level. *The Search for Common Ground*, 1971, on the other hand, discusses the biological, social, natural, and historical basis for the quest for unity and community within the human family. In *The Luminous Darkness* Thurman pulled together many of the themes on racism, segregation, and discrimination which are scattered throughout his earlier works, particularly *Jesus and the Disinherited*, *Deep River*, and *The Negro Spiritual Speaks of Life and Death*. In the later two works, Thurman examined the significance of the religion of Jesus, slave religion, and religion in general as spiritual resources for the oppressed. Racism is one expression of the abuse of power in an oppressive society. But Thurman is most clear about the fact that racism, as embodied in segregation, is not simply a social problem for the oppressed. As he noted, "the cost of segregation is corrosion of the spirit and the slow deadly corruption of the soul. [The soul] is overcome by evil."[13]

Racism, discrimination, prejudice, and bigotry are social cancers, and they eventually destroy every aspect of the social and political fabric of a people. More fundamentally, however, these forces are cancers to the human soul, individually and collectively. They destroy the spirit of a race, a nation, a people, as well as individuals. Thurman called segregation a sickness which robs all persons of their most valuable spiritual commodity, their true sense of humanity. Thus segregation is not simply a socio-economic system, it is:

> a mood, a state of mind, and its external manifestation is external.
> The root of the evil, and evil it is, is in the human spirit. Laws which
> make segregation illegal may or may not attack the root of the evil.[14]

As a mood and a state of mind, racism, discrimination, prejudice, and bigotry's roots are deep within the human spirit and psyche. This is not to deny the efficacy of the law in dealing with the social dimensions of racism, prejudice, and segregation, as Thurman goes on to note.

> [Laws'] great function is to deny the binding character of the external
> symbol by giving it no legal standing. . . The law cannot deal with
> the human spirit directly. This is not within its universe of
> discourse. [15]

Originating within the human spirit, racism and prejudice are willful moods of defiance against the good will of humankind. Thurman describes these defiant moods as walls within the human mind and spirit. They are walls which destroy other persons.[16]

Oppression: The Stifling of Human Potential

The great tragedy in all forms of oppression is that it represents a stifling of God-given potential. This stifling can occur in a multiplicity of ways: socio-economic, political, psycho-spiritual, and ethical. Individual oppression is expressed particularly through forces that affect individual behavior but over which the individual often has no control. Thurman said that each individual is born into a world of "facts" over which she/he has no control, for instance, racial identity, social class, culture, nationality, educational opportunities, and political realities. Individuals come to self-awareness in a world and at a time when all of these factors have already been determined. The task of every human life, however, is to seek "wholeness" and "self-actualization". The socio-economic and political world in which one lives will shape whether and how one approaches the quest for wholeness and self-actualization. Social realities and institutions can function as liberating forces, but often they become agents of human oppression and bondage.[17]

The experience of oppression is greater than this. There is a "cosmic" dimension. Thurman argued that there is meaning and purpose in the entire movement of history, just as there is in human lives. Just as individuals are born with purpose and potential, so is the cosmos. According to Thurman, all things move toward a kind of "telos," otherwise known as potential. He defined potential as, "that which has not yet come to pass but is always coming to pass."[18] This goal-seeking quality is central to all living reality, human institutions, etc.

> [T]he "intent" of creation is that life lives on constantly seeking to realize itself in established forms, patterns, and units. Expressed in this way, it must not be thought that life is static, something that is set, fixed, determined.[19]

Thus Thurman saw within the very structure of human life and within history a whole-making motif. This quality of "aliveness" is central to every fabric of Thurman's thought.

> The development of a quality of human life that would give to all the rest of living a sensitiveness, a depth of being, which would put man in the fullest possession of all his powers; in other words [it would] make man whole.[20]

Wherever and whenever these experiences of wholeness occur in the cosmos, we see expressions of an actualized sense of community, or liberated existence.

> The degree to which potential in any expression of life is actualized marks the extent to which such expression of life experiences wholeness, integration and community.[21]

Walter E. Fluker correctly notes that Thurman's view of this process is based on a triadic conception of the interrelation of God, the individual, and the world (which includes nature, human history, society, and government.)[22] Granting this view, we will discuss in greater detail how Thurman envisioned the life, teachings, and religion of Jesus as agents of human liberation.

The Human Response to Oppression

Thurman believed that the oppressive social and political realities do not necessarily maintain "absolute control" over the individual. Rather, the individual is always capable of maintaining control over that aspect of his/her life which is most important in shaping his/her identity, that is the "inner self." Therefore, an individual can resist and combat oppression as long as he/she remembers that,

> out of the heart are the issues of life and that no external force,
> however great and overwhelming, can at long last destroy a people
> if it does not first win the victory of the spirit against them.[23]

It is possible for individuals and groups to maintain a degree of "freedom, integrity," and "liberated" existence, despite the devastating power of oppressive forces. The control of the human spirit is the true domain where authority over individuals and groups is won or lost. This control was, as we shall see below, what Thurman considered to be Jesus' greatest attainment. Jesus was a member of a community under a system of socio-economic and political domination which its members had little hope of overcoming. Within and in spite of this context, Jesus offered to his generation a sense of freedom, which was all encompassing and which touched every level of human existence. Jesus pointed his followers to a level of psycho-spiritual and ethical freedom.

> Again and again [Jesus] came back to the inner life of the individual.
> With increasing insight and startling accuracy, he placed his finger
> on the "inward center" as the crucial arena where the issues would
> determine the destiny of his people.[24]

Let us note here that Thurman did not downplay the power and tyrannical impact of socio-economic and political realities. His primary concern was providing a more thorough understanding of these forces.[25]

Thurman wanted to demonstrate that the quest for community influenced
every level of human existence, as did the experience of oppression.
He discussed this subject in great detail in *The Search for Common
Ground,* wherein he described certain utopian social visions. He wrote:

> Community as the Utopian dream is a part of the basic aspiration of
> the human spirit. It is not important at any particular time and place
> that the Utopia does not become literal fact; it reveals, however,
> what the imagination of man has to say about the true possibility of
> the human spirit.[26]

Community is a potential that is present in the very processes of life
themselves. In recognizing this potential, this inclination, that
individuals begin to know and experience true liberation and freedom
in history. All other manifestations of human freedom are secondary
to this one.[27]

Jesus of Nazareth and the
Resources for Human Liberation

What specifically about the life, ministry, and religious experiences
of Jesus speaks most profoundly to the oppressed? Thurman identified
several key facts in direct response to this question. The first fact is
that Jesus was a member of an "oppressed minority group." He was
a first century Palestinian Jew. As such, Jesus lived and operated
within a repressive political system, experiencing oppression firsthand.
Thus Jesus' message to the disinherited was forged within an oppressive
social context. The second significant fact is that Jesus consciously
shaped an alternative ethic distinctively addressed to the oppressed
within his community. The third factor centers on the "economic"
forces surrounding Jesus' life and ministry. Jesus, in addition to being
politically oppressed, was economically impoverished. In his poverty,
Jesus represented God's identification with the great masses of poor
and oppressed people on the planet. For this reason, Thurman said that
the birth of Jesus was a symbol of the "dignity" of the politically and
economically disinherited, thus demonstrating God's concern for their
plight and place. Likewise, Thurman posited that the crucifixion of
Jesus represents the ultimate punishment that an organized and
oppressive society exacts upon those who would dare to challenge its

destructive system. In this area of Thurman's thought, we go directly
to the heart of his interpretation of the person and work of Jesus.

Jesus' Religious Experience and Message: Agents of Divine Liberation

Thurman argued that religion, particularly the religion of Jesus, is
"a basis for integrating all of the individual acts and moments of a
persons' life."[28] He believed that every aspect of an individual's life is
influenced by the quality of his/her religious experience. This is a part
of the dynamic quality of religious experience. A true religious experience, though intimately personal, always moves the individual back
towards the world of brokenness and non-fulfillment. It pushes him/
her back to the world, in quest for wholeness and fulfillment. This
dynamic movement is a part of what Thurman called the "genius" of
religious experience. True religious experiences transform the individual and push him/her towards a sense of ethical awareness for other
persons.

> There is a quality present at the very core of the religious experience
> that pushes against any mood of self-centeredness until the very
> boundaries of the self are transformed into a dimension of the Other,
> the more than self. Thus the ultimate validity of the privacy of the
> religious experience is its universality. This is the miracle and the
> paradox.[29]

Thurman's argument begins with Jesus' conception of God as that
which "bottoms" existence. As he said:

> [Jesus] started in his experience with God as primary fact. As a
> matter of fact, as God is the only authentic fact in existence, and
> everything else derived its meaning, its significance, its relevance,
> its purposes from this central fact.[30]

This points to what Thurman believed to be an unquestionable source
of power within Jesus' religious experience and its relevance to other
persons:

> But wherever the Gospel is preached, whatever may be the power of
> the written emphasis that it may have, this insistence on the part of
> Jesus manages to get through to the desperate and this is why his

religion, though not political or economic, is a reformist religion. The logic of it, what it does to underscore and to deepen and to make aware the dignity of the individual becomes the source of revolution and the source for social change.[31]

The impetus for social change, Thurman argued, emerged directly from the religion of Jesus itself. Thurman believed that Jesus' direct encounter with God became the basis for his sense of ethical responsibility to other human beings. No aspect of Jesus' life was unaffected by his religious experience. This was not merely a rhetorical claim for Thurman. He believed that Jesus' religious experiences had a revolutionary and transformative power. Fluker has correctly demonstrated that there is a "worldly" component to Thurman's mysticism and religious experience; they must have an impact on the world in which the recipients of such experiences live.[32] In Thurman's view, mysticism does not seek to "deny" or escape the world; rather it affirms and drives one back to the world. He insisted that the "realistic mystic" will always be driven back to the social world where the depth of one's religion will be revealed. Thurman used Rufus Jones' idea of an "affirmation mystic" to explain how mystical experiences are connected with transformative social practices.[33]

Thurman's insistence on the radically outward dimension of mystical experiences partly accounts for his comments regarding the radical significance of Jesus' psycho-spiritual and ethical claims. Regarding these claims, Thurman wrote:

> [I]t is my sincere and profound conviction that [Jesus] is the great enemy of our civilization and our culture. And if his will, as he experienced it, becomes operative in our society not a single stone will be left upon another.[34]

He went further in defining Jesus' challenge as a "terrible" religion:

> Our survival as a culture, I think, is contingent upon the degree to which we are able somehow to separate ourselves from His almighty insistence and his terrible religion.[35]

The religion of Jesus challenges all forms of oppression and inhumanity, including racism, classism, and religious bigotry, as perpetuated by individuals and groups. Individuals and groups often thrive on injustice and inhumanity, but religious experiences mitigate against these.

Thurman believed that the religion of Jesus would critique this and every other culture by which it is confronted. This "whole-making" principle is foundational to the nature of religious experience. Oppressed people share Jesus' liberating power when they embrace this type of religious experience.

Liberating Voices: Jesus' Message, the Slave Religious Tradition, and Human Liberation

In examining several of Thurman's works, we see more than a strong correlation between what he says about the black experience and his claims about the religion of Jesus. We see this in three of his texts, *Jesus and the Disinherited,* and *Deep River and The Negro Spiritual Speaks of Life and Death.* The point we will focus specifically upon is the liberating dimension of the black experience and the religion of Jesus.[36] In both the black and the New Testament communities, the oppressed responded to their environment in several ways, namely out of fear, deception, and hate. These are the attitudes that continually plague oppressed people. Jesus' message of liberation to the oppressed focused directly upon these issues. He used love and a message of reconciliation as a basis for providing the disinherited with a spiritually based, ethical model for overcoming negative psycho-spiritual and ethical forces. It is within the religion of Jesus that we find answers to these problems that so terrorized the oppressed. The religion of Jesus also provided the basis for an individual's ethical responsibility.[37]

For Thurman, two key hermeneutical keys emerge from Jesus' religious experience. First we see an affirmation of the unity of the human family and a strong belief in the notion that all people are children of God.[38] These two factors, infusing human life with a profound sense of meaning and purpose, are at the heart of Jesus' contribution to the psycho-spiritual and ethical vision of his contemporaries. Thurman based much of what he said on this issue on Jesus' proclamation in John 10:10 (RSV):

> The thief comes only to steal and kill and destroy; I came that they may have life, and have it abundantly.

This text demonstrates God's concern for the individual and the sense of meaning and purpose that is inherent in life:

This idea—that God is mindful of the individual—is of tremendous import in dealing with fear as a disease. In this world the socially disadvantaged man is constantly given a negative answer to the most important personal questions upon which mental health depends: "Who am I? What am I?"[39]

Knowing that one is a child of God, who wills and acts on behalf of the freedom of the oppressed, is a prerequisite for living a holistic life. This is the same basic principle of faith that Thurman discovered in the following slave Spiritual:

> Didn't my Lord deliver Daniel
> Deliver Daniel, deliver Daniel.
> Didn't my Lord deliver Daniel
> Then why not every man?
>
> He delivered Daniel from the lion's den
> Jonah from the belly of the whale,
> The Hebrew Children from the fiery furnace.
>
> Then why not every man?

The slaves believed that the God of the Bible was on their side, for they too were slaves and victims of oppression. Thurman posited that Jesus—just as the black slaves would do—helped people to grasp their role as children of God.

Jesus and the Disinherited

Jesus on Fear

Jesus' message on fear has direct relevance to the oppressed, for fear is one of the perennial "hounds of hell"[40] that constantly plague the oppressed. Thurman based his claims in this area on a reading of New Testament passages such as Luke 4:18 (RSV).

The Spirit of the Lord is upon me, because he hath anointed me to preach good news to the poor. He has sent me to proclaim release to the captives and recovering of sight to the blind, to set at liberty those who are oppressed, to proclaim the acceptable year of the Lord.

Fear can be conquered because God has willed the oppressed to be free; this was Jesus' message to his generation. The religion of the slaves, Thurman argued, suggested a similar focus:

> With untutored hands—with a sure artistry and genius created out of a vast vitality, a concept of God was wrenched from the Sacred Book, the Bible, the chronicle of a people who had learned through great necessity the secret meaning of suffering. This total experience enabled them to reject annihilation and affirm a terrible right to live.[41]

The true power by which the oppressed resist fear comes from God.

> The center of focus was beyond [the slaves] in a God who was a companion to them in their miseries even as He enabled them to transcend their miseries. And this is good news! Under God the human spirit can triumph over the most radical frustrations![42]

Thurman did not speak in abstract philosophical terms here with regard to the socio-psychological forces that continually hound the oppressed. Instead, he used the conditions of the African-American community in order to demonstrate his point. Given this concrete situation we may grasp the devastating impact of oppression. Yet, as Thurman indicated, we also see how the religion of Jesus, as well as the slave religious experiences, helped to mitigate against the negative powers which affect the oppressed. Thurman's study of the themes in African-American religion and the religion of Jesus, coupled with what he said about the social contexts in which these emerge, provide a concrete example of how religion affects the lives of the disinherited.

Jesus on the Problem of Deception

In discussing Jesus' view of deception, Thurman returned to the conditions of the oppressed in order to demonstrate his claim about the impact of religious experience upon human behavior. Thurman said that deception is a tactic employed both by the disinherited and by their oppressors. It provides a means whereby the oppressed can escape their temporary experiences of suffering and despair. Deception is the practice whereby the disinherited use cunning habits and devices in order to deceive their oppressors. Thurman explained the issue by referring to his conception of how black people in his native Florida viewed whites:

Behavior toward [whites] was amoral. They were not hated particularly; they were not essentially despised; they were simply out of bounds. It is very difficult to put into words what was at work here. They were tolerated as a vital part of the environment, but they did not count in. They were in a world apart, in another universe of discourse.[43]

This context changed the normal ethical situation: "To lie to them or to deceive them had no moral relevancy; no category of guilt was involved in my behavior."[44] Because there is no true social intercourse between the oppressed and the oppressors—which can only exist in a situation in which there is social equality—both groups are apt to secure their places through deceptive means. Thurman suggested:

The pattern of deception by which the weak are deprived of their civic, economic, political, and social rights without its appearing that they are so deprived is a matter of continuous and tragic amazement.[45]

It was Thurman's belief that, irrespective of the end of the socio-political scale one is on, the price of deception is high. If a person lies continually he/she becomes a lie and alters his/her sense of moral judgment. One who deceives will eventually become a deception. This is the problem with using deception as a tool for achieving one's goals in life. Deception obscures the truth, and as such it is a denial of the ultimate meaning and purpose of life.

Jesus offered the alternative to deception. Thurman said that deception betrays the plan of God.

The word—Be genuine!
Let your words be yea, yea; nay, nay!
All else obscures the truth,
Tempting man to betray the Eternal.

What a hard word for the weak!
It brings crashing down around their heads
The great fortress of defense
Against embattled power.[46]

Thurman insisted that Jesus was against deception in all forms, and the follower of Jesus is always commanded to resist it. For followers are always reminded of the words of Jesus, "What shall a man give in return for his life?" (Matthew 16:26f, RSV)

It is interesting that Thurman used the slave spiritual, "Everybody Talkin' about Heaven Ain't Goin' There," in order to explain his view of deception. He repeated what he says about the issue in *Jesus and the Disinherited*. Persons whose religious faith is only exercised and applied when it is convenient, such as the white slave masters and supporters of the institution of slavery, could not expect to receive the rewards that the slaves envisioned for the children of God. In any case, Thurman suggested that the only legitimate forces which can be used are morality and honesty, both of which can only be exercised with great humility and courage. The weak and the strong can only be legitimately related when courage and humility are exercised on both sides.

In discussing the issue of deception among the oppressed, Thurman proposed three alternatives available to individuals in responding to situations wherein deception is a moral option. As he said:

> The first alternative is to accept the apparent fact that, one's situation
> being what it is, there is no sensible choice offered. The individual
> is disadvantaged because he is a member of the "party in power,"
> the dominant, controlling group. His word has no value anyway.
> He cannot meet his opponent on equal terms, because there is no
> basis of equality that exists between the weak and the strong.[47]

In this instance the oppressed simply assumes that there are no grounds for moral interaction between the oppressed and their oppressors. Therefore, any decision that the oppressed make in protecting themselves from their oppressors, and preserving their lives, is justified. Deception, then, becomes only one expression of the attempt to preserve and perpetuate one's life. The problem with such thinking, however, is that it buys into the oppressors' most effective weapon, that is the degradation of life. In degrading the value of the lives and experiences of the oppressed, systems of oppression denigrate the sense of meaning and purpose that should naturally exist among oppressed people. The use of deception for temporary gain—that is, preservation—cheapens the eternal worth of the lives of oppressed people. To use Thurman's phrase, deception "tends to destroy whatever sense of ethical values the individual possesses. . . if a man calls a lie the truth, he tampers dangerously with his value judgments."[48] Deception destroys because it eventually destroys an individual's ability to make moral distinctions between good and evil, right and wrong, etc.

The second alternative stems from the first. This alternative involves essentially an attitude of compromise. When choosing this option, oppressed people selectively decide to affirm or not to affirm particular moral precepts and values according to a given situation. The situation will dictate whether and when one decides to be deceptive. But the situation of compromise is no Promised Land, because it too tampers with the essential meaning and value of life. In this system, life "becomes a grim game of wits, and the stakes are one's physical existence."[49] If life's value and purpose are reduced to a situation of matching wits for the purpose of realizing momentary control and gain, where is its eternal dimension?

This aspect of Thurman's analysis of the issue of deception is very fascinating, particularly when one tries to put the principle into the socio-historical situation of the African-American community, or of any oppressed community. One needs to return to Thurman's analysis of the religious situation in which Jesus lived in order to appreciate his analysis of deception. Jesus' socio-ethical mandates were among many alternatives which were available to the oppressed.   The radical, revolutionary Zealots, the disdainful Pharisees, and the compromising Sadducees all presented other options.   Deception and compromise could be justified in each of these traditions, for varying reasons. Jesus' religious and moral vision differed because his mandates and values were universal in intent and focus.   And Thurman wrote that the "greatest challenge that the religion of Jesus faces in modern life"[50] is that of helping oppressed people grasp the eternal worth and value of their lives. When viewed in this light, even compromise for the sake of gain is unrealistic.

So how does this mandate against deception apply to the revolutionary visions of great leaders such as Denmark Vesey, Nat Turner, Harriet Tubman, John Brown, and Sojourner Truth? All of these persons surely used deceptive means in order to fight the evils of slavery. Moreover, most mass movements for social and political equality employ questionable measures at one point or another. Is deception not justified in these cases? Thurman's response remains, any compromise with the demand for integrity eventually destroys life. Any deception eliminates the oppressed person's ability to attach eternal value to their lives.

> Even within the disinherited group itself artificial and exaggerated emphasis upon not being killed tends to cheapen life. That is to say, the fact that the lives of the disinherited are lightly held by the dominant group tends to create the same attitude among them toward each other.[51]

Thurman described the third alternative to deception as one of "complete and devastating sincerity." He quoted from one of the letters of Mahatma Gandhi to Muriel Lester in explaining this point.

> Speak the truth, without fear and without exception, and see everyone whose work is related to your purpose. You are in God's work, so you need not fear man's scorn. If they listen to your requests and grant them, you will be satisfied. If they reject them, then you must make their rejection your strength.[52]

This alternative mandates that the individual be totally truthful and honest in every aspect of life, irrespective of the cost. This is, according to Thurman, the key to the religion of Jesus. And it is Jesus' challenge to the oppressed, and likewise a message of empowerment for the oppressed. Jesus demanded, "Let what you say be simply 'Yes' or 'No'; anything more than this comes from evil." (Matthew 5:37, RSV)[53] This demand applies both to how human beings deal with each other as well as to their response to God. Thurman concludes:

> Unwavering sincerity says that man should always recognize the fact that he lives always in the presence of God, always under the divine scrutiny, and that there is no really significant living for a man, what ever may be his status until he has turned and faced the divine scrutiny.[54]

Anything else would lead to hypocrisy, deceit, and duplicity, the result of which is always as devastating to the deceitful person as it is to the person deceived. It would otherwise be an ethic of convenience.

Thurman's claims here are very similar to the moral reasoning of the great Enlightenment philosopher, Immanuel Kant. Kant argued that morality is the essence of religion, and that the foundation of all moral actions is the demand to do what is right for the sake of duty and duty alone.[55] Consequences, benefits, personal gratification, and other such benefits should never come in to play when one is deciding upon a moral action. Moreover, according to Kant, moral mandates are universal and unchangeable, they apply to all persons in all situations. Thurman strongly affirmed this idea:

> On the other hand there was the insistence in the religious insight of the Master and the categorical insistence derived from his religious experience that what God requires of man always, under all

circumstances, is sincerity. Sincerity is one of the virtues found in all religions of whatever category.[56]

We will return to this theme when we turn to Thurman's ideas about love within this context.

Jesus on Hatred and Despair

According to Thurman, the oppressed are always faced with the possibility of using hate as a weapon against their oppressors. Racial hatred is most often a result of unjust social arrangements. It emerges in situations in which there is forced social contact without genuine fellowship. This is inevitable in contexts where there is no equality; for without true socio-economic and political equality there can be no fellowship. Thurman made no excuses for the fact that expression of hatred between the races is inevitable in situations of oppression and deprivation. He said, for example:

> In the South, as long as the Negro is called John or Mary and seems to accept the profoundly humiliating position of an inferior status, fellowship within the zones of agreement is possible. It has not been uncommon for great personal sacrifices to be made for Negroes and all the weight of personal position and power put at their disposal. But always this has been done within the zones of agreement established and assured by the mutual horizon of the pattern.[57]

What is more important he indicated that:

> It is precisely because of this false basis of fellowship so often occurring that in the section of the country where there is the greatest contact between the races, there is apt to be the least real fellowship and the first step along the terrible road of bitterness and hate assured.[58]

Thurman believed that hatred often served as a tremendous source of self-validation and authentication for oppressed people. Its influence, however, is always negative and destructive; it contaminates the spirit and the mind of the person who hates and wills the annihilation of the person against whom it is directed. Hatred destroys the moral fiber of the human spirit. Therefore, Thurman urged black people to resist the temptation to hate their white oppressors. Instead of hating, he suggested that they follow the model of Jesus and learn to love in spite of circumstances. He argued that:

Every man is potentially every other man's neighbor. Neighborliness
is non spatial; it is qualitative. A man must love his neighbor directly,
clearly permitting no barrier between [59]

He also based his view of the subject of hate on a synthesis between the
religion and message of Jesus and the plight of the oppressed. The
religion of Jesus, he noted, offers two steps to overcoming hate. The
first step is for persons to "lay bare their lives to the scrutiny and to the
judgment and to the will of God."[60] This experience will cause a
fundamental change within the individual which will enable him/her to
counteract hate and to deal with another man even as God deals with
man.[61] The second step that Jesus offers in the struggle against the
power of hate involves "re-imaging" the spiritual and psychological
resources that oppressed people rely upon for the sake of survival. The
oppressed person learns:

> I must put at the disposal of the new creation in me all of the resources
> of my mind and personality, all of the resources that are at the disposal
> of the sensitive mind and spirit, the skills and the techniques and the
> methods that will enable me to reestablish the hated person into the
> human race. If I am unable to do this, all prayers, tears and the
> beating of breasts will not avail.[62]

This is without question an ethic which resists the forces of oppression
and the depressing attitudes which emerge from them.

Jesus and the Categorical Demand to Love

No aspect of Thurman's thought more strongly supports the
principal theses that we mentioned above than does his love ethic.
According to Thurman, the human family is essentially one and all
persons are children of God, and one should do all that is necessary to
preserve this unity, thus Jesus' categorical demand for love among all
persons. And Jesus' demand is at one and the same time the demand
that comes from all true religious experiences.

> And this is why, my friends, that to love your enemy, to love the
> person whose activities work against the furtherance of life and its
> maintenance is not an ethical act. It is not a political act, it is not a
> moral act, it is a spiritual act. I must desire to do this or else with all
> the techniques and the skills in the world I am sounding brass and a
> clanging cymbal.[63]

Thurman understood the love ethic to be a part of the "outward thrust" of religious experience. He believed that it was a contradiction to affirm the universality of the human family without loving all other human beings. Therefore, he said, "The religion of Jesus makes the love-ethic central."[64] Thurman noted that the teachings of Jesus represent the embodiment of the Hebrew Shema—Deuteronomy 6:4f—that emphatic command to love God, the self, and the neighbor. Love is the essence of the religious experience because love is essentially a spiritual expression, just as hate is a spiritual act.

Thurman explained Jesus' concept of love by noting that Jesus, in the context of the Jewish faith within which he was reared, radically altered the public conception of the meaning of "neighborliness." Jesus refused to define "neighborliness" in racial, socio-economic, ideological, or any other terms that seemed to impose limitations on human relationships. Jesus' command to love other persons was inclusive of all other human beings.

Thurman demonstrated Jesus' command to love one's enemies by referring to three types of enemies: the personal enemy, that is, a person who is a member of one's social-group; the enemies from within, one who would sell the soul of and destroy his/her community from within; and those persons on the outside of the community who are directly responsible for maintaining systems of oppression.[65] According to Thurman, each enemy is to be loved. Loving the first type of enemy simply entails becoming reconciled with the person. There are no social impediments to this event. Thurman used the position of the tax collector in the Jewish community to show how Jesus applied his principle of love to the second type of enemy, persons who even sell out and participate in the oppression of their own people. Loving this person would be a more demanding task, but this is required because, as Jesus said, "This man is not just a tax collector; he is a son of God."[66] The third type of enemy is one who is in the status of a political enemy; this is a person who is directly responsible for perpetuating another's oppression. The Roman authorities in Jesus' time represented this type of enemy. The key issue is, however, that irrespective of the type of enemy one may have, the ethical mandate—emerging from the depth of one's religious experiences—is indeed the same. One must first see the Roman authorities as individual persons in need of love and understanding; they must be seen as true human beings. As in other cases, Thurman used the racial circumstances in America to demonstrate the demand for love of "oppressive" other.

While he was careful not to suggest that one can have absolute love in circumstances where there is social oppression and inequality, it is equally clear that he did not think that one must wait until such a time as social equality occurs before the demand for love is met. The move towards love and the experience of community begins now, as the religious experience pushes individuals towards wholeness and community. This reflects the radical nature of Jesus' ethical challenge.

Let us close this segment by looking at how Thurman closed *Jesus and the Disinherited*. He repeated the question of the relevance of Jesus' message and ministry to those who are oppressed. He went on to say that after the oppressed recognize the limitation of fear, deception, and hatred:

> [They] will know for themselves that there is a Spirit at work in life and in the hearts of men which is committed to overcoming the world. It is universal, knowing no age, no race, no culture, and no condition of men. For the privileged and underprivileged alike, if the individual puts at the disposal of the Spirit the needful dedication and discipline, he can live effectively in the chaos dedication and discipline, he can live effectively in the chaos of the present the high destiny of a son of God.[67]

This is how Thurman believed that the religion and message of Jesus help to shape the lives of oppressed people as they struggle for liberation and freedom.

Conclusion

Let us conclude this chapter with a summation of how Thurman envisioned Jesus' life, religious experiences, and message as sources of liberation for the oppressed. First, Thurman began by examining the facts surrounding the birth of the historical Jesus. These facts place Jesus within the same socio-historical context as other oppressed people. Thurman believed that "facts" about the historical Jesus provide a primary impetus for how the disinherited view themselves. The socio-economic facts surrounding Jesus' life are also significant in relation to his death and other aspects of his life. Second, Jesus' religious experiences and message provide primary examples of how religious experiences help to shape one's vision of himself and of the socio-political realities which shape one's life. We have identified the "outward" thrust in all religious experiences, which lead towards social transformation and human liberation. It is in this nexus that we find the true power in Thurman's Christology; he demonstrated how religious experiences address the "multidimensional" sources of human oppression. He uncovered the true nature of human oppression as a force which touches every facet of human existence. Finally, we have examined how Thurman used the African-American experience in general and specifically the religious aspects of the tradition as the points of departure in his interpretation of the religion, life, and message of Jesus of Nazareth. We will move now in the final chapter of this study to discuss the distinctiveness of Thurman's Christology within the African-American religious tradition.

Notes

1   Howard Thurman, *Jesus and the Disinherited.* p. 13.
2   Thurman retired from Boston University in 1965, four years before the publication of the first texts on black theology, James H. Cone's *Black Theology and Black Power*, and Gustavo Gutierrez, *Liberation Theology* (Maryknoll, NY: Orbis Books, 1973). Thurman was not, however, totally out of touch with what was happening in black theology. He did, for example, write an encouraging review of J. DeOtis Roberts' text on *Liberation and Reconciliation* (Philadelphia: Westminster Press, 1971.) Moreover, in an interview with this author, as well as in some of his writings, Roberts credits Thurman for having been an important influence upon his personal and professional life. Interview with J. DeOtis Roberts, Eastern Baptist Theological Seminary, Telephone interview, 12 February 1989. Thurman also includes a reference to James Cone's *Black Theology and Black Power* in *The Search for Common Ground*. See the bibliography for the reference.
3   Stewart's reflections on Thurman are found principally in his dissertation "A Comparative Analysis of Theological Ontology and Ethical Method in the Theologies of James H. Cone and Howard Thurman" (Ph.D. Dissertation: Northwestern University, 1982); also see his article "The Concept of Liberation in Thurman's Thought" in Henry J. Young's *God and Human Freedom* (Richmond, IN.: Friends United Press, 1983). Stewart's work is very insightful and helpful. The dissertation, however, suffers from a lack of emphasis on the impact of the African-American religious tradition upon Thurman's thought. His use of the ontological categories and claims of Martin Heidegger, for example, seems to obscure Thurman's creative theological voice and contribution.
4   Stewart correctly notes that the principal difference between Thurman's view of self-actualization and Cone's view of liberation is that Thurman's was derived from a more ontological and metaphysical base as opposed to the more socio-scientific and political definition of liberation that one finds in Cone's works. Nevertheless he says that a proper analysis of the foundations of Thurman's thought will reveal a deeper link between his and Cone's work.
5   Howard Thurman, *Jesus and the Disinherited,* p. 7.
6   Ibid., p. 7.
7   Ibid.
8   While Thurman did not use this term, it does express his understanding of the direct connection that he envisioned between the psychological and spiritual realms of human experience as central motivational factors in shaping human behavior. It also helps to demonstrate the fact that Thurman believed that there is a specifically religious dimension to the experience of oppression. More will be said on these subjects below.

9   This issue is addressed in greater detail in the next chapter when we talk about Thurman's contribution to black theology.

10   Cornel West, *Prophesy Deliverance: An Afro-American Revolutionary Christianity* (Philadelphia: Westminster Press, 1982); see also his *Race Matters* (Boston: Beacon Press, 1993). Suffice it to say here that he helps us to better interpret Thurman's work. See also James H. Cone, *For My People* (Maryknoll: Orbis Books, 1984) p. 86.

11   Cone even admits that black theologians such as himself may have been too preoccupied with racial oppression in the early stages of their movement. James H. Cone, *For My People*, p. 88.

12   Thurman offered his most thorough treatment of the idea of community, and the sense of absence of community, oppression, in his text *The Search for Common Ground*. See Fluker's discussion of community for a more thorough understanding of how Thurman relates the different aspects of his view of oppression and of his view of community. See his *Community*, p. 30f.

13   Thurman, *The Luminous Darkness*, p. 26.

14   Ibid., pp. 89-90.

15   Ibid., p. 90.

16   Alonzo Johnson, "Howard Thurman and the Problem of Christian Racism: Confronting the Crisis of the Human Spirit." *Unity and Renewal: The Eradication of Racism*, eds. Sue Davies, et al (Grand Rapids: William B. Eerdmans Pub. Company, 1997).

17   The idea of self-actualization and self-authentication is also related to what Howard Thurman says about the meaning and experience of community. There are several sources that help to elucidate this point. Katie G. Canon's book, *Black Womanist Ethics* (Atlanta: Scholars Press, 1988) offers the first extended comparative treatment of the idea of community in Howard Thurman's and Martin Luther King's works. Walter E. Fluker's text, *They Looked for a City* (Washington, DC: University Press of America, 1989), offers the most thorough treatment of the subject. See especially the first three chapters of his text. Luther E. Smith's early work on Thurman should also be mentioned here; see his *Howard Thurman: The Mystic as Prophet*, see especially Chapter 6. See also Dennis W. Wiley's "Church." Chapters 3-5 are particularly helpful in illustrating the connection between Thurman's view of the Church and his view the experience of community and self-actualization.

18   Howard Thurman, *The Search For Common Ground* (New York: Harper & Row, 1971), p. 4.

19   Thurman, *The Search For Common Ground*, p. 4.

20   Howard Thurman, *Meditations of the Heart* (Richmond, Ind.: Friends United Press, 1979), quoted in Carlyle Felding Stewart, III, "The Concept of Liberation in Thurman's Thought," in Henry J. Young, *God and Human Freedom* (Richmond, Ind.: Friends United Press, 1983), p. 108.

21   Thurman, *Common Ground*, p. 4.

22   Fluker, *Community*, p. 30f.

23   Thurman, *Jesus and the Disinherited*, p. 21.

24   Ibid.

25   More will be said of this subject below.

26   Thurman, *Common Ground,* p. 54.

27   This will also be addressed in more detail when we speak about the Jesus' message to the oppressed masses of his generation.

28   Howard Thurman, "The Religion of Jesus and Social Change," 19 November 1950, N.P.

29   Howard Thurman, *The Temptations of Jesus,* 13.

30   Howard Thurman, "Jesus and the Disinherited," Part III, 25 January 1959. p. 4.

31   Howard Thurman, "Jesus and the Disinherited," Part V, 22 February 1959, p. 5.

32   Fluker, *Community*. p. 30. I also find Dennis Wiley's Chapter 5 to be helpful on this point. He emphasizes Thurman's connection between religious experience and the formation of true community. The Church for the Fellowship of all Peoples was an *experiment* in community.

33   See the fourth of his series of lectures on mysticism entitled "Mysticism and Social Change," p. 1.

34   Howard Thurman, "Jesus and the Disinherited," Part III, p. 7.

35   Ibid., p.7

36   Thurman gave more extensive attention to the subject of the social implications of his religious vision in several works. See his treatment of the connection between mysticism and social change in Howard Thurman, "Mysticism and Social Change," *Eden Theological Seminary Bulletin* (Spring, 1939); *The Luminous Darkness*; and *Common Ground*.

37   Note his claims about the spirituals. See *Deep River and The Negro Spiritual Speaks of Life and Death.*

38   Katie Canon describes Thurman's ethics as a theocentric ethic. See her text, *Black Womanist Ethics* (Atlanta: Scholars Press, 1988), see the chapter on Thurman and King.

39   Thurman, *Jesus and the Disinherited*. p. 49.

40   Ibid. p. 36.

41   Thurman, *Deep River*, pp. 127-28.

42   Ibid. p. 108.

43   Thurman, *The Luminous Darkness*. p. 3.

44   Ibid.

45   Ibid., p. 65.

46   Thurman, *The Mood of Christmas* (New York: Harper & Row Publishers, 1973; reprint Richmond, In.: Friends United Press, 1985), p. 114.

47   Thurman, *Jesus and the Disinherited*, p. 62.

48   Ibid., p. 64.

49   Ibid., p. 67.

50   Ibid., p. 68.

51   Ibid., p. 70.
52   Ibid.
53   Ibid. p.71.
54   Ibid.
55   Immanuel Kant, *Critique of Practical Reason*, trans. and with and introduction by Lewis White Beck (Indianapolis: Bobbs-Merril Educational Publishing, 1982)
56   Howard Thurman, " Jesus and the Disinherited," Part IX, p. 2.
57   Thurman, *The Luminous Darkness*, p. 39.
58   Ibid. p. 39
59   Thurman, *Jesus and the Disinherited*, p. 89.
60   Howard Thurman, "Jesus and the Disinherited," Part XI, p.5.
61   Ibid.
62   Ibid.
63   Thurman, "Jesus and the Disinherited" Pt. 12, p.6.
64   Thurman, *Jesus and the Disinherited*, p. 89.
65   Ibid., p. 91f.
66   Ibid., p. 95.
67   Ibid., pp. 108-109.

Chapter V

Howard Thurman and the African-American Quest for a Black Christ

> The Black Christ is He who threatens the structure of evil
> as seen in white society, rebelling against it thereby
> becoming the embodiment of what the black community
> knows that it must become. Because He has become black
> as we are, we now know what black empowerment is.
>
> —James H. Cone

In this chapter we will return to the subject mentioned earlier in the study, namely Thurman's rootedness within the African-American religious tradition. The idea of a "Black Christ" or "Black Messiah" is the point of reference for the discussion in this chapter. The search for a Black Christ has been a core component of black nationalist thought for the past two centuries. We will define Thurman's contribution to the African-American quest for a Black Christ and as such, locate his work within the tradition of black nationalist thought.

Black Nationalist Philosophy

Sterling Stuckey has defined black nationalism as a particular world view which:

> emphasized the need for black people to rely primarily on themselves in vital areas of life—economic, political, religious, and intellectual—in order to effect their liberation.[1]

John H. Brace, August Meier, and Elliot Rudwick subdivide black nationalists into several smaller groups (such as religious nationalists and cultural nationalists).[2] Despite the diversity of expressions, black nationalists are united by their emphasis on black pride, solidarity, and unity as the means of attaining black emancipation. Black nationalism also fosters a strong separatist impulse within the black community. Black nationalists accent the need for black people to organize themselves around their common sense of identity; such a vision necessarily thrives on the tactical need for black separatism. Marcus Garvey's UNIA group from the 1920s and the Minister Louis Farrakhan's Nation of Islam in the 1990s are the two most well known black nationalist groups of this century. Both of these groups have built their ideological program on strong religious ideals.

Our discussion thus far demonstrates that Thurman was not a separatist. He was an integrationist, both philosophically and methodologically. His idea of community—while affirming the need for racial distinctiveness and pride—was universal. There were no back-to-Africa, "black power," and black machismo themes in his thought. Whatever the concern for black survival and unity, Thurman was passionately committed to a world where all racial and religious groups would exist in unity. There is no circumvention of this fact. Some question why Thurman did not more readily identify with the central current within the black community. Why did he not espouse more of a Pan-Africanist vision, in the manner of W. E. B. DuBois and Marcus Garvey? We will briefly look at aspects of this subject.

Howard Thurman and the Black Nationalists' Agenda: Conceptual Ideals and Programmatic Visions

Black nationalists accent the idea of black genius and uniqueness. They also consistently attribute the problems of the African-American community to centuries of American slavery, segregation, and oppression. On these two salient points, Thurman would certainly agree with the black nationalists' tradition. His progressive and insightful interpretation of the slave Spirituals, coupled with his appropriation of themes from the black religious tradition, support this idea. More than any other theologian of his era, Thurman brought the black experience into the forefront of his theological project. He took every opportunity to show how the historical experiences of African-Americans, particularly their religious experiences, spoke to the prevailing situation in American life. Furthermore, Thurman's constructive interpretation of the black religious experience was the theological counterpart to the progressive thought of African-American intellectuals of the Harlem Renaissance and post-renaissance era. He was indeed a "Black Renaissance Theologian."[3]

The Harlem Renaissance was a major harbinger for black nationalist thought in the early twentieth century. It fostered black cultural nationalism, representing the dominant stream of African-American self-interpretation and re-imaging in this century. Themes ranging from the literary to the religious are in this tradition. The unifying principle within the tradition is the emphasis on black self-discovery and definition, which is the essence of black nationalism. Interestingly, no Thurman interpreter to date has taken seriously the task of understanding his brilliant theological contributions within the context of the spirit of the Harlem Renaissance era. George E. Kent says that the Harlem Renaissance, the mood, the personalities who supported it, and the vision revolved around one central theme.

> The single unifying concept which places the achievement of the Harlem Renaissance in focus is that it moved to gain authority in its portrayal of black life by the attempt to assert, with varying degrees of radicality, a dissection of sensibility from that enforced by American culture and its institutions. [T]he achievement of the writers was the breaking of ground, which left the soil in much more receptive condition for future tillers.[4]

The Harlem Renaissance writers offered a very articulate statement of the back nationalist emphasis on black pride and black solidarity. More than anything else, the Harlem Renaissance writers wanted to offer a positive and constructive portrayal of black life in America. Their perennial concern was their portrayal of black life.

There were other writers who, like Thurman, offered strong and credible interpretations of aspects of black religion, but none with the far-reaching implications of Thurman's work. His interpretation of the Spirituals, for example, was not as thorough as others' such as those by W.E.B. DuBois, John Lowell, Miles Mark Fisher, and Benjamin E. Mays.[5] Yet none of these scholars matched Thurman in his ability to lift the Spirituals to the highest level of significance as theological statements. Thurman's concern was to demonstrate how the Spirituals can function as alternative world views, offered from the vantage point of the black experience. In describing treatments of the slave Spirituals, Thurman suggested that other scholars should,

> examine the Negro spirituals as a source of rich testimony concerning life and death, because in many ways they are the voice. . . of a people for whom the cup of suffering overflowed in haunting overtones of majesty, beauty and power![6]

He posited that the true meaning of the Spirituals is located in their sense of "religious experience and spiritual discernment."[7] The significance of our claim is further verified when we recall the thematic connection between Thurman's treatment of the Spirituals and his understanding of the life and teachings of Jesus. In *Jesus and the Disinherited*, he provided a constructive ethic for oppressed people and the black experience is the point of departure. He used the black experience as an example of the tremendous sustaining power inherent in all religious experiences. If, as indicated in the preceding chapter, black religious experience is a liberating experience, it would follow that one would want to expose this liberating experience to others outside of this tradition. Thurman took this task to heart when he spoke to whites and blacks about the genius of the Negro Spirituals, and of black religion.

I accent this point because it helps to further verify Thurman's connection to the black nationalist spirit and ethos of the Harlem Renaissance period. He was not a resident of Harlem during the formal period of the Harlem Renaissance (1921-1934). Moreover, the

Renaissance period had actually ended before Thurman began to do extensive writing (in the mid-1930's). Despite these disclaimers, it is possible, however, to see Thurman's connection to the Harlem Renaissance mood at a much deeper level. He articulated this point in his description of the aim of his 1947 Ingersoll Lecture on Immortality at Harvard Divinity School, which was later published under the title, *The Negro Spiritual Speaks of Life and Death*.

> The indigenous insights inherent in the Negro spirituals bear significantly on the timeless search for the meaning of life and death in human experience. I sought to establish a beachhead of thought about the slave's religious creativity in the presence of those gathered in assembly in perhaps the most prestigious academic institution in our society, with the hope that the ideas generated would open the eyes of the blind and deliver those in another kind of bondage into new freedom. Thus, however briefly, they and the slave would stand side by side together as children of life.[8]

His point here is to depict the spiritual genius of African-American religion. It is offered as a perspective along side of other interpretations of the meaning of life and death. Toward accomplishing this task, Thurman put the insights of the Spiritual in dialogue with other religious perspectives. The Spirituals demonstrated the slaves' self-definition and their struggle against the odds to create a sense of peoplehood and community. Let us note that he delivered these Ingersoll Lectures, focusing on the religious insights of the Spirituals, at Harvard University. Clearly he believed that the songs of his foreparents could speak meaningfully to the religious imagination of his white audience. One might view Thurman's entire career in this light, given his long tenure of service in predominantly white institutions.[9] This ambassador role to which Thurman assigned himself further demonstrated his conviction that there was a truth in black religion which needed to be unfolded to the world. He likewise pointed to the need for African-Americans themselves to understand and appreciate their religious heritage and the insights of their ancestors. Thurman bemoaned the commercialization of the Spirituals, decrying the popular use of them as instruments of entertainment. In writing his books on the Spirituals, then, his aim was to help a new generation grasp their true insights and meaning.[10] Again, nothing was closer to the true spirit of the Harlem Renaissance than the attempt to depict the heart and meaning of the black experience in America. The gift that Thurman passed on to his contemporaries was that of helping to provide a creative hermeneutical model for understanding their religious heritage.

The other principal point of identification between Thurman and the black nationalist tradition deals with his emphasis on and response to racism and segregation. We recall that he deemed segregation—as well as all forms of racism, prejudice, bigotry, and xenophobia—the most crucial problem facing the American public. The heinous nature of these forces is strongly evident in their support for the sociopolitical system which perpetuated the oppression and disenfranchisement of the African-American community. The impact of these factors is even more profound on the psycho-spiritual level. They produce a disease-like pattern within human personalities. Thurman said, for example, that the system of segregation filled black people with a deep sense of inferiority, worthlessness, and fear; meanwhile, it infused the white community with a false sense of pride and superiority. He put it this way:

> The fact that the first twenty-three years of my life were spent in Florida and Georgia has left its scars deep in my spirit and has rendered me terribly sensitive to the churning abyss separating white from black. Living outside of the region, I am aware of the national span of racial prejudice and the virus of segregation that undermines the vitality of American life.[11]

Thurman went on to say that the American system of segregation and racial oppression was immoral— immoral because it rejected the principle of universality and the love ethic. To put it differently, segregation and racial oppression were a rejection of the gospel. The fundamental issue here is that Thurman saw segregation and other such problems as empirical manifestations of "spiritual" problems indicative of crises within the human spirit, mind, and personality, as noted above. What is more important, they indicate the tyranny of racism. Thurman's approach to segregation was definitely not simplistic. He emphasized that black people were the only group directly limited by the segregationists' system. White people were separated from blacks by choice, but they could and did go into the black community at will. Black people, on the other hand, were under the legal constraint of segregation.[12]

Thurman's proposal for overcoming the vestiges of racism was the adoption of the universalist ethic. In America this meant the adoption of a radical call for integration. He went even further in suggesting that the true embodiment of Jesus' love ethic in America would mandate the destruction of the system of racial and religious segregation. He bemoaned the lack of this type of attitude among American Christians:

> Historically in this country, the church has given the sweep of its moral force to the practice of segregation within its own community of believers. To the extent to which this has been done, the church has violated one of the central elements of its own commitment.[13]

Thurman was not sentimental or naive concerning the difficulties of his proposal; he certainly had to deal with these issues when considering the possibility of establishing an institution such as the Church for the Fellowship of All Peoples in 1943. This method of approaching the problems in the country focused on creating opportunities for institutional change within the country. Thurman envisioned the churches as a universal fellowship and laboratory that, while a non-political movement, prepares individuals to become agents of social transformation. Thurman participated in the 1963 March on Washington, but beyond this he had very little public involvement in the Civil Rights struggles of the 1960s.[14] He was not an activist, in the Martin Luther King, Jr., Marcus Garvey, or Malcolm X tradition.

Thurman was a product of Morehouse College, King's alma mater, and a classmate of Martin King, Sr. He remained close to the elder King throughout his lifetime. Thurman had very little direct contact with Martin Luther King, Jr. during King's adulthood. He noted, however, that King visited his home at least once during the final year of King's residency work at Boston University. Thurman also said that he visited King during his stay in Harlem Hospital. He was moved to visit King in the hospital because of his, Thurman's, concern about King's mental, spiritual, and physical health. Except for this encounter, their direct contact was limited.[15]

Thurman's tribute to King gives us a sense of the separate paths the two men took. Thurman wrote:

> Perhaps the ultimate demand laid upon the human spirit is the responsibility to select where one bears witness to the truth of his spirit. The final expression of the committed spirit is to affirm: I choose! and to abide.[16]

King was true to his spirit, which led him to pursue a career in the struggle for black rights; Thurman had great respect for King's vocational choice and for his method of affirming the race problem. As he said, "I felt myself a fellow pilgrim with [King] and with all the host of those who shared his dream and shared his vision."[17]

Despite this point of identification with King's vision, Thurman's approach to the subject of human oppression was different. Nothing makes this point more aptly than Thurman's assessment of the spiritual dimensions of the Civil Rights struggle. According to Thurman, the key to King's contribution was that he always

> . . . . spoke from within the context of his religious experience, giving voice to an ethical insight which sprang out of his profound brooding over the meaning of his Judeo-Christian heritage. And this indeed is his great contribution to our times. He was able to put at the center of his personal religious experience a searching ethical awareness.[18]

These are the words of a man whose personal approach to civil rights was less direct, and much less confrontational. The issue here is not a matter of making a choice between the methodologies of these two men; this would be a useless task. Walter E. Fluker is closer to the truth in suggesting that Thurman and King complement each other. He says that Thurman's more spiritualized, personal, and individualistic approach to civil rights should be viewed as a corrective balance to King's aggressive and organized practice of nonviolent direct action. King's method, on the other hand, also gives balance to Thurman's less aggressive approach. Both persons, at any rate, made the connection between religious experiences and the demand for social transformation. Their goals were the same but the methods were different.[19]

The Quest for a Black Christ in African-American Religion and Literature

The Religious Quest

The focus in this segment of the chapter now shifts to Thurman's connection to the Black Christ debate. As a symbol of the black nationalist-liberationist vision in African-American thought, the notion of a Black Christ is a central rallying point.[20] There are three phases to this movement that we will examine: the religious phase (represented by Henry M. Turner and Marcus Garvey);[21] the literary phase (represented by Countee Cullen and Langston Hughes); and the quest in black theology (as articulated by Albert Cleage, Jr., J. DeOtis Roberts, and James H. Cone).

Early in the nineteenth century, Robert Alexander Young offered a strong rationale for the quest of the Black Messiah. His "Ethiopian Manifesto" states categorically why blacks needed a Savior who was black like themselves: Only a black Savior—born of an enslaved black mother, could understand the plight of black slaves and, subsequently, save them.[22] Like many others, Young could not conceive of a God who did not make the conditions of oppressed people a number one priority for action and liberation.

In a similar manner, Bishop Henry McNeal Turner argued that a black God was an essential component of the black struggle for freedom. In a 1898 speech, he declared that:

> We have as much right biblically and otherwise to believe that God is a Negro, as you bukra, or white, people have to believe that God is a fine looking, symmetrical and ornamented white man. For the bulk of you and all the fool Negroes of the country believe that God is a white-skinned, blue-eyed, straight-haired, projecting-nosed, compressed lipped, and finely robed white gentleman sitting on a throne somewhere in the heavens . . . We do not believe there is any hope for a race of people who do not believe they look like God.[23]

Notice that Turner's central concern was principally that of establishing the "right" of black people to envision God in their own image. In so doing, blacks would be engaging in the same action that all cultures and groups have done. It is to be expected that people would "create" God in their own image. However, Turner would argue that blacks did not exercise this right and they have suffered because of it. He believed that this vision was a practical, psychological, and theological necessity, as the survival of the black community was at issue in this connection.

Turner's views were echoed by his younger contemporary, Marcus Garvey. Garvey, a Jamaican-born Pan-Africanist, came to the United States in 1916, at the urging of Booker T. Washington. Within five years, Garvey had become one of the most visable, if not the most visible black leader in the country. He based his entire movement on a quest for black independence, unity, and strength. The centerpiece of his project was his search for a black God. He articulated this idea in the following statement:

> If the white man has the idea of a white God, let him worship his
> God as he desires. If the yellow man's God is of his race, let him
> worship his God as he sees fit. We, as Negroes, have found a new
> ideal. Whilst our God has no color, yet it is human to see everything
> through one's own spectacles, and since the white people have seen
> their God through white spectacles . . . We Negroes believe in the
> God of Ethiopia, the everlasting God—God the Father, God the Son,
> and God the Holy Ghost, the one God of all ages. That is the God in
> whom we believe, but we shall worship Him through spectacles of
> Ethiopia.[24]

Several key issues emerge from this quote. To begin with, like Turner,
Garvey noted that all people have the right to envision God in their
own image. Both men also believed that black people have suffered
unduly in America because they had inculcated the Euro-centric views
of God. Turner, however, did not insist that God be literally "black."
The key issue for him was the declaration of the rights of oppressed
people, particularly their images of God. Moreover, Turner never made
any claims about the "racial" or "color" characteristics of the other
members of the Trinity. Garvey, on the other hand, based his entire
thesis on the claim that Jesus of Nazareth was a true black man, an
Ethiopian in every sense of the term.

Further, neither Turner nor Garvey offered an extensive critique
of the traditional Christian view of the incarnation, the resurrection of
Jesus, nor the doctrine of the Trinity. Garvey's African Orthodox
Church was a duplication of the core beliefs and structure of the Roman
Catholic Church, with the central difference being Garvey's Pan-
Africanist vision. Turner remained faithful to the central theological
claims of the Methodist tradition, in which he was a leading bishop.[25]
It is also noteworthy that neither Garvey nor Turner challenged the
substance of western Christological and Trinitarian dogmas; they choose
instead to critique the symbols and images through which these dogmas
were interpreted.

The "Black Christ" in
African-American Literature

That Thurman's theological project is linked to the Harlem
Renaissance era has already been discussed. The quest for a Black
Christ, as seen in the literature of this period, provides more substance
for this claim. If the general thrust among Harlem Renaissance writers

was to present enlightened images of the black community, the religious dimension was essential to this picture. Thus it is of interest to look at some of the religious insights of the Harlem Renaissance writers.[26] Benjamin E. Mays has done an important job of this. He identifies members of the black literati, such as Countee Cullen and Langston Hughes, as individuals who attempted to bring ideas about God "up to date, and fill them with meaning that touches life situations."[27]

Each writer attempted to bring Christian symbols, claims, ideas, and beliefs into dialogue with the socio-political realities and plight of the oppressed masses in America. This inevitably lead to the need for images of God which reflected the condition of black people and which emerged from the souls and spirits of black folk. Any other religious perspective would have been outdated and meaningless. Cullen's satirical poem expresses this idea graphically:

> In His own time, He will unfold
> Your milk and honey, streets of gold,
> High walls of jasper. . . phrases rolled led
> Upon the tongues of idiots.
> What profit then, if hunger gluts.[28]

This passionate bit of satire offers a profound challenge to the idea of a just and loving God, so strongly affirmed in black popular religion. One also notices this emphasis in Cullen's statements about Christ.

But Christ who conquered Death and Hell What has He done for you who spent A bleeding life for His content Or is the white Christ, too, distraught By these dark skins His Father wrought.[29]

Behind Cullen's reflections was the hope for a Black Christ.

> Wishing He I served were black,
> Thinking that it would not lack
> Precedent of pain to guide it,
> Let who would or might deride it,
> Surely then this flesh would know,
> Yours had borne a kindred woe.
> Lord, I fashion dark gods, too,
> ———————————
> Lord, forgive me if my need
> Sometimes shapes my human creed.[30]

Note the emphasis here on the idea that the "need" (for divine liberation) shapes the creed (one's theological claims). Cullen's concern is a prayer for divine intervention in the suffering of oppressed people:

> Our Father, God; our Brother,
> Or are we bastard kin,
> That to our complaints your ears are closed,
> Your doors barred from within?
> Our Father, God, our Brother, Christ, Retrieve my race again;
> So shall you compass this black sheep.
> The pagan heart. Amen.[31]

This is a plea for a Christ who shares the plight of the oppressed—a Black Christ, if you will.

Langston Hughes, Cullen's contemporary, offered a similar plea and critique. Like Cullen, Hughes was very knowledgeable of the popular currents in black spirituality, particularly their vision of God. He called this vision into question with some incisive and pointed questions. Hughes' writings contain at least three different conceptions of Jesus. His autobiographical reflections record his youthful fascination with the hope of experiencing Jesus' salvific power as well as his frustrations with not having had such an encounter. Hughes' reflections on the idea of a Black Christ indicate a more critical element in his thought. "Goodbye Christ" contains some of his more radical statements:

> Listen Christ,
> You did all right in your day I reckon But that day's gone now.
> They ghosted you up a swell story, too,
> Called it Bible—
> The popes and the preachers've
> Made too much money from it
> They've sold you to too many
> Kings, generals, robbers, and killers—
> Even to the Tzar and the Cossacks
> Even to Rockefeller's church
> Even to the Saturday Evening Post.
>
> Christ Jesus Lord God Jehovah,
>
> Beat it on away from here now. Make way for a new guy with no religion at all.

A real guy named
Marx Communist Lenin Peasant Stalin,
Worker Me—
Go ahead on now.
You're getting in the way of things Lord
And please take Saint Becton or the Consecrated Dime
And Step on the gas, Christ
Don't' be so slow about moving;
Move

The world is mine from now on—
And nobody's gonna sell me
To a king or a general
Or a Millionaire
Go ahead on now.[32]

These verses from Hughes' poem demonstrate his fascination with Marxist claims about the impotence of religious faith. Hughes later explained that the purpose of this poem was to challenge Christian churches and to call them to task for ignoring the racial situation in America. It was a way of saying that churches were out of touch with reality and, as such, they were to be challenged, if not ignored.[33] He believed that America's racist and oppressive system was an affront to the spirit of Christianity.[34]

We can look elsewhere in order to further connect with Hughes' statements about the Black Christ. "Christ in Alabama" offers further insight:

Christ is a Nigger, Beaten and black—
O, bare your back.

Mary is his Mother— Mammy of the South,
Silence your mouth.

God's His Father—
White Master above, Grant us your love.

Most holy bastard of the bleeding mouth: Nigger Christ
On the cross of the South.[35]

Hughes took the oppression within the African-American community as the point of departure for his understanding of the Jesus. He suggested that the Christian gospel is validated in accordance with its identification with the plight of black people. Christ had to become a part of the black condition; there had to be a "Nigger Christ." Here again we see how questions concerning the conditions of black people have been brought into the forefront of twentieth century conversations about who Jesus was.

The challenge of black nationalists such as Turner and Garvey and the visionary claims of Harlem Renaissance thinkers Cullen and Hughes are all central in the Black Christ debate. None, however, went as far as Howard Thurman, their younger contemporary, in radically challenging the substance of western God-talk. Thurman's project called in to question the lack of socio-political relevance in popular religious practices and radically critiqued traditional doctrines such as the incarnation, resurrection, and miracles of Christ. Moreover, Thurman called the doctrine of the Trinity into question. There are no references in Thurman's writings to the traditional interpretations, for example, of the work of the Holy Spirit in the life and ministry of Jesus. We have already noted that Thurman attributed Jesus' uniqueness entirely to the depth of his religious experience. Thurman's rare references to the work of the Holy Spirit lack the full Trinitarian implications traditionally assigned to this doctrine.[36]

Moreover, Thurman refused to confine his religious vision to the claims and concerns of the Christian tradition. In this he went far beyond his contemporaries, who choose to critique their traditions from within and only to challenge aspects of their claims. Garvey's African Orthodox Church was a duplication of the Catholic Churches, with black saints, a black God, and a black Christ. Turner was likewise indebted to the mainstream of Christian thought. In this sense, Turner, Garvey, Hughes, and Cullen remained rather traditional in their basic theological beliefs. While they challenged aspects of the tradition, such as the failure to address social issues and the heavy reliance on European images, their critiques were intentionally limited. On the contrary, Thurman was in search of a more creative vision of the religious life, of which Christian faith was one component.

We see evidence of Thurman's vision and the far-reaching implications thereof in the establishment of the Church for the Fellowship of All Peoples in 1943. Thurman wrote:

> Here at last I could put to the test once more the major concern of my life: Is the worship of God the central and most significant act of the human spirit? Is it really true that in the presence of God there is

neither male or female, child nor adult, rich nor poor, nor any classification by which mankind defines itself in categories, however meaningful?[37]

Throughout his career Thurman demonstrated a willingness to experiment both with liturgical symbols and with the theological claims of the Christian tradition. He was more than willing to pursue the meaning of his religious experiences even to their most far-reaching conclusions in dialogue with persons from other religions and cultures. The motto of CFAP helps us to understand that while Thurman remained firmly rooted in the Christian community, he was willing to pursue truth elsewhere.

> I declare to share in the spiritual growth and ethical awareness of men and women of varied national, cultural, racial, and creedal heritage united in a religious fellowship.[38]

This is not to suggest that Turner and Garvey had no appreciation for other religious traditions; rather it simply indicates the degree to which Thurman was willing to pursue dialogues with persons from other religious traditions. Thurman was a "spiritual technologist" or a "Shaman" of the Spiritual, to use Mozella G. Mitchell's phrase. Thurman described religious truths as universal "facts" which are not limited to any particular religious communion. As he said:

> The things that are true in any religion are found in that religion because they are true; they are not true because they are found in the religion. It is not the context that determines the validity or the truth of the insights. Wherever [truths] are found they are true without special reference to the context in which they are observed.[39]

Thurman's beliefs about the power and universal significance of religious experience led him to his strong criticism of traditional Christian dogma.[40]

The very conception of the idea of a Black Christ is also an area of emphasis where Thurman differs from black nationalists like Turner and Garvey. We have already noted that both Turner and Garvey categorically believed that a "Black Christ" was a necessary counterpart to the black struggle for freedom. Thurman, on the other hand, made no claims about the "blackness" of Christ. He was familiar with the popular claims about the "Black Christ" early in his career and at later stages in the development of the black theology movement.[41] But in his case, Thurman thought that it was essential to note Jesus' ethnic and racial identity, thus his strong emphasis on Jesus' Jewish heritage.[42] Unlike Garvey, Thurman did not say that the historical Jesus was an African man. We also note that neither Cullen nor Hughes said that Jesus was of an African heritage; the key issue for both of them was the idea that black peoples' conception of God should be developed in relationship to their condition of oppression and suffering. They were not as literal as Garvey on this point. In any case, Thurman found Garvey's claim to be questionable in terms of historical accuracy. In focusing on Jesus' racial identity, Thurman stressed the idea that God's revelation is made known through the particularity of specific human cultures and communities. The key issue, however, was to emphasize that Jesus was a "poor Jew."[43] It was Jesus' Jewishness and his poverty that made him relevant, Thurman believed, to the suffering black people. He said that Jesus' plight as a poor person "placed him initially with the great mass of men on earth."[44] He focused upon how Jesus' liberation ethic addressed conditions of poor people. They can see in Jesus a person who transcended all of the limitations imposed upon him by society.

> It means that against the background of anonymity [Jesus] emerged articulate, and particular. . . .[H]is answer becomes humanity's answer and his life the common claim. In him the miracle of the working paper is writ large, for what he did all men may do.[45]

So Thurman's focus was upon how Jesus destroyed the multidimensional forces of human oppression which the oppressed encounter. In this regard the religion and message of Jesus took on very significant roles.

Thurman, Black Theologians, and the Quest for a Black Christ

The search for a black Messiah was particularly crucial in the development of the black theology movement. The theologians whose works we will examine—Albert B. Cleage Jr., James Hal Cone, and J. DeOtis Roberts—are, in varying degrees, responding to the nationalist impulses of the 1960s.[46]

Albert B. Cleage, Jr.

Cleage, a militant black nationalist minister, earned his revolutionary stripes in the Civil Rights struggles of the black community in Detroit. He has been in ministry there for several decades. Cleage's Christology emerged out of the context of his Pan-Africanist and black nationalist vision for the formation of a "Black Nation." He wanted to demonstrate how God is revealed in the realities of the world, particularly the "world" where black people struggle for their dignity and self-definition. Cleage's Christology, then, begins with what he believes to be the "facts" about the historical Jesus, the Black Christ. The fact, as he saw it, is that:

> Jesus was a revolutionary black leader, a Zealot, seeking to lead a Black Nation to freedom so the Black Church must carefully define the nature of the revolution.[47]

And, further, that Jesus "was the non-white leader of a nonwhite people struggling for national liberation against the rule of a white nation, Rome."[48] This is no minor claim in Cleage's work. His entire project is based on the concept of "nationhood" he gathered from studying the Old Testament. According to Cleage, the biblical story of Israel was the literal story of a black nation. The Bible is thus a book dedicated to the freedom of the black nation.

Cleage follows Garvey in the belief that the historical Jesus was an African. As the product of a black nation, Jesus was the incarnation of God among the chosen people. His mission was that of showing his people the way to freedom within human history. Thus, Cleage's belief in the Black Christ was not merely an affirmation of a symbolic notion. He believed in the literal interpretation of the concept.

Cleage also believed that the idea of a black Christ was a psycho-spiritual necessity for black people. In further connection with Garvey and with Turner, he contended that African-Americans needed a black God in order to support their struggle against self-hatred. He put it this way: "Black people cannot build dignity on their knees worshipping a white Christ."[49]

Cleage believed that the problems of black people could be explained in terms of the complete socio-economic and political exploitation of the black community in America and in the world community. He believed this systematic domination of black people could only be counteracted through the affirmation of the idea of a black nation, the central element of which was the espousal of the idea of a Black Christ. The Black Christ was the embodiment of the highest ideals of Cleage's black nationalist religion.

James H. Cone

Cone came to national prominence in the late 1960s. His emergence took place on the strength of his provocative text, *Black Theology and Black Power* (1969). His Christology revolved around one principal claim, which he described in the following manner:

> Christianity begins and ends with the man Jesus—his life, his death and resurrection. He is the Revelation, the special disclosure of God to man, revealing who God is and what his purpose for man is. In short, Christ is the essence of Christianity.[50]

For Cone, the Christian vision of God and conception of human freedom and liberation finds its fullest expression in the life, death, and resurrection of Jesus of Nazareth. He makes this point very graphically in his definition of theology.

> [Theology is a] rational study of the being of God in the world in light of the existential situation of an oppressed community, relating the forces of liberation to the essence of the gospel, which is Jesus Christ.[51]

Cone noted that the biblical witness about the historical Jesus is the essential starting point for Christology because it points towards the God who is revealed in Jesus as the liberator of the oppressed. The historical Jesus was a participant in the black struggle for freedom; thus Cone definitively affirmed the relevancy of the Christian message to the conditions and aspirations of black people.

Kelly D. Brown has correctly noted that Cone's is an ontological approach to the question of the Black Christ.[52] While Cone believed in the idea of a Black Christ, his definition of "blackness" in general and the blackness of Christ in particular is ontological and metaphysical as opposed to literal, as was the case with Garvey and Cleage, both of whom believed in the literal blackness of Christ. Cone also stood in opposition to J. DeOtis Roberts' claim that the idea of the Black Christ is simply an expression of the "psychocultural" needs of African-Americans. [53] In rejecting Roberts' approach, Cone argued that Jesus is black.

> [People believe in the Black Christ] not because of some cultural or
> psychological need of black people, but because and only because
> Christ really enters into our world where the poor, the despised, and
> the black are.[54]

This particular emphasis allowed Cone to critique both Roberts and
Cleage. Cone, despite his respect for Cleage's black nationalist agenda,
raised questions about Cleage's "literal" claim that Jesus was an
African.[55] For Cone, Cleage's thesis was questionable on historical
and theological grounds. Cone chose to define blackness both in racial
and in nonracial terms. He argued that blackness in the complete sense
refers to the oppression, suffering, and tragedies of history, by which
the poor are bitterly victimized. Blackness is, rather, a condition of
life; a condition through which God was revealed in the Exodus, and
into which Jesus was born. Given this particular approach, Cone, unlike
Cleage or Garvey, admitted the provisional nature of his claim about
the Black Christ.[56] The key issue for Cone was the connection between
the idea of the Black Christ and the universal experience of suffering.
God became incarnate in Jesus Christ and identified with the despair
and tragedies of history, that is, with human oppression.[57] This,
according to Cone, is the true meaning of God's revelation in Jesus
Christ.[58]

J. DeOtis Roberts

The middle road between Cleage's and Cone's Christologies was
charted by J. DeOtis Roberts. Most of Robert's writings in black
theology have centered on his attempts to correct some of the more
controversial aspects of Cone's theology. More specifically, Roberts
challenged Cone's statements about the compatibility of the Christian
gospel with the black power philosophy. His Christology reflects this
very important aspect of his thought. Robert's Christology combined
the quest for a Black Messiah with the idea of a cosmic (universal)
Christ. He offered a Christ for black people who is also the Christ for
all people. He put it this way:

> The genius of the Christian religion is that it is at once particular and
> universal, personal and social. . . Particularism and universalism
> have their place in the context of the Christian faith.[59]

For Roberts, the search for a more particular definition of who Jesus is
must emerge in this context. To talk about Christ for black people is to
talk about the role of the Black Messiah in black faith. He wrote:

> [T]he universal Christ is particularized for the black Christian in the black experience of the black Messiah, but the black Messiah is at the same time universalized in the Christ of the Gospels who meets all men in their situation. The black messiah liberates the black man. The universal Christ reconciles the black man with the rest of mankind.[60]

The universal Christ, in Robert's thought, is the biblical depiction of Jesus Christ as the incarnation of God, and as the one who brings salvation to human beings and reconciles them to God and to each other. The Black Christ represents an expression of one aspect of the meaning of the universal Christ.

The idea of a Black Christ was, for Roberts, a symbolic claim, which emphasizes the fact that all people have a right to view God in their own image. It is a symbol or a myth that black people need in combating their oppression.[61] Roberts critiques, on the one hand, Cleage's literal conception of the Black Christ as an inaccurate fact on historical ground. He critiques Cone in general for an insufficient emphasis on the doctrine of reconciliation and for being too narrowly Barthian and Christocentric in his work.[62] Roberts insisted that black theologians should be less tied to western theological concepts and more open to dialoguing with African traditional religions. According to Roberts, there needs to be an openness to Eastern modes of thinking about God.[63]

Conclusion: Continuities and Discontinuities

There are several factors which need to be addressed when examining potential areas of dialogue between Thurman and his younger contemporaries in the field of black theology. To begin with, it is clear that each of the writers considered in this segment joined Thurman in the quest for an interpretation of the Christian faith which takes the conditions of the black community to heart. Each theologian—for his own reasons—challenged the Christian community to deal with the racial contradictions in American life. All agree that the systems of race, class, political, and sexual (for some) oppression are incompatible with the spirit of Jesus of Nazareth. In this sense, each theologian viewed Jesus in a liberationist perspective. This is to say that they believed that Jesus' life, religion, message, death, and resurrection stand as symbols of God's identification with the conditions of all oppressed people.

Here Thurman parts company with his fellow black theologians. While he would not be at odds with their quest for a Black Christ, he does not engage in the debate. His principle concern was not the question of Jesus' race; rather he wanted to demonstrate the relevance of Jesus' life to suffering people in general. By no means was the race question irrelevant to him, nothing could be further from the truth. But Thurman was a universalist, for whom the discussion of the particularities of the black experience was simply an entry point into the broader discussion of the human experience. Moreover, Thurman's discussion of Jesus' Jewishness addressed the question of racial rootedness. Again, however, even here the experiences of Jesus, the poor Jew, were relevant as a means of understanding the universal plight of suffering peoples.

Thurman's view of the universal Christ is another significant issue. (We have discussed this issue at length in Chapter III.) The point that needs to be noted here is that it is possible to identify a "Christ" element in Thurman's thought. It reflects his understanding of what the historical Jesus "attained" through his encounter with God. Jesus' religious experiences helped to "make" him the "son" of God. For Thurman, however, there was no Trinitarian Christ, no universal, cosmic, Savior, in the traditional sense. Thurman stands in opposition to Cone and Roberts on this point. Cone and Roberts are close in terms of their mutual use of the Trinitarian conceptions of the person of Jesus, as outlined in the Bible and in the Christian tradition. Cone, for example, drew heavily on the Nicene and Chalcedonian traditions in the development of his Christology. For him, the historical Jesus is simultaneously the Son of God and the Second Person of the Trinity.[64] Thurman's Jesus was elected to be the son of God, in the same sense that all other persons can be.

Albert Cleage was clearly the most radical among the theologians we have studied, but it is interesting that he too remained traditional. This is particularly true with reference to the ambiguous appropriation of Trinitarian ideas in his sermons and prayers. We have noted Thurman's reluctance to pray to or worship Jesus, or even to pray in Jesus' name. Cleage, on the other hand, evoked the name of Jesus Christ throughout his book, *The Black Messiah* and deemed him the Son of God and the Black Messiah. For instance, he prayed:

> Help us that we may follow in the footsteps of the Black Messiah, thy Son, our Lord and Savior, Jesus Christ. . .Help us to come forward and say: "I am not ashamed to worship a black Christ."[65]

He evoked the biblical notion of the "spirit" of God in his prayers, as well, as he requested a "persuasive touch of [God's] spirit."[66]

The third and final aspect to note here is the degree to which Thurman differed from black theologians in terms of their use of the birth, death, and resurrection continuum in the search for a Black Christ. Cone and Roberts were similar in their reference to the doctrine of the incarnation, the meaning of the political nature of the death of Jesus, and the supernatural implications of the doctrine of the resurrection. For them, the reality of the incarnation and the truth of the resurrection ensured, on the one hand, that Jesus was indeed the Son of God, and on the other hand, they affirmed that God's liberation and reconciliation of the oppressed has been completed. The act of reconciliation which was accomplished by Jesus restored human beings to God and reconciled them with each other.[67] Their temporal and eternal freedom were made complete through Jesus' life, death, and resurrection.

Thurman offers a different view of the incarnation. Jesus was not the incarnation of the second person of the Trinity, rather, for Thurman the idea of the incarnation pointed to God's election of the conditions of oppressed people as the context of divine revelation. The incarnation was not to be taken literally, but should be viewed as a symbol of divine identification with the conditions of the oppressed.

We find general agreement between Cone, Roberts, and Thurman on the idea that the death of Jesus represented an act of supreme oppression to the oppressed Jewish community of the first century. Each also saw the direct connection between this event and the oppressed conditions of the African-American community. Thurman did not, however, speak about the death of Jesus as an act of atonement for human sins and brokenness. Finally, Thurman understood the resurrection primarily as a source of spiritual and psychological power for all people. It reminds them of the aliveness of life. It is a symbol of the resilient power that is inherent in life. He found no need to argue for a literal view of the resurrection; he was satisfied to point to the symbolic power of the event. In this regard, he differed from Cleage, who connected the resurrection theme to the idea of the resurrection of the Black Nation. While not as overtly political as Cleage in his view of the resurrection, Thurman clearly demonstrated the significance of the event as a source of power for the oppressed.

Notes

1 Sterling Stuckey, *The Ideological Origins of Black Nationalism* (Boston: Beacon Press, 1972), p. 1.

2 See John H. Bracey, August Meier, and Elliot Rudwick *Black Nationalism in America* (New York: The Bobbs-Merril Company, Inc., 1971), p. xxvi. Stuckey argues against the practice of dividing the black nationalist groups up into smaller groups.

3 I presented this theme in an unpublished lecture entitled "Howard Thurman: Black Renaissance Theologian," delivered at the annual meeting of the Southeastern Commission of the American Academy of Religion, 17 March 1990, Charlotte, NC. I will say more about this theme below in talking about Thurman's view of the Black Messiah.

4 See his article in Arna Botemps, ed. *The Harlem Renaissance Remembered* (New York: Dodd, Mead & Company, 1972), p. 27.

5 James H. Cone offers a very helpful comparative discussion of each writer's interpretation of the spirituals. See his *Spirituals and the Blues* (New York: Seabury Press, 1982). Note especially chapter 2.

6 Thurman, *Deep River* p. 11.

7 Ibid.

8 Thurman, *With Head and Heart*. p. 217.

9 A full elaboration of this point is beyond the scope of this study. Suffice it to say, however, that a significantly large portion of Thurman's distinguished career was spent in predominantly white institutions and working with largely white organizations and groups. We recall for example his work with the Fellowship Church over nine years, and his thirteen years with Boston University. This is in addition to the tremendous amount of time that he spent lecturing to white groups and working with entities such as the YMCA. He was very much the ambassador of the African-American religious community.

10 See his discussion in *Deep River,* p. 5.

11 Howard Thurman, *The Luminous Darkness* (New York: Harper & Row Publishers, 1965), p. x.

12 See Ibid., p. 8; and Wiley, "Church," Chapter 6.

13 Ibid., p. 104

14 Thurman, *The Luminous Darkness*, p. 23; *With Head and Heart,* p. 255.

15 Dean Lawrence Carter of Morehouse College in Atlanta, GA., has noted that Thurman and King did at least have several telephone conversions, which were usually initiated by Thurman. Interview with Lawrence Carter, Morehouse College, Atlanta, GA., 10 November 1989. Moreover, Lerone Bennett has also indicated that King traveled with a copy of *Jesus and the Disinherited* in his briefcase. See his *What Manner of Man* 2nd revised edition (Chicago: Johnson Publishing Co., 1976). Thurman also referred to this fact. *With Head and Heart*, p. 255.

16 Thurman, *With Head and Heart*. p. 255.

17 Ibid.

18 Thurman made these remarks during his tribute to King, on the occasion of King's death. Ibid., p. 223.

19 See Fluker, *They Looked for a City*, p. 174f.

20 Kelly D. Brown, "Who Do They Say That I Am?" A Critical Examination of the Black Christ (Ph.D. Dissertation, Union Theological Seminary, 1988), pp. 19-20. See also her expanded version of this study, Kelly D. Brown Douglass, *The Black Christ* (Maryknoll, NY: Orbis Books, 1994).

21 This theme is raised in Randall Burkett, *Garveyism as a Religious Movement: The Institutionalization of a Black Civil Religion* (Metuchen, NJ.: Scarecrow Press, Inc., and the American Theological Library Association, 1978).

22 Robert Alexander Young, "The Ethiopian Manifesto," in Sterling Stuckey, *The Ideological Origins of Black Nationalism* (Boston: Beacon Press, 1972), pp. 33-34.

23 See his speech in Bracey, *Nationalism*, pp. 154, 164.

24 Marcus Garvey, *Philosophy and Opinions of Marcus Garvey: Or Africa for Africans*, compiled by Amy Jacques Garvey; with a New Introduction by E. U. Essien Udom, 2 vols. (London: Frank Cass and Company Limited, 1967), p. 33.

25 See John Bracey's discussion of this issue in his *Nationalism* , p. 192.

26 See Warrington Hudlin's article in Arna Botemps, ed. *The Harlem Renaissance Remembered* (New York: Dodd, Mead & Company, 1972), p. 269.

27 Benjamin E. Mays, *The Negro's God as Reflected in His Literature* (New York: Russell & Russell, 1938), p. 185.

28 Countee Cullen, *The Black Christ and Other Poems* (New York: Harper & Brothers Publishers, 1929) pp. 84-85.

29 Ibid., pp. 104-105.

30 Countee Cullen, *Color*, Afro-American Culture Series (New York: Harper & Brothers, 1925; reprint ed., New York: Arno Press and the New York Times, 1969, p. 40.

31 Countee Cullen, *On These I Stand* (New York: Harper & Row, 1927), pp. 11-12.

32 Langston Hughes, ed., *Good Morning Revolution*, an introduction by Faith Berry, foreword by Sanders Redding, (New York: Lawrence Hill & Company, 1973), p. 36.

33 Ibid., p. 133.

34 He later offered several disclaimers regarding this poem. See Ibid. See also *The Langston Hughes Reader* (New York: George Brazeller, Inc. 1958) pp. 127-28. He expresses a much deeper respect for orthodox piety and theology in his novel, *Not Without Laughter* (New York: Alfred A. Knopf, 1963).

35 Hughes, *The Langston Hughes Reader*, p. 405.

36 Thurman makes several such references. Thurman, *Footprints of a Dream,* p. 136, and *The Temptations, of Jesus* p. 23.

37 Thurman, *With Head and Heart,* p. 144.

38 Ibid., p. 143.

39 See Thurman's unpublished collection, at Boston University, see box # 49/6A. See Mitchell's discussion of this aspect of Thurman's thought in her, *Spiritual,* Chapter 2.

40 See his interview with Ron Eyre in *Critic's Corner,* n.p. n.d. p. 211.

41 Note Thurman's discussion of the connection between Jesus and the black slaves in his lecture "Negro Spirituals and the Black Madonna," paper presented at the Black House, Blaisdell Institute, Claremont, CA 10 November 1975. Here he demonstrated the spiritual relationship between slave religion and the religion of Jesus. Moreover, Thurman was very familiar with the works of James Cone and the even more radical nationalist theology of Albert Cleage. He read Cleage's *The Black Messiah* (New York: Sheed and Ward, 1968) and highly recommended it, as well as Cone's *Black Theology and Black Power* (New York: Seabury, 1969) to other students of religion. See the reference to it in the recommended reading list of Thurman's *Common Ground.* Thurman was familiar with Cleage's work in Detroit. Prior to this he became acquainted with him during the early days of the Fellowship Church. Dr. Charles Johnson, the noted sociologist, had introduced Cleage to the Dr. Alfred Fisk, the co-founder of Fellowship Church. Cleage worked at the church before Thurman arrived in San Francisco. See the discussions about Cleage's work with the church in *The First Footprints* (San Francisco: Lawton and Alfred Kennedy, 1975.)

42 This is one of several principal points that he believed to be at the heart of shaping who Jesus was. We have examined these areas in the preceding chapter.

43 Thurman, *Jesus and the Disinherited*, p. 14.

44 Ibid., p. 17.

45 Ibid., p. 112.

46 We will not offer a full discussion of any of these theologians in this study; our concern here is simply to look at their Christologies. Major J. Jones, also a noted black theologian from this period, offers some helpful insights on the subject of a black theological view of Christ. See especially his *The Color of G.O.D.* (Macon, GA.: Mercer University Press, 1987), note Chapter 6.

47 Albert Cleage, *The Black Messiah* (Kansas City, Kansas: Sheed Andrews and McMeel, Inc., 1968), p. 3.

48 Ibid.

49 Ibid.

50 James H. Cone, *Black Theology and Black Power*, (New York: Seabury Press, 1969), p. 34.

51 James H. Cone, *A Black Theology of Liberation* (New York: Seabury Press, 1969), p.34.

52 Brown, *Black Christ*, p. 104.

53 James DeOtis Roberts, *A Black Political Theology* (Philadelphia: Westminster Press, 1974), p. 137. See Cone, *God of the Oppresse*d, (New York: Seabury Press, 1975), p.136.

54 Cone, *God of the Oppressed*, p. 136.

55 James H. Cone, *For My People* (Maryknoll, NY: Orbis Books, 1984), p.36.

56 Cone, *God of the Oppressed*, pp. 135-137. See also his *A Black Theology of Liberation*, p.32.

57 See Dwight N. Hopkins' *Black Theology USA and South Africa* (Mary knoll, NY: Orbis Books, 1989), note particularly Chapter 2.

58 See his *God of the Oppressed*, chapter 10.

59 J. DeOtis Roberts, *Liberation and Reconciliation* (Philadelphia: Westminster Press, 1971), p. 130.

60 Ibid., p. 14.

61 Roberts, *Liberation and Reconciliation*, p. 134.

62 See his *Political*, chapter 1, for more on his debates with Cone.

63 See his *Black Theology in Dialogue* (Philadelphia: Westminster Press, 1987) for an account of his most recent comments in this area.

64 As quoted in Carlyle Felding Stewart, *God, Being and Liberation*. Note his discussion in chapter three, pp. 147-150.

65 Cleage, *The Black Messiah*, p. 114.

66 Ibid.

67 See Cone's *A Black Theology of Liberation*, p. 134.

Chapter VI

"Who Do the People Say That I Am?" Personal Perspectives Regarding Christology

In the previous chapters of this study the focus has been exegetical and expository. I have analyzed the primary components of Thurman's interpretation of the life, teachings, and ministry of Jesus of Nazareth. The book is organized in a manner which best reflects Thurman's theological vision and methodology, quoting his literal words and thoughts wherever possible. I trust that the reader has indeed heard his voice in this text. My own approach to the subject of Christology differs from Thurman's on several critical points, but I have tried to be as objective as possible in presenting his views. The remaining task of this study is to summarize, and to discuss some of the implications of Thurman's thought for my own theology. In discussing the implications of Thurman's thought, I will both appropriate and critique relevant aspects of his theology. In so doing, I hope to present some relevant theological claims for the late 1990s.

Summary

Thurman's most significant Christological claim was his contention that Jesus' primary role was that of a deliverer, liberator, of the disinherited. More than simply a good teacher or a role model, Jesus identified with the oppressed by becoming one of them. As such he understood their oppression in its broadest, multidimensional sense. And Jesus remains at the center of Christian faith because he was the "word made flesh": he became the son of God through obedience, suffering, moral discipline, and religious experience. He was an oppressed man in a despised community, yet he was chosen by God as an instrument of freedom for all people. For Thurman the meaning of Jesus' birth, life, teaching, death, and resurrection is grounded in their representation of God's identification with human suffering. In Jesus' birth, God elected the poor masses as vehicles of divine revelation; in Jesus' teaching, God gave the poor a practical theological vision for the attainment of their freedom; in Jesus' death, God demonstrated the price that is to be paid for the strength of conviction. Through Jesus' resurrection, God vindicated the oppressed from the penalties of their subservient status.

A passionate concern about the relevancy of the Christian gospel to the problem of human suffering in general, and in particular the plight of the African-American community, runs throughout Thurman's work. As an African-American theologian, Thurman's racial plight was the context within which he understood the meaning of Jesus' life, teaching, and death. He was uncompromising in this effort to bring the issue of human fulfillment and the quest for justice into the foreground of Christian Christ-talk. For this reason he unequivocally insisted that America, with its history of segregation, racism, and oppression could not claim to be a true Christian nation. Likewise, churches complicit in this situation were not living up to the truths of the gospel. The separation between persons of different religious traditions, social classes, and races, within and outside of the Christian faith, was also of great concern to Thurman. Such separations would suggest that God does not favor the human quest for unity. Thurman insisted that a legitimate interpretation of Jesus would not lead to the divisions within the human community; it should instead be a unifying force.[1]

The basic claims outlined in this study provide the core of Thurman's beliefs on the subject of Jesus as a unifying force developed over the course of his career. He began to outline the central themes of *Jesus and the Disinherited*, his principal statement on Jesus, as early as 1935. It was published in 1949, while Thurman was living in San Francisco and serving at the pastor of the Church for the Fellowship of All Peoples. Ten years later, in 1959, Thurman presented a series of lectures on the same subject. Though his profession and geographical location, as well as the circumstances within the world, had changed, his basic insights about how the religion of Jesus addresses the problem of oppression in general and specifically the experiences of fear, deception, hate, and love remained the same. Further evidence of this line of continuity in Thurman's thought can be found in his text, *The Luminous Darkness*, which contains his direct attempt to come to terms with turmoil in American life and the mandates of the Civil Rights movement of the 1950s and 1960s. His statements about the connection between hate, despair, and segregation, as articulated earlier in *Jesus and the Disinherited*, are repeated there.

The area of Thurman's interpretation of Jesus which does show considerable development, however, is his treatment of Jesus' "religion" and "religious experiences." In his later writings on Jesus, we see a much stronger "comparative" emphasis in his thought. He was not content speaking about Jesus in isolation from the broader religious world, particularly the Eastern religious traditions. In *Jesus and the Disinherited*, for example, he does not provide us with a clear understanding of his theory of religious experience and mysticism, which are so central to his general religious vision.[2] Moreover, there is no mention made of a theory of religious experience in this work, but it would be made throughout his later works, particularly *The Creative Encounter*, *The Growing Edge*, *Disciplines of the Spirit*, and *The Search for Common Ground*.

As discussed in Chapter Two, Thurman attributed the primacy to Jesus' humanity. He attempted to depict Jesus as a full human being, without any claims about his divine nature, preexistence, or superiority to other human beings. Thurman's Christology was not rooted in traditional Trinitarian language, theology, experience. Moreover, I have described this issue in relation to Thurman's theory of religious experience. In a lecture at Fellowship Church in 1950, for example, he focused on "The Religion of Jesus and Social Change." In this series, for example, he spoke at length about the specific aspects of Jesus' religion. A similar focus is found in his series on "A Faith to Live By," where Jesus' tradition is presented as one among several, each of which depict prophetic models for living. In each of these writings, Thurman was careful to depict Jesus as a model of true religious faith.   Like Buddha, the Brahmin Mystics, and others, Jesus was a model for how people experience God. Moreover, as a man among other humans, Jesus provided a prime example of how human beings should face suffering and temptation, as he described in Thurman's *The Temptations of Jesus*. This work began as a preaching series at Boston University's Marsh Chapel in 1962.   The climax in the development of Thurman's interpretation of Jesus was offered in his 1978 lectures on "The Religion of Jesus." In those lectures Thurman outlined with great clarity what it means to view Jesus as the subject of religious experience, as opposed to the object of religious devotion.[3]

Shaping the Christological Dialogue: Social Context, Scripture, and Tradition

Liberation theologians, post-modernists, and others have all helped us to understand that theology is a human enterprise. God does not write theology, individual persons and religious communities perform this task. Theology is not a neutral science, it always reflects, wittingly or unwittingly, the socio-cultural and political life of its creators. For Christians, God's revelation is found in the Bible and the life, teachings, and ministry of Jesus.

As human reflection on God's revelation, theology emerges from the social world of the theologian. The theologian writes from the vantage point of the world as she/he experiences it. But, according to James H. Cone,

> {The} truth of Jesus Christ, whom we meet in our social existence,
> is not exhausted by the questions we ask. The meaning of Christ is
> not derived from nor dependent upon our social context.[4]

Rather, Cone suggests that Christological discussions rely upon three primary elements: the social context of the theologian, Scripture, and Tradition (the history of Christian thought).[5]

Cone's central concern here is for the objectivity of Christian theology. If theology only reflects the questions and concerns of the racial, ethnic, social, and ecclesial group which is writing it, it cannot legitimately be said to be reflections on God's self-revelation. Theology always includes, but must also extend beyond, the individual or collective human experiences. Therefore, the theological enterprise must also include an analysis of the Bible and of the history of Christian thinking about particular doctrinal issues, that is, tradition. In shaping my own Christology, Cone's suggested trifold foci essential.

My Social Context

My own spirituality, theology, and vision of the world are deeply rooted in socio-cultural and religious traditions of the African-American community. I grew up in the rural town of Goose Creek, South Carolina. I was educated in the public schools of this town during the civil rights and post-civil rights era. While the legal separation of the races had ended, the world in which I grew up remained segregated. I lived with my family in an all black community, surrounded by my immediate family. I lived there for the first eighteen years of my life, before going to Orangeburg, SC for four years to attend Claflin College.

My religious experiences were shaped within the confines of Calvary Church of God in Christ, where my father was and remains the pastor. Calvary remains my home church, though I pastor elsewhere. Thus the Church of God in Christ tradition has significantly shaped my life, theology, and spirituality. I have benefited from the great wisdom of the history of the Christian church, as I have studied it over my career. Moreover, I have learned much in recent years from my explorations into the mythical and theological systems of people of faith from various religious communities around the world. Teaching and researching within the university setting has afforded me this luxury. Yet I am continually reminded of Thurman's statement:

> My roots are deeply rooted in the throbbing reality of the Negro idiom and from it I draw a full measure of inspiration and vitality. I know that a man must be at home somewhere before he can feel at home everywhere.[6]

Being "at home" for me means being spiritually, culturally, and socially rooted in the "Negro idiom", or the "African-American experience". Being rooted in the African-American experience helps to put flesh on my theological vision. It is impossible for me to talk about the meaning of Christian faith in general, and in particular the meaning of Jesus of Nazareth, without consideration of the historical and current experiences of this community, as well as of the history of Christian thought.

Like Thurman, my concern, as an African-American Christian theologian, is to relate the truths of the Christian gospel to the life and death issues of this community. I have addressed this issue, as did Thurman, Cone, and a host of others, by affirming that Jesus brought good news for the disinherited. From the New Testament community down to our own time, the life and message of Jesus has brought power and meaning to those who suffer. (This issue is explained more fully in Chapter Four as a response to the multidimensionality of human oppression.) Jesus' good news for the disinherited is presented as an answer to the human experience of oppression in its broadest sense. Oppression is understood to include economic, political, cultural, as well as psychological and spiritual realities. Likewise, the message of liberation for the oppressed must address each of these dimensions of oppression.

For the past few decades, discussions in black and womanist theologies have concentrated primarily on questions related to racial, gender, and economic oppression, with varying degrees of emphasis. In recent years, however, there have been attempts to push the discussions about oppression and liberation to a much deeper existential level, including the psychological and spiritual dimensions of human experience. This is particularly noted in the works of writers such as Cornel West, Michael Dyson, Lerone Bennett, and others.

One example of this current is seen in the work of Cornel West. West described the current crises in the African-American community in terms of nihilism, which is to be understood

> not as a philosophic doctrine that there are no rational grounds for
> legitimate standards or authority; it is, far more, the lived experience
> of coping with a life of horrifying meaninglessness, hopelessness,
> and (most important) lovelessness.[7]

West's description of nihilism includes far more than the social and economic aspects of human oppression. He articulates the psycho-spiritual and emotional aspects of the experience. His definition is similar in scope to what Michael E. Dyson's claims about black male suicide, Lerone Bennett's notion of the crisis of the African-American spirit, and what is described elsewhere as fatalism. In his book, *Reflecting Black*,[8] Dyson discusses the socio-cultural conditions surrounding the problem of black male suicide. He links it to the feelings of powerlessness, despair, hopelessness, oppression and benign neglect.

Bennett has described the central problem of the African-American community as a crisis of spirit. For Bennett, spirit is not a religious concept, but is rather the prevailing sense of purpose, meaning, and will which dominate a particular historical epoch. What he has described is the loss of a communal will to survive. As he said:

> The danger is real and pressing. For the first time in our history, the inner fortresses of the Black Spirit are giving away. For the first time in our history, we are threatened on the level of the spirit on the level of our most precious possession, on the level of the soul.[9]

Bennett goes on to describe the "signs" of the crisis:

> The signs of crisis are everywhere. The homicide rate in the Black community has reached such an astronomical rate that young Black males are rapidly becoming an endangered species . . . [W]e are losing a whole generation of people. And this fact, which is cultural, political and economic at the same time, constitutes the gravest challenge we have faced in this country since the end of slavery.[10]

Further exploration of the themes of oppression and liberation include recent discussions of fatalism in the medical community. Fatalism has been described as the belief that death is inevitable when cancer is present.[11] Fatalism is one of the major deterrents to participation in particular screening and preventative measures. Fatalism is not simply a response to cancer mortality, it is also linked to perceptions of hopelessness, powerlessness, worthlessness, and social despair.[12] This is a central connection. Fatalism cannot be separated from the general socio-economic experiences of the community.

As with the other maladies that I have discussed, fatalism is not a religious concept, but it is closely linked to other facets of human spirituality, which is the heart of religion.[13] Nihilism, suicide, the crisis of the African-American spirit, and fatalism are all responses to, and cannot be separated from, the lived-experiences of oppression. People are not born with a genetic predisposition to feelings of despair, hopelessness, lovelessness, and powerlessness; these are learned reactions to perceived experiences of failure and devastation. In any case, fatalism, the crisis of spirit, and nihilism are all expressions of the lived-experiences of the African-American community.

The lived-experiences of too many African-Americans point them all too emphatically to the reality of despair and deprivation. A black baby born in 1994 had an average life expectancy of 69.6 years, more than seven years less than a white child born at the same time. Blacks can expect to die at higher rates from illnesses such as cancer (prostate and breast), diabetes, HIV infection, chronic liver deterioration, and heart disease. In 1992, for example, black men were dying of heart disease at a rate of 264 per 100,000 persons, as compared to 190 per 100,000 for white men. In 1993-94 214 black men out of every 100,000 had AIDS, compared with 39.6 per 100,000 for white males. Among black females the rate is 63.6 per 100,000 compared to 3.7 white women per 100,000 with AIDS. And only about 74 percent of blacks have some form of health insurance, as opposed to 86 percent of whites.[14] Poverty, education, racism and other factors are referenced by scholars as major contributors to these grim realities.

Couple these facts with the reality of the growing gap between the rich and the poor in America. Between 1968-1996 the estimated average income for the bottom 20 percent of workers rose only 8 percent while the top 20 percent of earners saw a 44 percent increase in their income. More than 30 percent of the African-American community lives in poverty and they are twice as likely to be unemployed than their white counterparts. Further, a disproportionately high number of African-American kids who experience failure in school and are more frequently labeled as learning disabled or troubled kids.[15] And African-Americans know all to well the startling impact of the increase in juvenile crime over the past decade. From 1982 to 1993 the murder rate among juveniles increased by 128 percent. Adult arrest rates over that same period rose 8.6 percent. From 1988-1992 aggravated assaults increased among juveniles by more than 80 percent. And they comprise more than 23 percent of the victims of violent crime.[16]

Though these statistics may not seem overwhelming in and of themselves, they collectively point to a pattern of destruction, decay, and devastation that African-Americans face daily. There is no singular cause or cure for these problems. They reflect the socio-economic, political, spiritual, and moral conditions of the time. As a product of this social context and segment of the American public, it is impossible for me to reflect theologically and write about God's revelation in Jesus without speaking to these realities. The African-American community is not America's only oppressed community but its problems are tremendous and awesome. The proposal that I will offer in the remaining sections of this study critically and constructively uses Thurman as a means of addressing these problems. It is my hope that this call for an understanding of the social and existential basis of the African-American struggle will contribute to the ongoing discussions among black theologians, womanist theologians, and black churches respectively.

Scripture

The social context of the theologian is a starting-point for shaping and understanding Christology. We must be reminded, however, of Cone's admonition. According to Cone, the meaning of Jesus' life, message, and mission is established today in the "dialogical tension between social context and Scripture."[17] The reference to Scripture links the social conditions of today with the biblical depiction of the historical Jesus. The biblical depiction of Jesus is essential because it provides an objective reference-point within which to frame a discussion of Jesus' meaning in the present. Scripture demonstrates who the historical Jesus was and the nature of his ministry of reconciliation. I believe that without the guidance of Scripture, any Christology is easily reduced to a kind of mythological docetism or to mere Jesusology, divorcing the work of Christ from the actions of the historical Jesus, as he is described in Scripture. There is also the danger of reducing the life and ministry of Jesus to that of a natural man. A carefully reading of the New Testament would call either extreme into question. In Scripture we come face-to-face with the historical Jesus, who was the Christ of Christian faith and upon whose life the New Testament Church was built. My Christology diverges from Thurman's most radically on this point. My views are thoroughly biased towards the full story of biblical and traditional Christology.

The New Testament makes no claim of objectivity, in the modern sense of the term. New Testament writers were not seeking to write biographies of Jesus or a history of early Christianity. Rather they were telling a story of faith, affirming their convictions about the meaning of Jesus' birth, life, teaching, death, and resurrection. And they expressed their beliefs are expressed in various linguistic and substantive ways. Thus there is no singular Christology in the New Testament; instead there are various Christological strands and themes throughout the New Testament. All of these strands and themes converge unapologetically on the assumption that Jesus of Nazareth was their Lord and Christ. He was the cornerstone of their faith, their Messiah, and the sole reason for their creation of a new religious community. This was a result of their radical reinterpretation of Judaism. New Testament writers depicted Jesus as a true man. But he was an extraordinary man, his life set apart by phenomenal events and experiences, such as his birth, miracles, death, and resurrection. We find these events throughout the New Testament. For example, Matthew's narrative affirms the Virgin Birth:

> "Behold, a virgin shall conceive and bear a son, and his name shall be called Emmanuel" (which means, God with us). When Joseph woke from sleep, he did as the angel of the Lord commanded him; he took his wife, but knew her not until shehad borne a son; and he called his name Jesus. (Matthew 1: 23-25, RSV)

Matthew casts the Jesus story in Messianic terms. The following is Matthew's account of how Herod responded to the news of Jesus' birth:

> Now when Jesus was born in Bethlehem of Judea in the days of Herod the king, behold, wise men from the East came to Jerusalem, saying, "Where is he who has been born king of the Jews? For we have seen his star in the East, and have come to worship him." When Herod the king heard this he was troubled, and all Jerusalem with him; and assembling all the chief priests and scribes of the people, he inquired of them where the Christ was to be born. (Matthew 2: 1-4, RSV)

Even the Gospel of Mark, alone among the gospels in omitting references to either the Virgin Birth or the preexistence of Jesus, affirms that it is the "gospel of Jesus Christ, the Son of God" (Mark.1.1, RSV). Mark begins with the ministry of John the baptizer, who baptized Jesus and attested to his messianic role. John the baptizer introduced Jesus as the one who would "baptize you with the Holy Spirit" (Mark.1.8, RSV). Luke presents the most elaborate statement on the events surrounding the birth of Jesus, as described in the first two chapters of his gospel. And, like Matthew, Luke too presents the Virgin Birth as a key who Jesus was.

Unlike the Synoptic gospels, the Johannine gospel identifies Jesus as the preexistent, divine Logos. John's gospel is perhaps the most emphatic in placing Jesus' life and work in the tradition of the divine Logos.

In the beginning was the Word, and the Word was with God, and the Word was God. He was in the beginning with God; all things were made through him, and without him was not anything made that was made. . . . And the Word became flesh and dwelt among us, full of grace and truth; we have beheld his glory, glory as of the only Son of the Father. . . . For the law came through Moses; grace and truth came through Jesus Christ. (John 1:1-3; 14; 17 RSV)

John clearly delineates Jesus' role in relation to the Father and in relationship to the Jewish law. His Jesus is on a divine mission from the very inception of his existence. The Pauline epistles are famous for their lack of reference to the life of the historical Jesus. Yet throughout his writings, Paul expressed his loyalty to Jesus Christ as the definitive authority in Christianity. All of the Pauline epistles, for example, begin with his affirmation of allegiance and servanthood to Jesus Christ.

The significance of these references is that they remind us of the Christologies of the New Testament. New Testament writers were clearly convicted of Jesus' messianic mission. They demonstrated this in their claims about principal aspects of his life specifically his birth, his ministry, his miracles, his death, and his resurrection. These beliefs provide a central framework on which to build current Christological perspectives. My own Christology grows out of my reading of the Christological traditions of the New Testament.

Pneumatology and Christology

The doctrine of the Holy Spirit or pneumatology, is at the heart of New Testament Christology. My own Christology differs from Thurman's on this point. Thurman's Christology reflects more of the Old Testament monotheism than it does the complexities of New Testament Christology. For example, Thurman gives very little attention to the Pauline and Johannine literature in shaping his Christology. I, on the other hand rely heavily on the Pauline and Johannine material, as they are at the core of Christian tradition. Thurman spoke at great length about Jesus' religious experience and his ultimate acts of submission to God. But Thurman did not link these religious experiences to the person and work of the Holy Spirit, as understood biblically and historically.

The failure to link these religious experiences to a doctrine of the Holy Spirit limits the potential impact of his Christology. Thurman's Christology significantly. This is unfortunate because his treatment of Jesus' religious experience is closely related to the biblically-based pneumatological focus that I will describe here. Like Thurman, I too argue that Jesus' messianic mission evolved significantly over the course of his ministry. But the question is, how did this growth take place? In the New Testament, the Holy Spirit supports the growth and maturation of Jesus' messianic mission.

As a Pentecostal, I hold the doctrine of the Holy Spirit is essential and to personal spirituality and to Christology. In seeking to combat issues such as fatalism, nihilism and the crisis of the African-American spirit, a pneumatological Christology becomes an essential means of empowerment. It brings the liberating message and ministry of Jesus, as empowered by the Holy Spirit, in contact with the desperate plight of the African-American community. The church of today must seek this tradition of faith and power and use it to address the pressing problems of our world.

I take seriously the idea which is put forth throughout the book of Acts, particularly 2:38, ". . . Repent, and be baptized every one of you in the name of Jesus Christ for the forgiveness of your sins; and you shall receive the gift of the Holy Spirit." The Holy Spirit is God's gift to the believer individually and to the church in general. The Holy Spirit bestows God's charismatic presence within persons and institutions, as Paul described in I Corinthians 12. Thus a New Testament based Christology makes a pneumatology essential.

In the New Testament church, the Holy Spirit, working in conjunction with the written Word, represented the Hands of God at work in the world.[18] The Virgin Mary's conception, according to Matthew, was the work of the Holy Spirit. The book of Luke's annunciation makes this point emphatically:

> And behold, you will conceive in your womb and bear as son, and you shall call his name Jesus. He will be great, and will becalled the Son of the Most High. . . And Mary said to the angel, "How can this be, since I have no husband?" And the angel said to her, "The Holy Spirit will come upon you, and the power of the Most High will overshadow you; therefore the child to be born will be called holy, the Son of God." (Luke 1:31-31; 34-35, RSV)

According to Luke, The birth of Jesus was confirmed by revelation of the Holy Spirit to Simeon. The Spirit revealed to Simeon that the he would live to witness the birth of the Christ. Simeon was inspired by the Spirit and it was he who blessed the baby Jesus and pronounced his messianic mission. When Jesus was baptized, John's John the baptizer's testimony confirmed that Jesus received the Spirit in order that he might impart the Spirit to his followers.[19]

> And John bore witness, "I saw the Spirit descend as a dove from heaven, and it remained on him. I myself did not know him; but he who sent me to baptize with water said to me, 'He on whom you see the Spirit descend and remain, this is he who baptizes with the Holy Spirit.' And I have seen and have borne witness that this is the Son of God." (John 1:32-34, RSV)

When Jesus began his public ministry, following his period of temptation, he was "full of the Holy Spirit" (Luke 4:1, RSV). The Spirit, according to Mark and Luke, drove him into the wilderness in order to face Satan's temptation. Being full of the Holy Spirit, he was prepared to begin his ministry of liberation to his community, preaching the good news to the poor, releasing the captives, giving sight to the blind, setting the oppressed free, and proclaiming the year of the Lord. Jesus' spirit-empowered ministry brought the Kingdom of God into the lives of the oppressed. He did not confront the world as a mere man or as a raging prophet; he was able to speak to the conditions of his world because he was full of the Spirit. This is what made him different. He grew into his messianic role as he continued to be influenced by Holy Spirit.

In the Johannine literature the Holy Spirit is called is the Paraclete, *Parakletos,* whose role is inextricably tied to the messianic work of Jesus Christ. The Johannine Paraclete is the Holy Spirit in a highly specialized role as "the personal presence of Jesus in the Christian while Jesus is with the Father."[20] The Paraclete is said to perform several central functions in the church, all of which are extensions of the earthly ministry of Jesus. The roles are variously described in the gospel of John.

> {Jesus said,} "If you love me, you will keep my commandments. And I will pray to the Father, and he will give you another Counselor, to be with you for ever . . . But the Counselor, the Holy Spirit, whom the Father will send in my name, he will teach you all things, and bring to your remembrance all that I have said to you. (John 14: 15-16; 26, RSV)

Elsewhere in John, Jesus provides further description of the Paraclete's role: "But when the Counselor comes, whom I shall send to you from the Father, even the Spirit of truth, who proceeds from the Father, he will bear witness to me" (John 15:26, RSV). Moreover, the Paraclete will be distinguished by his effort to "convince the world of sin and of righteousness and of judgment" (John 16:8, RSV). Finally, John says that the Paraclete is said to offer no new revelation and have no independent authority; his principal task is that of guiding the disciples into the truths of Jesus and to glorify Jesus, just as Jesus had glorified the Father (John 16:13) After his resurrection Jesus passed on his ministry of liberation to his disciples, passing on to them the power to forgive sins. The prelude to this however, was that he breathed upon them and prayed that they would "Receive the Holy Spirit." (John 20:22b; RSV). This latter point is essential because it helps us to grasp how Jesus' ministry of liberation was passed on to his followers, namely, through the impartation and work of the Holy Spirit.

All of these references point to an undeniable pattern in New Testament thinking regarding the triadic connection between God, Jesus, and the work of the Holy Spirit. And we can see that   is no mere coincidence that the Holy Spirit became the driving force in the creation and work of the New Testament Church. The Spirit was the power which gave the Church the ability to implement the mandates of Jesus. Christians could have liberating ministry and fellowship because they, like Jesus, were full of the Holy Spirit. The New Testament community saw the work of the Holy Spirit as the foundation for the creation of a new world order. The Day of Pentecost was the birthday of the Church, which commenced with the outpouring of the Holy Spirit.[21] For Luke, the outpouring of the Holy Spirit upon the church was a visible sign of God's continual work of salvation in the midst of human history.[22] The descent of the Spirit was signified by a supernatural event.   Luke described it in this manner:

> When the day of Pentecost had come, they were all together in one place. . . And there appeared to them tongues as of fire, distributed and resting on each of them. And they were all filled with the Holy Spirit and began to speak in other tongues, as the Spirit gave them utterance. (Acts 2:1-4, RSV)

The Spirit's work was not incidental it was central to God's redemptive work in history.   The Apostle Peter's sermon on that day further confirms this fact. He saw the coming of the Spirit as a confirmation of Jesus' messianic mission.

> Men of Israel, hear these words: Jesus of Nazareth, a man attested
> to you by God with mighty works and wonders and signs which God
> did through him in your midst, as you yourselves know—this Jesus,
> delivered up according to the definite plan and foreknowledge of
> God, you crucified and killed by the hands of lawless men. But God
> raised him up, having loosed the pangs of death, because it was not
> possible for him to be held by it. (Acts 2:22-24, RSV)

The "Day of Pentecost" was a foundational event in the formation of
the New Testament church and the establishment of their ministry of
liberation. It was the context for the empowerment of persons whose
task it was to serve the institutional life of the Church.[23] The work of
the Spirit in the creation of the Church is similar to the image of the
Spirit's work which is described in the Genesis creation story. As "the
Spirit of God was moving over the face of the waters" (Genesis 1:2b,
RSV) the work of creation began.

So Scripture and tradition point us toward the conclusion that
pneumatology must be a key element in shaping any thorough
Christology. George C. L. Cummings is instructive in noting that a
pneumatological Christology prevents persons from objectifying the
work of God in persons, places, and institutions.[24] Like Cummings
and Theo Witvliet, the Dutch theologian, I believe that pneumatological
emphasis is sorely lacking in much of liberation theology.[25] As God's
liberating presence in history, the Holy Spirit assures that God's work
will be done through the believing community, the church. And church
is here understood as universal, invisible institution. This is not a call
for narrow-minded, pneumatocentric-biblicism. Rather, I simply
suggest that the New Testament writers were intentional in making the
link between Jesus' liberating ministry and the ministry of the church.
For them this link was assured through the work and agency of the
Holy Spirit.

Thurman viewed Jesus' religious experiences as the sources of his
strength and as the context within which to understand Jesus' divinity.
This is one area of his thought that I fully appreciate. The emphasis on
religious experience places the reality of Jesus' humanity and his need
for spiritual empowerment center-stage in Thurman's Christology. A
pneumatological Christology differs slightly from this in that it views
Jesus' spiritual maturation as the result of his encounter with the Holy
Spirit, and in this way his maturation was not simply a matter of
personal choice or natural evolution. Jesus was under the influence of
the Holy Spirit and this alone was the source of his power. This is not

a contradiction of Thurman's thesis as such, but it does seek to ground the idea of Jesus religious experience specifically in the work of the Holy Spirit. I believe this emphasis follows more closely the full wisdom of the New Testament writers. A pneumatologically-based Christology does not limit God's revelation to the person and work of Jesus of Nazareth or to the church. If the Holy Spirit is truly God's Spirit, then this Spirit imparts God's power and carries on God's liberating work in the cosmos. Wherever the work of freedom, liberation, justice, peace, and the quest for human fulfillment takes place in the world, the power of the Holy Spirit is at work. And, as the gospel of John reminds us, the Spirit testifies only of the truths of God, as articulated through Christ (John 16:13).

While they did not employ the full-fledged Trinitarian language that would later be sacrosanct in Christian history, the New Testament writers were clear that the Holy Spirit existed in special relationship with God and in the ministry Jesus. New Testament discussions about the Holy Spirit are more often than not tied to the life, teachings, and ministry of Jesus of Nazareth. The Holy Spirit is variously described as an expression of power, love, and influence of the divine, for example, Romans 8:1f;15:30. For Paul the Holy Spirit is the vehicle through which God shares divine knowledge and power with other persons, particularly the church. Galatians 4:6, for example, declares that "God has sent the Spirit of his Son into our hearts." The Holy Spirit is the Spirit of God carrying out God's will in the world. Just as the Spirit was active and alive in Jesus' life and ministry, helping him to destroy the powers of Satan, so too does the Spirit today empower believers to carry on Jesus' ministry in the world. In this sense, a pneumatological Christology is eschatological in scope. This is to say that it is structured with a view towards the future. The present and future work of liberation in the Church grow out of the realities of God's divine actions in the past.

Today the church must address the existential, socio-economic, political, and cultural powers of destruction through the liberating power of the Holy Spirit, effecting what Leonard Lovett has called "pneumatological liberation."[26] The call for a pneumatological liberation is rooted in the belief that the pressing problems of the world, particularly those of the African-American community, cannot be properly addressed and corrected without the power and vitality of religious faith. Social, economic, cultural, and political problems are real and relevant, but they alone comprise only segments of the human dilemma. A pneumatological emphasis must include a discussion of the psycho-spiritual and existential dimensions of human experience, which are universally present. Again, this is what I believe New Testament writers were pointing to when they grounded Jesus' ministry in the power and work of the Holy Spirit. The Apostle Paul said it best:

> In Jesus Christ, then, I have reason to be proud of my work for God. For I will not venture to speak of anything except what Christ has wrought through me to win obedience from the Gentiles, by word and deed, by the power of signs and wonders, by the power of the Holy Spirit, so that from Jerusalem and as far round as Illyricum I have fully preached the gospel of Christ. . . (Romans.15:17-19 RSV)

The New Testament offers specific testimonies about how the first generations of Christians viewed Jesus. Their views provide the framework within which later Christologies would develop. Scripture remains important in my own Christology because it exposes us to the spirituality and beliefs of the early Christian community. This brings me to the last of the three components that I noted above from James H. Cone's discussion of the formation of a Christology: tradition.

Tradition

Cone notes the centrality of tradition (of Western Christianity and of the black church) in the development of a Christology for our times. Tradition presents a picture of how the church has understood particular doctrines throughout the centuries. Tradition, as Cone affirms, also includes the faith claims of African-American Christians, as they have understood the world. In Chapters Two, Three, and Four we noted some of the great Christological controversies which emerged in the first three centuries of Christian history. Doctrinal confessions such as the Nicene and Chalcedonian Creeds were attempts made by the Christian community to make sense of its confession of faith in God's redemptive work through Christ.

In the debates leading up to the Council of Nicaea in 325, A.D. many questions were raised about the meaning of Jesus' divinity, or more specifically, Jesus' relationship to God. In the official position, as indicated by the Nicene Creed, Jesus was declared to be the Son of God. He was described as being *homoousios*, of one substance, with

God the Father, as opposed to the Arian notion of Jesus as a creature. Later, in A.D. 381 at the Council of Constantinople the Holy Spirit too was declared to be divine, being described as the Lifegiver who is to be worshipped and glorified along with the Father and the Son.

Following the Nicene and Constantinople resolutions, the church confronted directly the question of the two natures of Christ. The issue at hand concerned the degree to which he was both human and divine. The Council of Chalcedon, 451 A.D., was the setting wherein some of the major Christological issues would be resolved, for a period of time at least. The resolution presented the following conclusions as the standard of Christian doctrine:

> . . .{Our} Lord Jesus Christ is one and the same Son, the same perfect in Godhead and the same perfect in manhood, truly God and truly man, the same of a rational soul and body, consubstantial with the Father in Godhead, and the same consubstantial with us in manhood, like us in all things except in sin; begotten from the Father before the ages as regards His Godhead, and in the last days, the same, because of us and our salvation begotten from the Virgin Mary, the *Theotokos* , as regards His manhood; one and the same Christ, Son, Lord, only-begotten, made known in two natures without confusion, without change, without division, without separation, the difference of the natures being by no means removed because of the union. . . [27]

There are several key phrases here which were developed in opposition to the heretical writings of Apollinarius, Nestorius, and Eutyches.[28] Phrases such as Jesus having a "rational soul" (a critique of Apollinarius), Mary as *Theotokos*, Mother of God, "as regards His manhood", (a critique of Nestorius), and "in two natures" (a critiques of Eutyches), are the keys to this statement. As with the preceding Councils, the Chalcedon conclusion did not settle all of the potential questions regarding the relationship between Jesus' two natures,[29] but it set the standard for what the church could say about the two natures of Jesus Christ.

By the fifth century, the doctrine of the Trinity was firmly established in the West. The common understanding was, simply put, that there is a unity, quality, and spiritual coherence among the three "persons" of the Godhead, with a spiritual coherence between the three. With scriptures such as Matthew 28:19 and II Corinthians 13:14, the Western church declared that God is one being or nature. Moreover, the doctrine of God was expressed in Trinitarian language and substance.

The key issue for my consideration is the fact that the early church, and later generations of Christians definitely understood God, Christ, and the Holy Spirit in relation to each other. The function of each person is interrelated, and this is principally revealed in Jesus' life.

The notion of a Trinitarian revelation seeks simply to be true to the faith heritage and experience of Christians throughout the past two thousand years. Such a notion does not attempt to limit the revelation to this community or to suggest that God is limited to a specific mode of revelation. The great mysteries of religious faith defy such reductionism. Nor is my Trinitarian emphasis simply for the preservation of Christian orthodoxy. Rather, it is a rational method of explicating the Christian understanding of how God's revelation in the Old Testament is related to their view of Christ, and the continuing revelation of God within and outside of the Christian community. . The Trinity establishes God's mode of acting in the world throughout history. A Christology devoid of Trinitarian grounding looses touch with this theological idea and the wisdom of Scripture. As a serious Christian, I find this to be problematical. In essence, the doctrine of the Trinity is an evangelical doctrine, fundamental to what the church can say about God's revelation in human history. For the Trinity fixes God's relationship with the world in terms of creation, redemption through Christ, and the continual work of liberation in the world through the agency of the Holy Spirit, which was the essence of Jesus' ministry. And this work knows no institutional, doctrinal, racial, socio-economic, or cultural barrier. It is real and essential because it is Jesus' good news to the disinherited. And this is, for me, the key to a meaningful Christology.

Gender Issues in the Christological Debate

The significance of Jesus' gender has been a key issue in feminist and womanist theology for the past couple of decades. Some theologians have asked whether or not the traditional references to the Fatherhood of God and the maleness of Jesus contribute to the oppression of women. The notion of the Fatherhood of God, as understood in Trinitarian language, coupled with the traditional ideas about Jesus' ontologically-based "two natures", is often viewed as the objectification of male power. This has led some women theologians to reject the doctrine of the traditional Trinitarian and Christological doctrines.[30]

Like some womanists and feminists, I agree that traditional Western Trinitarian and Christological formulas may indeed contribute to the perpetuation of oppressive patriarchal structures and institutions. They may indeed mask male bias and a quest for power. Yet I believe, as I have described above, that the Christological and Trinitarian resolutions of the Western Christian tradition do have theological merit. And my views were not shaped within the secure comforts of the academy. Rather they were formed in the social context of the African-American community and nurtured in my Pentecostal spirituality.

The significance of the Trinity, the meaning of the humanity/divinity of Christ, and the significance of his birth, life, ministry, and death does not rest on the issue of gender. The truth about the Trinity, in my opinion, does not stand or fall on the basis of the notion of the Fatherhood of God. Nor is it based on the maleness of Jesus Christ. The doctrine of the Trinity helps us to interpret how God reveals God's self to human beings throughout history. This doctrine is derived from the church's experience of God in the world, and not on vain speculation. The historical fact is that Jesus was a male. But his status as Lord and Christ, and his liberating role in the African-American community has nothing to do with gender and everything to do with his message and ministry. Jesus was the liberator of the oppressed because his life, message, and ministry showed us God's manner of acting in the world.

In Chapter One, I described some the primary folk beliefs in African-American religious history regarding Jesus. I referred to Harold Carter's claim that in traditional black prayers, no distinction was made between the persons of the Trinity. Things which may be biblically attributed to God, may in these prayers and songs be attributed to Jesus or the Holy Spirit.[31] Thurman corroborates this theme in his discussion of the theological basis of the slave Spirituals.[32] Thurman noted that the Spirituals do not include many specific references to the work of the Holy Spirit, and they often use the names of God and Jesus interchangeably. The composers of the Spirituals did not trouble themselves with metaphysical distinctions between the persons of the Godhead:

> Whether the song uses the term Jesus, or the oft repeated Lord, or Savior, or God, the same insistence is present—God is in them, in their souls, as they put it , and what is just as important, He is in the facts of their world. In short, God is active in history in a personal and primary manner.[33]

I believe Thurman is absolutely correct on this matter; the slaves, and later their descendants, meant to demonstrate that God is present in works in their world. They were concerned about the pragmatic power and meaning of the idea of believing in a true God. Neither gender nor the divine title matters absolutely, what is essential is the liberation they provide. The affirmation of faith in Jesus in the black community was a resource against the deification of white oppression and black suffering. Black slaves created their own world of beliefs, values, and spirituality. In this world, Jesus was a supreme power who assured that "trouble will not last always." In the world that they created, the slaves knew that what was most important was Jesus' redeeming work on their behalf, it was most important for them to know that he was their liberator. And so, in the early stages of this tradition, particularly during the slavery period, people prayed intermittently to God, Jesus, and the Holy Spirit without fear of contradiction.

As a life-long member of an African-American Pentecostal community, and a student of the theology of the same, I can recall no extensive discussions wherein the question of Jesus' maleness was ever used as a defense of male domination. What I do recall is a strong Jesus-centered piety which anchored the very heart and soul of the faith in the experience of Jesus' redemptive influence and work. The central ritual event in the church of my youth was the *Tarry Service*, which took place weekly. Seekers, people who were seeking to be converted, and full members alike were required to *seek the Lord* for salvation and baptism of the Holy Spirit. Tarrying is a ritual which took place around the altar. The seekers would begin by either kneeling or standing before the altar and praying in a cadence that varied from slow to fast, soft to loud, with less to more fervor. One had to tarry until she/he got it. There were prayer warriors, mothers, missionaries, and others who stood by and assisted the seeker in tarrying. Throughout the process the seeker would ritual chant "Jesus", "Jesus", "Jesus", continually. Eventually other phrases followed such as "save me Lord", "Thank you Jesus!", and "hallelujah!" Tarrying usually took place in a festive atmosphere aided by singing, musical instrumentation, and shouting. All of this took place as people prayed and worship with the passion and belief that God was present among them in the person of the Holy Spirit. And this event —the presence of God— should be celebrated in the fullness. This is a "Jesus" tradition, anchored in the person and work of the Holy Spirit. The reality of the power of God which operated in history sets believers free today to receive and celebrate the Good news that Jesus brought to the disinherited.

Concluding Reflections

As a Christian theologian, I am deeply committed to the Christian community and to its mission in the world. This community and its mission are anchored in an understanding of the meaning and significance of Jesus' birth, life, teaching, death, and resurrection. My contributions to this subject, Christology, revolve around several proposals and areas that I have addressed in this study.

To begin with, I have proposed that Christology must be rooted deeply within the socio-political realities of particular communities. Individual theologians and religious communities alike cannot afford to be oblivious to the social realities of the world in which they live. We can thank liberation theologians for their uncompromising emphasis on this idea. Irrespective of one's bent—either towards the traditions of the past or the eschatological hopes of future generations—Christian theological reflections must remain in dialogical partnership with the world as we know and experience it today. Theologians need not become sociologists or political scientists, but they must seek to be prophetic. This is to say that they must be willing to relate their theological claims to the questions and concerns of the oppressed within their communities. The Christian gospel must be meaningfully related to conditions all over the globe, wherever people are suffering and are in need of good news.

Two-thirds of the inhabitants of the world live in abject poverty, suffer from endless brutalities, and know nothing of the basic human rights and freedom that we take for granted in America. Moreover, Christianity remains, in the scope of human history, a young religious community, and there are billions of suffering people who have never heard the Christian message. The possibilities for shaping a liberating Christology are endless, some of the most creative work in liberation theology is being done in this area. Further, understanding the need to relate the gospel to prevailing social conditions will help Christian churches throughout the world to remain faithful to their prophetic mission. In my own Christology I have attempted to address the message of Jesus to some of the most pressing realities of the African-American community.

In addition to the centrality of social context, one's Christology must be developed in dialogical communication with the primary text of the Christian community, the Bible. Though I am neither a biblicist nor a fundamentalist, my theological perspectives are unapologetically rooted in the Bible. The Bible must continue to guide future Christological reflections because it is the written word of God. As such the Bible must be a principal point of departure for Christian theology. My emphasis on the centrality of the Holy Spirit in Christological reflections is rooted in the biblical revelation. The doctrine Holy Spirit is not an ancillary idea which can be relegated to the periphery of Christological discussions. It is rather at the center of the conversation. Likewise, this will remain true in the future.

In the Christian community biblical revelation is mediated through tradition. Tradition is understood both as an affirmation of the entire history of Christian thought and in relationship to the faith claims of specific racial and ethnically-defined religious groups. I am a folk theologian and my theological perspectives are equally steeped in the socio-cultural and religious traditions of my community. In Chapter One, for example, I discuss some of the central folk beliefs and experiences within the African-American community which inform my Christology. Practices such as seekin' the Lord, an African-American folk tradition, have roots in African traditional religions and culture. This raises the question of the relationship between the Christian understanding of Jesus Christ to the truth and reality claims of other religious traditions. Thurman's Christology, focusing as it does on Jesus' teachings, offers some hope in this regard. He was far ahead of his time in terms of his understanding of the whole process of interreligious dialogue. In addressing the gospel to the disinherited, Thurman knew no racial, ethnic or religious barriers. The good news for the disinherited was good news for all people. In the Introduction, I used the following quote: "what is true in any religion is found in that religion because it is true. It is not true because it is found in that religion."[34] This is a prophetic statement. I trust that what I have said here was indeed "good news" for the reader.

Notes

1   He points to the Kyber Pass experience as a central point in the evolution of his view of the possibilities for establishing a fellowship that cuts across religious, racial, and cultural barriers. See his discussion of this in his text, *Footprints of a Dream*. p. 137.

2   Similar points are made *The Mood of Christmas* and in *Disciplines of the Spirit*, see   particularly Chapter 4 of the latter.

3   Thurman's response to the Civil Rights era was certainly not from the vantage point of a political scientist; rather he addresses it in light of his religious vision. "The Religion of Jesus" revealed his deep conviction that the social problems in America had a "spiritual" base. Further, he demonstrated the religious resources for overcoming these problems. See especially the conclusion to this text on pages 2-113, *The Luminous Darkness* (New York: Harper and Row, 1965).

4   James H. Cone, *God of the Oppressed*. p. 110.

5   James H. Cone, *God of the Oppressed*. p. 108.

6   Howard Thurman, *The Luminous Darkness* (New York: Harper and Row Publishers, 1965), p. x.

7   Cornel West, *Race Matters*. p. 14.

8   Michael E. Dyson *Reflecting Black* (Minneapolis: University of Minnesota Press, 1993).

9   Lerone Bennett, "Crisis of the Black Spirit," *Ebony Magazine* (October 1977), p. 80. Luther E. Smith has done much to make the connection between Thurman's idea of religious experience and social transformation. He actually uses Bennett's article in one of his treatments of Thurman. See his "Black Theology and Religious Experience," *The Journal of the Interdenominational Theological Center*   p. 71.

10 Ibid.

11 Powe, B.D. & Johnson, Alonzo, "Fatalism among African Americans: A Philosophical Perspective", *Journal of Religion and Health,* 1995, 34:119-125.

12 Ibid.

13 Ibid.

14 Thrity Umrigar, "Health in Black & White," *The State*, 28 May, 1996.

15 Powe, "Fatalism", p. 121

16 *Safe Streets* (Washington, DC: Safe Streets, 1996).

17 James H. Cone, *God of the Oppressed*. p. 113.

18 Jose' Comblin *The Holy Spirit and Liberation* (Maryknoll, NY: Orbis Books, 1989), p. 45.

19 Ibid. p. 140.

20 *The Gospel According to John (xiii-xxi)* The Anchor Bible. Introduction, Translation and Notes by Raymond E. Brown (Garden City, NY: Doubleday & Company, Inc., 1980), p. 1139.

21 Comblin, *The Holy Spirit and Liberation*. p. 144.

22 Brevard Childs, *The New Testament as Canon: An Introduction* (Philadelphia: Fortress Press, 1984), pp. 108-109.

23 James A. Forbes' *The Holy Spirit and Preaching* (New York: Harper and Row, 1987) is an excellent demonstration of this kind of emphasis.

24 George C. L. Cummings *A Common Journey: Black Theology (USA) and Latin American Liberation Theology* (Maryknoll, NY: Orbis Books, 1993). p. 150.

25 See Theo Witvliet *The Way of the Black Messiah* (Oak Park, IL.: Meyer Stone Books, 1987). J. DeOtis Roberts and Major J. Jones have both begun to bring the idea of pneumatology into the dialogues in black theology, but neither one has gone far enough in their analysis of the New Testament idea of Spirit Baptism as a liberating theological and ecclesiological symbol. Moreover, they have not linked the idea of eschatology thoroughly with an eschatological view, which is at the heart of the black Pentecostal witness. See Robert's *Dialogue* ; and Jones' *The Color of G.O.D.* Jose' Comblin has done a great service to liberation theologians with his emphasis on the connection between Spirit Baptism and eschatology. See his text, *The Holy Spirit and Liberation* (Maryknoll, N.Y.: Orbis Books, 1987).

26 This idea of a "pneumatological" approach to liberation theology has been suggested by Leonard Lovett. See his above-mentioned dissertation.

27 See, for example, J.N.D. Kelly, revised edition, *Early Christian Doctrines* (New York: Harper & Row, 1978), pp. 339-340.

28 See Ibid., note especially Chapter XII.

29 Ibid.

30 For a very good discussion of how some of these topics are addressed by womanists and feminists, see Jacquelyn Grant, *White Women's Christ and Black Women's Jesus*, note especially her discussion in Chapter II.

31 Harold A. Carter, *The Prayer Tradition of Black People*. p. 50.

32 See my reference to this in footnote 48 of Chapter One. This section of the book also contains my full discussion of black folk Christology.

33 Thurman, *Deep River and the Negro Spiritual Speaks of Life and Death*. p. 126.

34 See footnote number 6 of the Introduction.

Bibliography

Howard Thurman

Books

Thurman, Howard. *The Centering Moment*. Richmond, IN: Friends United Press, 1975.

——. *The Creative Encounter*. Richmond, IN: Friends United Press, 1972.

——. *Deep is the Hunger*. New York: Harper, 1951; Reprint Edition, Friends United Press, 1975, p. 172.

——. *Deep River: An Interpretation of Negro Spirituals*. Mills College: The Eucalyptus Press, 1945.

——. *Deep River & The Negro Spirituals Speak of Life and Death*. Richmond, IN: Friends United Press, 1975.

——. *Disciplines of the Spirit*. Richmond, IN: Friends United Press, 1977.

——. *For the Inward Journey*. New York: Harcourt Brace & Jovanovich, 1984.

——. *Footprints of a Dream: The Story of the Church for the Fellowship of All People*. New York: Harper & Brothers Publishers, 1959.

——. *The Greatest of These*. Mills College, CA: Eucalyptus Press, 1944.

——. *The Growing Edge*. Richmond, IN: Friends United Press, 1980.

——. *The Inward Journey*. Richmond, IN: Friends United Press, 1980.

——. *Jesus and the Disinherited*. Richmond, IN: Friends United Press, 1981.

——. *The Luminous Darkness: A Personal Interpretation of the Anatomy of Segregation and the Ground of Hope*. New York: Harper & Row Publishers, 1965

——. *Meditations for Apostles of Sensitivity*. California: The Eucalyptus Press, 1947.

——. *Meditations of the Heart*. Richmond, IN: Friends United Press, 1979.

——. *The Mood of Christmas*. New York: Harper & Row, 1973.

——. *Mysticism and the Experience of Christian Love*. Wallingford, Pa.: Pendle Hill Pamphlet 115, 1961.

——. *The Negro Spiritual Speaks of life and Death*. New York: Harper & Brothers, 1947.

——. *The Search for Common Ground: An Inquiry into the Basis of Man's Experience of Community*. New York: Harper & Row, 1971.

——. *The Temptations of Jesus*. Richmond, IN: Friends United Press, 1981.

————. *With Head and Heart.* New York: Harcourt Brace & Jovanovich, 1979.

————. Editor, *A Track to the Water's Edge: The Olive Schreiner Reader.* New York: Harper & Row, 1973.

————. Editor, *The First Footprints: The Dawn of the Idea of the Church for the Fellowship of All Peoples: Letters Between Alfred Fisk and Howard Thurman, 1943-1944.* San Francisco: Lawton and Alfred Kennedy, 1975.

Contribution to Books/Articles

Thurman, Howard. "And When Thou Prayest." *Sermons From An Ecumenical Pulpit.* Chapter 9. Edited by Max F. Daskam. Boston: Starr King Press, 1956, pp. 80-90.

————. "Exposition to the Book of Habakkuk." *The Interpreter's Bible.* Vol. 6. Edited by George A. Buttrick, et al. Nashville: Abingdon Press, 1956, pp. 979-1002.

————. "Exposition to the Book of Zephaniah." *The Interpreter's Bible.* Vol. 6. Edited by George A. Buttrick, et al. Nashville: Abingdon Press, 1956, pp. 1013-1034.

————. "Fascist Masquerade." *The Church and Organized Movements.* Chapter 4. Edited by Randolph Crump Miller ("The Interseminary Series"). New York: Harper & Brothers, 1946, pp. 82-99.

————. "Finding God." *Religion on the Campus.* Edited by Francis P. Miller. New York: Association Press, 1927, pp. 48-52.

————. "God and the Race Question." *Together.* Chapter 12. Compiled by Glenn Clark. Nashville: Abingdon Cokesbury Press, 1945, pp. 118-120.

————. "Good News for the Underprivileged." *The Negro Caravan.* Edited by Sterling A. Brown. New York: The Citadel Press, 1949, pp. 685-692; reprinted from the 1935 article in *Religion in Life.*

————. "The Greatest of These." *The Preaching Pastor.* Edited by Charles F. Kemp. St. Louis: Bethany Press, 1966, pp. 123-127. Reprinted from Thurman's book *The Growing Edge*, pp. 24-28.

————. "Introduction." *Why I Believe There Is a God: Sixteen Essays by Negro Clergymen.* Chicago: Johnson Publishing Co., Inc., 1965, pp. v-xi.

————. "Judgment and Hope in the Christian Message." *The Christian Way in Race Relations.* Chapter 12. Edited by William Stuart Nelson. New York: Harper & Brothers, 1948, pp. 229-235.

————. "From the Luminous Darkness." *Viewpoints From Black America.* Edited by Gladys J. Curry. Englewood Cliffs, NJ: Prentice-Hall Inc., 1970, pp. 207-212. Reprinted from Thurman's book *The Luminous Darkness.* pp. 192-209.

———. "The Meaning of Purpose in Religious Experience." *Religion Ponders Science.* Chapter 15. Edited by Edwin P. Booth. New York: Appleton-Century, 1964, pp. 266-278.

———. "The Meaning of Spirituals." *The Negro in Music and Art.* Edited by Lindsey Patterson. New York: Publishers Co., 1967.

———. "Mysticism and Ethics." *The Journal of Religious Thought* (Summer Supplement 1979), pp. 23-30.

———. "Mysticism and Social Change." *Eden Theological Seminary Bulletin* (Spring 1939) pp. 3-34.

———. "The Religion of Jesus and the Disinherited." *In Defense of Democracy.* Edited by T. H. Johnson. n. p., n.d., pp. 125-135.

Single Sermons, Addresses, and Articles

Thurman, Howard. "America in Search of a Soul." Paper Presented during the Robbin's Lecture Series, University of Redlands, Redlands, CA, 20 January 1976.

———. "The American Dream." Sermon Preached N.P. 6 July 1958.

———. "Christ's Message to the Disinherited." *Ebony* Centennial Issue, (September 1963): pp. 58-62.

———. "The Christian Minister and the Desegregation Decision." *Pulpit Digest* (May 1957): pp. 13-19.

———. "The Church and the Administrator." *California Elementary Social Administrators Association Yearbook.* 1953, pp. 162-164.

———. "The Church, The State and Human Welfare," Paper presented at the 34th Annual Convocation of The School of Religion, Howard University, Washington, D. C., 14 November 1950.

———. "Deep River." *Pulpit Digest* (January 1956): pp. 81-97.

———. "Desegregation, Integration, and the Beloved Community," Paper presented, N.P., n.d., pp. 125-135.

———. "The Discipline of Reconciliation." *Journal of Religion and Health* (October 1963): pp. 7-26. Reprinted from Thurman's book *Disciplines of the Spirit.* pp. 104-127.

———. "The Fellowship Church of All Peoples." *Common Ground* (Spring 1945): pp. 29-31.

———. "Footprints of the Disinherited." Sermon preached at The Eliot Congregational Church, Roxbury, Mass. 31 May 1972.

———. "Freedom Under God." Paper presented at the 2nd Century Convocation of the Washington University, Pullman, Washington., February 1955.

———. "For a Time of Sorrow." *The Christian Century* (July 26, 1953): p. 867.

———. "God and the Modern World." Paper presented, N.P. 29 June 1970.

———. "Good News for the Underprivileged." *Religion in Life*, (Summer 1935): pp. 403-409. Reprinted in *The Negro Caravan*. Edited by Sterling A. Brown. New York: The Citadel Press, 1949, pp. 685-692.

———. "The Great Incarnate Words." *Motive Magazine* (January 1944): p. 24.

———. "The Ground of Hope." *The Saturday Evening Post,* (January/ February 1980): pp. 42,44,47, and 114.

———. "Howard University and the Frontier of Human Freedom." Paper presented at Howard University, Washington, D.C. n.d.

———. "Human Freedom and the Emancipation Proclamation." *Pulpit Digest* (December 1962): pp. 13-16, 66.

———. "I Will Light Three Candles." *Parents Magazine* (December 1949): p. 26.

———. "The Idea of God and Modern Thought." Paper presented, n.p., 23 November 1965.

———. "Interracial Church in San Francisco." *Social Action*, 15 February 1945, pp. 27-28.

———. "Keep Awake!" *The Christian Century Pulpit* (June 1937): pp. 125-127.

———. "Man and the Moral Struggle." Paper presented n.p., n.d. (Typewritten.)

———. "The Meaning of Human Freedom." Paper presented at the Eighth Annual Fight for Freedom Fund Dinner, Detroit Chapter-National Association for the Advancement of Colored People, Detroit, Michigan. 29 April 1962.

———. "The Moment of Crisis in Paul," n.p., n.d.

———. "The Negro in the City." Paper presented at Howard University, Washington, D.C. n.d.

———. "Negro Spirituals and the Black Madonna." Paper presented at Black House, Blaisdell Institute, Claremont, CA, 16 October 1975.

———. "The New Heaven and the New Earth." *The Journal of Negro Education* XXVIII (1958): 115-119.

———. "Peace Tactics and a Racial Minority." *The World Tomorrow* (December 1928): pp. 505-507.

———. "The Powers of the Spirit and the Powers of This World." Paper presented to the 34th Annual Convocation of the Howard University School of Religion, Washington, D.C., 14 November 1950.

———. "Putting Yourself in Another's Place." *Childhood Education* (February 1962): pp. 259-60.

———. "Putting Yourself in Another's Place." *Child Guidance in Christian Living* XXII (February 1963): p. 9. Reprint of the 1962 article in Childhood Education.

———. "The Quest for Stability." *The Woman's Press,* April 1949.

———. "Religion in a Time of Crisis." *The Garrett Tower.* Garrett Biblical Institute. Evanston, IL August 1943.

———. "The Religion of Jesus—Jesus and God." Paper presented at the Second Christian Church Indianapolis, IN. 6 November 1978. (Typewritten.)

———. "The Religion of Jesus." Parts II & III. Papers presented at the Second Christian Church Indianapolis, IN. 7,8 November 1978. (Typewritten.)

———. "The Religion of Jesus and Social Change." Parts I-II. n.p. 19,26 November 1959. (Typewritten.)

———. "Religion: Our Nation's Heritage." Paper presented to the Association for the Study of Afro-American History Week. N.D., n.p. (Typewritten.)

———. "Religious Ideas in Negro Spirituals." *Christendom* (Autumn 1939), pp. 515-528.

———. "The Search for Common Ground." *Perspective: A Journal of Pittsburgh Theological Seminary* XIII (Spring 1972): 127-137.

———. "The Search for God in Religion." *The Laymen's Movement Review* (November-December 1962).

———. "The Sources of Power for Christian Action." Paper presented, n.p., n.d. (Typewritten.)

———. "What We Can Believe In?" *The Journal of Religion and Health* 12 (April 1973): 111-119.

———. "What Shall I Do With My Life?" *The Christian Century Pulpit* (September 1939): pp. 210-211.

———. "Whitney Young's Eulogy." A Eulogy delivered at Riverside Church on the occasion of the death of Whitney Young, New York, N.Y., 16 March 1971.

Book Reviews

———. Review of J. Deotis Roberts' *Liberation and Reconciliation: A Black Theology*. In *Religious Education* (November-December 1971): 464-466.

———. Review of William Douglass Chamberlain's *The Manner of Prayer*. In *The Journal of Religious Thought* I (1943-1944): 179.

———. Review of Douglas V. Steer's *On Beginning From Within*. In *The Journal of Religion* (October 1944): 284-285.

———. Review of Richard I. McKinney's Religion in Higher Education Among Negroes. In *Religion in Life* (Autumn 1946): 619-20.

Biographical Information

Burden, Jean. "Howard Thurman." *The Atlantic Monthly* (October 1953): 40-44.

Jenneso, Mary. *A Course for Intermediates on the Negro in America, Based Primarily on Twelve Negro Americans*. New York: Council of Women for Home Missions and Missionary Education Movement, 1936.

Ploski, Harry. *The Negro Almanac: A Reference Work on the Afro- American*. New York: The Bellwether, 1976.

Williams, Ethel L. *Biographical Directory of Negro Ministers*. 3rd ed. Boston: G. K. Hall, 1975.

Yates, Elizabeth. *Howard Thurman: Portrait of a Practical Dreamer*. New York: The John Day Co., 1964.

Bibliography and Bibliographical Essays

Massey, James E. "Bibliographical Essay: Howard Thurman and Rufus M. Jones, Two Mystics." *Journal of Negro History* (April 1971): 190-95.

———. "Howard Thurman and Olive Schreiner of the Unity of All Life: A Bibliographical Essay." *Journal of Religious Thought* Vol. 34 (Fall-Winter 1977): 29-33.

Sims, Janet L. *Howard Thurman: A Selected Bibliography*. Howard University, Noorland-Spingarn Research Center, (1976).

Essays, Articles and Books on Howard Thurman

Bennett, Lerone, Jr., "Howard Thurman: 20th Century Holy Man." *Ebony Magazine*, February 1978, p. 68.

———. "Crisis of the Black Spirit," *Ebony Magazine*, October 1977, p. 80.

Brown, Sterling A., ed. "Howard Thurman." *Negro Caravan*. New York: Arno Press, 1969.

Corbett, Jan. "Howard Thurman: A Theologian of Our Time." *American Baptist* (December 1979): 10-12.

Eyre, Ronald. "An Interview With Howard Thurman and Ronald Eyre." *Critics Corner* N.D. 208-213.

Fluker, E. Walter. *They Looked For A City*. Lanham, MD.: University Press of America, 1989.

Gandy, Samuel L., ed. *Common Ground: Essays in Honor of Howard Thurman on the Occasion of His Seventy-fifth Birthday*. November 18, 1975, with foreword by Kenneth I. Brown and Benjamin E. Mays, Washington, D.C.: Hoffman Press,1976.

Gloster, Hugh M., ed."Van Vechten Vogue." in *Negro Voices in American Fiction*. Chapel Hill: University of North Carolina Press, 1948.

Goodwin, Mary E. "Racial Roots and Religion: An Interview With Howard Thurman." 9 (May 1973): 533.

Martin Luther King Jr., Center. *Debate and Understanding*.Boston: Boston University, Martin Luther King Jr., Center, 1982.

Matthews, Basil L. "Whole-Making: Tagore and Thurman." *Journal of Religious Thought* 62-72.

Mitchell, Mozella G. *The Human Search: Howard Thurman and the Quest for Freedom*, Martin Luther King, Jr. Memorial Series in Religion, Culture and Social Development. New York: Peter Lang, 1992.

———. *Spiritual Dynamics of Howard Thurman's Theology*. Bristol, IN: Wyndham Hall Press, 1985.

Stewart, III, Carlyle Fielding Stewart. *God Being and Liberation*. Washington, D.C.: University Press of America, 1989.

Smith, Luther E. "Black Theology and Religious Experience." *The Journal of the Interdenominational Theological Center*. 7:1 (Fall 1980): 52-72.

———. Howard Thurman: *The Mystic as Prophet*.Washington, D.C.: University Press of America, 1982.

Young, Henry, e.d., *God and Human Freedom*. Richmond, IN., Friends United Press, 1983.

Films

"The Life and Thought of Dr. Howard Thurman" Landrum Bolling, Interviewer.British Broadcasting Company, 1978.

"Transcript of Howard Thurman Documentary." Howard Thurman Educational Trust.

Theses and Dissertations

Fluker, Walter. "A Comparative Analysis of The Ideal of Community in the Works of Howard Thurman and Martin Luther King Jr." Ph.D. dissertation, Boston University, 1988.

Johnson, Alonzo. "Good News for the Disinherited: The Meaning of Jesus of Nazareth in the Writings of Howard Thurman." Ph.D. dissertation, Union Theological Seminary, 1990.

Mitchell, Mozella G. "The Dynamics of Howard Thurman's Relationship to Literature and Theology." Ph.D. dissertation, Emory University, 1980.

Moxley, Irvin. S. "An Examination of the Mysticism of Howard Thurman and Its Relevance to Black Liberation." D.Min. dissertation, Louisville Presbyterian Theological Seminary, 1974.

Payne, Lewis. "The Social Mysticism of Howard Thurman." Master's thesis, Howard University, 1978.

Pollard, Alton III. "Howard Thurman and the Challenge of Social Regeneration: Transformed, Always Transforming." Ph.D. dissertation, Duke University, 1987.

Smith, Luther E. "An American Prophet: A Critical Study of the Thought of Howard Thurman." Ph.D. dissertation, St. Louis University, 1979.

Stewart, Carlyle F. "A Comparative Analysis of Theological Ontology and Ethical Method in the Theologies of James H. Cone and Howard Thurman." Ph.D. dissertation, Northwestern University, 1982.

Wiley, Dennis W. "The Concept of the Church in the Works of Howard Thurman." Ph.D. dissertation, Union Theological Seminary, 1988.

Background Material

Ahlstrom, Sidney, Editor. *Theology in America.* New York: The Bobbs-Merril Co., Inc., 1967.

Athanasius, "On the Incarnation." in *The Library of Christian Classics*, Vol. III, Edward R. Hardy in collaboration with Cyril Richardson, Editors Philadelphia: Westminster Press, 1954.

Articles, Books and Dissertations

Appiah-Kubi, Kofi and Sergio Torres, Editors. *African Theology En Route.* Maryknoll, N.Y. Orbis Books, 1979.

Boff, Leonardo. *Jesus Christ Liberator.* Translated by Patrick Hughes. Maryknoll, New York: Orbis Books, 1984.

Bornkamm, Gunther. *Jesus of Nazareth.* Translated by Irene and Frazier McLuskey with James M. Robinson. New York: Harper and Brothers Pub., 1960.

Braaten, Carl. *The Future of God.* New York: Harper & Row Publishers, 1969.

Bartsch, H.W., Editor. *Kerygma and Myth.* Translated by R. H. Fuller, New York: Harper Torchbooks, 1961.

Botemps, Arna. Editor. *The Harlem Renaissance Remembered.* New York: Dodd, Mead & Company, 1972.

Brown, Kelly D. "'Who Do They Say That I Am?' A Critical Examination of the Black Christ." Ph.D. dissertation. Union Theological Seminary, 1988.

Brown, Raymond E. *Jesus God and Man.* New York: MacMillan Pub. Co., Inc., 1967.

Bultmann, Rudolf. *Jesus Christ and Mythology.* New York: Charles Scribner's Sons, 1958.

———. *Jesus and the Word.* Translated by Louise P. Smith and Erminie H. Lantero. New York: Charles Scribner's Sons, 1934.

Braaten, Carl E., & Harrisville, Editors and translators. *The Historical Jesus & the Kerygmatic Christ.* New York: Abingdon Press, 1964.

Bracey, John H. Jr., August Meier and Elliot Ruddick, Editors. *Black Nationalism in America.* Indianapolis: Bobbs Merrill Educational Publishing, 1970.

Burkett, Randall. *Garveyism as a Religious Movement.* Metuchen, NJ: The Scarecrow Press, Inc. and the American Theological Library Association, 1978.

Cannon, Katie G. *Black Womanist Ethics.* Atlanta: Scholars Press, 1988.

Carter, Harold. *The Prayer Tradition of Black People.* Valley Forge: Judson Press, 1976.

Childs, Brevard. *The New Testament Canon: An Interpretation.* Philadelphia: Fortress Press, 1984.

Cobb, John B. Jr. *Christ in a Pluralistic Age*. Philadelphia: The Westminster Press, 1975.

Cleage, Albert B., Jr. *The Black Messiah*. Kansas City, Kansas; Sheed Andrews and McMeel, Inc., 1968.

Cone, James H. *Black Theology and Black Power*. New York: The Seabury Press, 1969.

——. *God of the Oppressed*. New York: The Seabury Press, 1975.

——. *Liberation*. The C. Eric Lincoln Series in Black Religion. New York: J. B. Lippincott Company, 1970.

——. *For My People*. Maryknoll, NY: Orbis Books, 1984.

——. *The Spirituals and the Blues*. New York: The Seabury Press, 1972.

Cauthen, Kenneth. *The Impact of American Religious Liberalism*. New York: Harper & Row, 1962.

Cross, George. *Creative Christianity*. New York: The MacMillan Company, 1933.

——. *Christian Salvation*. Chicago: University of Chicago Press, 1925.

——. *What Is Christianity?* Chicago: University of Chicago Press, 1918.

Cullen, Countee. *The Black Christ and Other Poems*. New York: Harper & Row Brothers Publishers, 1929.

——. *Color*. Afro-American Culture Series, New York: Harper & Brothers, 1925; Reprint Edition. New York: Arno Press and the New York Times, 1969.

——. *On These I Stand*. New York: Harper & Row Brothers, 1927.

Cullman, Oscar. *The Christology of the New Testament*. Translated by Shirley C. Guthrie, Charles A.A. Hall. Philadelphia: The Westminster Press, 1959.

Douglass, Kelly Brown. *The Black Christ*. Maryknoll, N.Y. Orbis Books, 1994.

Du Bois, W. E. B. *The Gift of Black Folk*. New York: John Reprint Corporation, 1924.

Earl, Riggins. *Dark Symbols, Obscure Signs*. Maryknoll, N.Y. Orbis Books, 1993.

Eckhart, Meister. *Meister Eckhart*. Translation by Raymond B. Blakney. New York: Harper Torchbooks, 1941.

Fisher, Miles Mark. *Negro Slave Songs in the United States*. New York: Citadel Press, 1953.

Forbes, James A. *The Holy Spirit and Preaching*. New York: Harper and Row, 1987.

Fosdick, Harry Emerson. *A Guide to Understanding the Bible*. New York: Harper & Brothers, 1938.

——. *The Modern Use of the Bible*. New York: Macmillan Company, 1924.

Frazier, E. F. *The Negro Church in America* and C. Eric Lincoln *The Black Church Since Frazier*. New York: Schocken Books, 1974.

Fredriksen, Paula. *From Jesus to Christ.* New Haven: Yale University Press, 1988.

Fuller, Reginald H. *Who is This Christ.* Philadelphia: Fortress Press, 1983.

Garvey, Marcus. *Philosophy and Opinions of Marcus Garvey: or Africa for Africans.* Compiled by Amy Jacques Garvey, with E. U. Essienudom, 2 Vols. London: Frank Cass and Company Limited, 1967.

George, Carol. *Segregated Sabbaths: Richard Allen and the Emergence of Independent Black Churches, 1760-1840.* New York: Oxford University Press, 1973.

Goldsmith, Peter. *When I Rise Crying Holy.* New York: AMS Press, Inc., 1989.

Genovese, Eugene. *Roll, Jordan, Roll: The World the Slaves Made.* New York: Vintage Books, 1976.

Grant, Jacquelyn. *White Women's Christ and Black Women's Jesus.* Atlanta: Scholars Press, 1989.

Grillmeier, Aloys. *Christ in Christian Tradition.* Volume 1. Translated by John Bowden. Atlanta: John Knox Press, 1975.

Gutierrez, Gustavo. *A Theology of Liberation.* Translated by Sr. Caridad Inda and John Egleson. Maryknoll, New York: Orbis Books, 1973.

Handy, Robert T. *A Christian America.* New York: Oxford University Press, 1971.

———. ed. *The Social Gospel in America.* New York: Oxford University Press, 1966.

Harvey, Van A. *Handbook of Theological Terms.* New York: MacMillan Publishing Co., 1964.

Hodgson, Peter C., *Jesus—Word & Presence.* Philadelphia: Fortress Press, 1971.

Hopkins, Dwight N. *Black Theology USA and South Africa.* Maryknoll, NY.: Orbis Books, 1989.

Hopkins, Dwight N. and Cummings, George C. L., Editors. *Cut Loose Your Stammering Tongue: Black Theology in the Slave Narratives.* Maryknoll, NY: Orbis Books, 1991.

Hopkins, Dwight N. *Shoes That Fit Our Feet.* Maryknoll, NY: Orbis Books, 1993.

Horsley, Richard A. *Bandits, Prophets, and Messiahs.* New York: Harper & Row, 1985.

Hughes, Langston. *Good Morning Revolution.* Edited with an Introduction by Faith Berry, and foreword by Saunders Redding. New York: Lawrence Hill & Company, 1973.

———. *Not Without Laughter.* New York: Alfred A. Knopf, 1963.

———. *Scottsboro Limited.* New York: The Golden Stair Press, 1932.

———. *The Big Sea.* American Century Series. New York: Hill and Wang, 1963.

Johnson, Alonzo. "Howard Thurman and the Problem of Christian Racism: Confronting the Crisis of the Human Spirit." *Unity and Renewal: The Eradication of Racism*, edited by Susan Davies, et al. Grand Rapids: William B. Eerdmans Pub. Company, 1997.

Johnson, Alonzo and Paul Jersild, Editors. *Ain't Gonna Lay My 'Ligion Down: African American Religion in the South*. Columbia, S.C. The University of South Carolina Press, November, 1996.

Johnson, C. H., Editor. *God Struck Me Dead*. Boston: Pilgrim Press, 1969.

Johnson, James Weldon & Rosamond, Compilers. *The Book of American Negro Spirituals and the Second Book of Negro Spiritual*. New York: The Vikins Press Publishing Co., 1949.

Jones, Major J. *The Color of G.O.D.* Macon, GA.: Mercer University Press, 1987.

Jones, Rufus M. *The Faith and Practice of Quakers*. Philadelphia: Philadelphia Yearly Meeting, 1927.

———. *New Eyes for Invisibles*. New York: The MacMillan Co., 1943.

———. *New Studies in Mystical Religion*. New York: The MacMillan Co., 1927.

———. *The Radiant Life*. New York: The MacMillan Co., 1944.

———. *Social Law the Spiritual World*. Chicago: The John C. Winston Co., 1904.

———. *The Trail of Life in College*. New York: The MacMillan Company, 1929.

Joyner, Charles. *Down by the Riverside*. Urbana: University of Illinois Press, 1984.

Jurgens, William A. *The Faith of the Early Fathers*. Collegeville, MN: The Liturgical Press, 1970.

Kant, Immanuel. *Critique of Practical Reason*. Translated with Introduction by Lewis White Beck. Indianapolis: Bobbs-Merril Educational Publishing, 1982.

Katz, Bernard. Editor. *The Social Implications of Early Negro Music in the United States*. New York: Arno Press, 1969.

Keck, Leander E. *A Future of the Historical Jesus*. Nashville: Abingdon Press, 1971.

Kaesemann, Ernst. *Jesus Means Freedom*. Translated by Franke Clarke. London: SCM Press, 1961.

———. *New Testament Questions for Today*. Translated by W. J. Montague. Philadelphia: Fortress Press, 1969.

———. *Perspectives on Paul*. Translated by Margaret Kohl. Philadelphia: Fortress Press, 1971.

Katz, William Lore, Editor. *Five Slave Narratives*. New York: Arno Press and the New York Times, 1969.

Kelly, J.N.D., Revised Edition, *Early Christian Doctrine*. New York: Harper & Row, 1978.

Knox, John.   *The Humanity and Divinity of Christ*.   Cambridge, Eng.:
    Cambridge University Press, 1967.

Leith, John H. *Creeds of the Churches*. Atlanta: John Knox Press, 1973.

MacQuarrie, John.   *Principles of Christian Theology*. New York: Charles
    Scribner's Son., 1966.

Mays, Benjamin E. *The Negro's God*. Westport, CN: Greenwood Press,
    Publishers, 1938.

Mitchell, Henry. *Black Preaching*. San Francisco: Harper & Row, Publishers,
    1970.

Niebuhr, H. Richard.   *Christ and Culture*. New York: Harper Coldphon
    Books, 1951.

———. *The Meaning of Revelation*. New York: Macmillan Publishing Co.,
    Inc., 1941.

Niebuhr, Richard R. *Schleiermacher on Christ and Religion*. New York:
    Charles Scribner's Sons, 1964.

Norris, Richard A. *The Christological Controversy*. *Sources of Early Christian
    Thought*. Philadelphia: Fortress Press, 1980.

Pannenberg, Wolfhart. *Jesus, God & Man*. Translated by L. L. Wilkens and
    D. A. Priebe. Philadelphia: Minster Press, 1968.

Pinckney, Alphonso. *Red, Black and Green, Black Nationalism in the United
    States*. Cambridge, Eng.: Cambridge University Press, 1976.

Pittenger, W. Norman. *The Word Incarnate*. New York: Harper & Row,
    1959.

Pitts, Walter F., Jr., *Old Ship of Zion*. New York: Oxfrod University Press,
    1993.

Powe, B.D. & Johnson, Alonzo, "Fatalism Among African Americans: A
    Philosophical Perspective", *Journal of Religion and Health* 34:2 (Summer
    1995): p. 119-125.

Raboteau, Albert J. *Slave Religion*. New York: Oxford University Press, 1979.

Rahner, Karl; Vorgrimler, Herbert.   *Dictionary of Theology*. New York:
    Crossroad, 1981.

Rawick, George P. *From Sundown to Sunup*. Contributions in Afro-American
    and African Studies, No. 11. Westport: Greenwood Publishing Company,
    1972.

Robins, Henry B. *Aspects of Authority in the Christian Religion*. Boston: The
    Griffith & Rowland Press, 1927.

Roberts, J. Deotis. *Black Theology in Dialogue*. Philadelphia: Westminster
    Press, 1987.

———. *A Black Political Theology*. Philadelphia: Westminster Press, 1974.

———. *Liberation and Reconciliation*. Philadelphia: Westminster Press, 1971.

Robinson, James M.   *A New Quest of the Historical Jesus*. Philadelphia:
    Fortress Press, 1959.

———. *Christology Reconsidered*. London: SCM Press, 1970.

Sanders, E. P. *Jesus and Judaism*. Philadelphia: Fortress Press, 1985.

Scroggs, Robin. *Christology in Paul and John*. Proclamation Commentaries. Philadelphia: Fortress Press, 1988.

Sobel, Mechal. *Trablin' On*. Westport, CN: Greenwood Press,. 1979.

Simkhovitch, Vladimir G. *Toward the Understanding of Jesus*. New York: The MacMillan Co., 1921.

Schweitzer, Albert. *The Quest of the Historical Jesus*. New York: Macmillan Pub., Co., 1968.

Schillebeeckx, Edwaud. *Jesus an Experiment in Christology*. Translated by Hubert Hoskins. New York: Crossroad, 1979.

———. *Christ the Experience of Jesus as Lord*. Translated by John Bowden. New York: Crossroad, 1980.

Schleiermacher, Friedrich. Editor H. R. Mackintosh and J. S. Stewart. *The Christian Faith*. Philadelphia: Fortress Press, 1976.

Smith, Theopholis. *Conjuring Culture*. New York: Oxford University Press, 1994.

Stuckey, Sterling, Editor. *The Ideological Origins of Black Nationalism*. Boston: Beacon Press, 1972.

Troeltsch, Ernst. *The Absoluteness of Christianity and the History of Religions*. Introduction by James Luther Adams. Translated by David Reid. Richmond: John Knox Press, 1971.

Townes, Emilie M. *A Troublin in My Soul*. Maryknoll, NY: Orbis Books, 1993.

Van Dusen, Henry P. *The Vindication of Liberal Theology*. New York: Charles Scribner's, 1963.

Vermes, Geza. *Jesus the Jew: "A Historian's Reading of the Gospel"*. Philadelphia: Fortress Press, 1973.

Wainwright, Geoffrey. *Doxology:The Praise of God in Worship, Doctrine, and Life*. New York: Oxford University Press., 1980.

Weinel, Heinrich, and Widgery, A.G. *A Jesus in the Nineteenth Century and After*. Edinburgh: T. & T. Clark. 1914.

West, Cornel. *Prophesy Deliverance: An Afro-American Revolutionary Christianity*. Philadelphia: Westminster Press, 1982.

———. *Race Matters*. Boston: Beacon Press, 1982.

Wiles, Maurice. *The Making of Christian Doctrine*. Cambridge, Eng.: Cambridge University Press, 1967.

———. *The Remaking of Christian Doctrine*. London: SCM Press, 1974.

Williams, Delores. *Sisters in the Wilderness*. Maryknoll, NY.: Orbis Books, 1993.

Wilmore, Gayraud S. *Black Religion & Black Radicalism*. Maryknoll, New York: Orbis Books, 1973.

Witvliet, Theo. *The Way of the Black Messiah*. Oak Park, IL.: Meyer Stone Books 1987.

Yetman, Norman R. Editor. *Life Under the Peculiar Institution*. New York: Holt, Rinehart and Winston Inc.1970.

Index

Page numbers followed by *n* indicate notes.